DECISION-AIDING SOFTWARE
Skills, Obstacles and Applications

Free Diskette!!!!

Each table in this book corresponds to a data file on a floppy disk which is available without charge. For example, Tables 1.2 through 1.4 correspond to a data file called SHRTPROB which is on a master file called DAS1. Each data file or spreadsheet matrix shows goals to be achieved on the columns, alternatives available for achieving them on the rows, and relations between goals and alternatives in the cells in order to choose or explain the best alternative, combination, allocation, or predictive decision-rule. The same disk also contains the P/G% decision-aiding program. The program and tables can be run on any IBM-compatible computer. One can thus manipulate the tables in this book by determining the effects on one's tentative conclusion produced by changes in the goals, alternatives, relations, or other inputs.

Mail your request to: Stuart S. Nagel, 361 Lincoln Hall, University of Illinois, Urbana, IL 61801, USA.

Pleased send me the **free** diskette
Name _____
Street/Number _____
City/State _____ Zip _____

POLICY STUDIES ORGANIZATION SERIES

General Editor: Stuart S. Nagel, Professor of Political Science, University of Illinois at Urbana-Champaign

NEIGHBOURHOOD POLICY AND PROGRAMMES: Past and Present
Naomi Carmon (*editor*)

HUMAN RIGHTS: Theory and Measurement
David Louis Cingranelli (*editor*)

THE DISTRIBUTIONAL IMPACTS OF PUBLIC POLICIES
Sheldon H. Danziger and Kent E. Portney (*editors*)

PUBLIC POLICY AND AGRICULTURAL TECHNOLOGY:
Adversity despite Achievement
Don F. Hadwiger and William P. Browne (*editors*)

MARKET-BASED PUBLIC POLICY
Richard C. Hula (*editor*)

PROMOTING PRODUCTIVITY IN THE PUBLIC SECTOR: Problems,
Strategies and Prospects
Rita Mae Kelly (*editor*)

THE POLICY IMPACT OF UNIVERSITIES IN DEVELOPING REGIONS
Fred Lazin, Samuel Aroni and Yehuda Gradus (*editors*)

DECISION-AIDING SOFTWARE: Skills, Obstacles and Applications
Stuart S. Nagel

GLOBAL POLICY STUDIES: International Intervention toward Improving Public
Policy
Stuart S. Nagel (*editor*)

GOVERNMENT INNOVATION POLICY: Design, Implementation, Evaluation
J. David Roessner (*editor*)

Decision-Aiding Software

Skills, Obstacles and Applications

Stuart S. Nagel
Professor of Political Science
University of Illinois

Palgrave Macmillan

ISBN 978-1-349-11659-1   ISBN 978-1-349-11657-7 (eBook)
DOI 10.1007/978-1-349-11657-7

© Policy Studies Organisation, 1991
Softcover reprint of the hardcover 1st edition 1991

First published in the United States of America in 1991

ISBN 978-0-312-04212-7

Library of Congress Cataloging-in-Publication Data
Nagel, Stuart S., 1934–
Decision-aiding software: skills, obstacles, and applications/
Stuart S. Nagel.
p.   cm.
ISBN 978-0-312-04212-7
1. Decision-making—Data processing.   2. Decision support systems.
I. Title.
HD30.23.N35   1990   90–32087
658.4'03'0285536—dc20   CIP

Dedicated to promoting more effective, efficient and equitable decision-making

Contents

Contents

List of Tables and Tutorial Screens

List of Tables and Tutorial Screens

Tutorial Screens

Preface

The essence of decision-aiding software is that it consists of various forms of microcomputer programming designed to enable users to process a set of (1) goals to be achieved, (2) alternatives available for achieving them, and (3) relations between goals and alternatives in order to choose the best alternative, combination, allocation, or predictive decision-rule.

Decision-aiding software should be distinguished from at least two other kinds of software that are relevant to making decisions, but do not process goals, alternatives, and relations in order to arrive at prescriptive conclusions. One related type of software is information retrieval software. It can be very useful for determining such things as the amount of money spent on a certain expense item in a certain year, the court cases that are relevant to a given subject matter, or any kind of information that might be contained in a statistical almanac, encyclopedia, or other compendium of information. Another related type of software is office practice software which can be useful for word processing reports, filing and retrieving in-house information, or doing bookkeeping relevant to financial matters. That kind of software is useful for better organizing the decision-making processes of a government agency, a law firm, or any kind of office. Such software, however, does not process goals, alternatives, and relations to arrive at prescriptive conclusions.

Decision-aiding software can take a variety of forms. The most common might be the following:

1. **Decision-tree software** for making decisions under conditions of risk such as whether to go on strike or accept a management offer. A decision-tree is usually pictured as looking like a tree on its side with branches and sub-branches. The branches generally represent alternative possibilities that depend on the occurrence or non-occurrence of probabilistic events.
2. **Linear-programming software** for allocating money, time, people, or other scarce resources to activities, places, tasks, or other objects to which the resources are to be allocated. In terms of form rather than function, linear programming involves maximizing or minimizing an objective function or algebraic equation

subject to constraints generally in the form of inequalities like "greater than" or "less than".

3. **Statistical software** for predicting how a future event is likely to occur, such as a trial, an election, or a weather occurrence in light of past events or expert opinions. Statistical software generally involves calculating averages or predictive equations in which decisions or other outcomes are related to factual inputs.

4. **Spreadsheet-based software** in which the alternatives tend to be on the rows, the criteria on the columns, relations in the cells, overall scores for each alternative in a column at the far right, and a capability for determining what it would take to bring a second-place or other-place alternative up to first place.

5. **Rule-based software** which contains a set of rules for dealing with a narrow or broad field of decision-making. The user gives the computer a set of facts, and the computer applies the rules to the facts in order to determine which alternative decision should be or is likely to be decided. Such software is sometimes referred to as artificial intelligence (AI) or expert systems, but the other forms of decision-aiding software also have characteristics associated with AI and expert systems.

6. **Multi-criteria decision-making** (MCDM) software, which emphasizes multiple goals to be achieved, as contrasted to decision trees, linear programming, and statistical regression analysis which emphasize a single objective function or a single dependent variable.

7. **Decision-aiding software** that focuses on a specific subject matter, as contrasted to the above types of software which cut across all subjects. Subject-specific software could relate to how to decide where to drill an oil well, how to deal with crisis situations in flying a plane, or any other specific decision-making situations.

8. **Software that is useful for generating alternatives, goals, or relations**, but that does not process those elements in order to draw a conclusion.

Any specific decision-aiding program can fit into any number of these categories since they are not mutually exclusive. This book emphasizes software which has a spreadsheet base with multi-criteria decision-making that can be applied to any subject matter. A big advantage of spreadsheet-based software is that it can be used to aid in making various types of decisions in a manner that is simpler – and possibly more valid – than more specifically focused software. For example, its flexibility enables it to aid in making decisions that involve:

1. **Risk analysis**, possibly better than decision-tree software.
2. **Allocation analysis**, possibly better than linear-programming software.
3. **Prediction analysis**, possibly better than statistical-regression software.
4. **Elaborate if–then rules**, possibly better than rule-based expert systems software.
5. **Specific subjects**, possibly better than subject-specific software.
6. **Idea generation**, possibly better than idea-generation software.

The book is divided into three main parts plus an overview (Part I) at the beginning and supplementary materials section (Part V) at the end. Part II deals with the skills that decision-aiding software enhances. These skills include:

1. **Choosing among alternatives**, where each alternative is a lump sum choice, meaning that one cannot generally choose parts or multiples of such an alternative. The situation can involve mutually exclusive alternatives, or it can allow for combinations.
2. **Allocating scarce resources** such as money, time, or people to such objects as places or activities. The allocating can be with or without minimum or maximum constraints on how much each object can receive.
3. **Explaining and predicting behavior** including individual cases or relations, either in the past or the future.
4. **Teaching decision-making**, as well as actually making or prescribing decisions.

Part III deals with the kinds of obstacles that decision-aiding software helps overcome. These obstacles include:

1. **Multiple dimensions on multiple goals.** This is sometimes referred to as the "apples and oranges" problem, although the problem appears to become more difficult if the goals are more abstract, like freedom and equality. The measures may simultaneously involve hours, miles, dollars, 1–5 scales, pounds, pollution units, and other measures.
2. **Multiple missing information.** In its simplest form, this problem

involves knowing the benefits and costs for a number of alternatives with the exception of one benefit or one cost. In its more challenging form, many benefits, costs, probabilities, and other inputs are unknown.

3. **Multiple and possibly conflicting constraints.** In its simplest form, there are a number of constraints that need to be met simultaneously, but they do not conflict. In its more challenging form, there may be minimum allocations required for each budget category, but the sum of the minimums adds to more than the maximum budget constraint.

4. **The need for simplicity in drawing and presenting conclusions** in spite of all that multiplicity. This is where spreadsheet-based software can be especially helpful because it can be relatively easy to manipulate and interpret in comparison to decision-trees, pay-off matrices, systems of simultaneous equations and inequalities, and arrow diagrams.

Part IV of the book deals with applications to diverse fields. These applications include:

1. **Public policy problems**, such as inflation–unemployment, consumer policy, labor relations, agriculture, housing, environment, poverty, race relations, crime, education, energy, health care, civil liberties, world peace, and governmental reform.

2. **Law problems**, such as contracts, property, torts, family law, criminal law, constitutional law, economic regulation, international law, civil procedure, and criminal procedure.

3. All fields of knowledge, such as physics, chemistry, geology, astronomy, biology, psychology, sociology, economics, political science, history, philosophy, language–literature, and the arts.

Those who read through this book and learn about decision-aiding software are likely to benefit in various ways. Those benefits include:

1. Being **more explicit** about goals to be achieved, alternatives available for achieving them, and relations between goals and alternatives.

2. Being stimulated to think of **more** goals, alternatives, and relations than one would otherwise be likely to do.

3. Being able to handle **multiple** goals, alternatives, and relations

without getting confused and without feeling the need to resort to a single composite goal or a single go/no–go alternative.

4. Being encouraged to **experiment** with changes in the inputs into one's thinking to see how one's conclusions are affected.
5. Being better able to **achieve or more than achieve** one's goals when choosing among alternatives or allocating scarce resources.
6. Being better able to **predict** future occurrences and **explain** past occurrences.
7. Being better able to **teach** decision-making and other related skills to students in courses that involve controversial issues.
8. Being able **more effectively to handle** multi-dimensionality, missing information, and multiple constraints as surmountable obstacles to systematic decision-making.
9. Being more able to deal with **diverse subject matters** as a result of having a cross-cutting decision-analytic framework that is easy to use.
10. Becoming more capable of **systematic decision analysis**, even when the software is not available.

One of the most exciting developments regarding the future of decision-aiding software is the idea of being able to achieve super-optimum solutions. Such a solution is one that is better than what each side in a controversy had originally proposed as its best alternative using each side's own goals and their relative weights. For example, in the 1988 election campaign George Bush proposed retaining the minimum wage at $3.35 in order to stimulate business. Michael Dukakis proposed raising the minimum wage to $4.00 in order to help labor. A super-optimum solution might be to allow business firms to pay as low as $3.00 an hour where they agree to hire the elderly, the handicapped, mothers of pre-school children, or other unemployed people and also agree to provide on-the-job training. The workers, however, receive $4.50 an hour with the government paying a $1.50 minimum wage supplement to the $3.00 business base. Business comes out ahead of its best expectations ($3.35) of being able to retain the present minimum wage. Labor comes out ahead of its best expectation of getting $4.00 an hour. The taxpayer is also better off if unemployed people are put to work who might otherwise be receiving public aid, food stamps, Medicaid, public housing, and maybe committing crimes. They can now become income-receiving taxpayers. This is a super-optimum solution where everybody comes out better off. It should be distinguished from a compromise solution which would be between $3.35 (Bush) and $4.00 (Dukakis) an hour. Super-optimum solutions are facilitated by thinking in terms of multiple goals and alternatives using spreadsheet-based decision-aiding software.

There are many people who should be acknowledged for the contributions they have made to the development of this book. They include people with whom I have collaborated in developing decision-aiding software such as David Garson of North Carolina State University, John Long of the University of Illinois, and Miriam Mills of New Jersey Institute of Technology. They also include people with whom I have worked at the University of Illinois as part of my research and teaching activities and the management of the Policy Studies Organization. Those people in recent years have included in alphabetical order Madelle Becker, Dawn Ehrenburg, Mary Glasgow, Kay Lust, Carla Manning, Kate Morrow, Vicky Pierce, James Prevo, Janet Ware, and Pat Young. Special thanks should go to Joyce Nagel who is the Business Manager of the Policy Studies Organization and the Vice President of Decision-Aids, Inc., among other roles.

Thanks should also be given to the many people who have participated in various experiments involving decision-aiding software. It is hoped that this book will help move such software out of the experimental realm into the realm of everyday usage. That could occur either explicitly by way of the software, or implicitly by way of internalizing the decision-making ideas contained in this book.

STUART S. NAGEL

Part I
An Overview of
Decision-aiding Software

1 A Microcomputer Program for Decision-making

The purpose of this chapter is to show how microcomputer software can aid in overcoming key methodological problems in program/ policy evaluation.

Five key methodological problems involve how to deal with:

1. evaluation criteria being measured on **different dimensions**
2. **missing or imprecise information** concerning criteria, alternatives, relative weights of the criteria, or relations between criteria and alternatives
3. alternatives that are **so many** one cannot determine the effects of all of them
4. **minimum and maximum constraints that may be conflicting** on the criteria and/or the alternatives
5. **the need for simplicity** in drawing and presenting conclusions in spite of all that multiplicity and potential complexity.

The most relevant software for program/policy evaluation is software in the general category of multi-criteria decision-making (MCDM). That software is designed to process a set of:

1. criteria or goals **to be achieved**
2. alternatives, programs, policies, or decisions for **achieving the goals**
3. **relations between** the **criteria** and the **alternatives**.

The purpose of the processing is to choose the best alternative or combination in light of the criteria, alternatives, and relations.

The most relevant MCDM program is probably the one called Policy/Goal Percentaging (P/G%). It is called thus because it relates policies to goals, and because it uses part/whole percentaging to deal with the problem of goals being measured on different dimensions. The program is available from the author at no charge to buyers of this present book on *Decision-Aiding Software: Skills, Obstacles, and*

3

Table 1.1   The main menu for the P/G% program

POLICY EVALUATION P/G%
*** Choose an option ***
1. File management
Master file = das1
Data file = SHRTPROB
2. Data management
3. Primary analysis
4. Threshold / Convergence analyses
5. Save present data

Applications. The program will run on IBM-compatible hardware with at least 192K of memory.

To illustrate how such microcomputer software can help in overcoming those methodological problems, this chapter will mainly use an example problem of trying to choose between two anti-crime programs where one program is better on crimes solved, and the other is better on civil cases processed. The programs are simply called Policy 1 and 2, without giving the policies further substantive content, which might distract from the methodological purposes of this chapter.[1]

THE MAIN MENU AND THE INPUT DATA

Table 1.1 shows the main menu of the program. That menu provides for five options or activities which can be exercised by pressing a *1*, *2*, *3*, *4*, or *5* on the keyboard. To return to this main menu at any time, press the *F9* button on the left side of the keyboard.

The Main Options

The five parts of the main menu can be briefly defined as follows:

1. *File management* enables the user to make changes in existing data or to create a new file.
2. *Data management* enables the user to make changes in existing data or to create new data mainly regarding (1) the goals or

criteria to be achieved, (2) the alternatives for achieving them, or (3) the relations between goals and alternatives.

3. *Primary analysis* shows the initial conclusion as to the overall scores or the allocation percentages of the alternatives.
4. *Threshold analysis* tells the user what it would take to bring a second-place or other-place alternative up to first place. "Convergence analysis" tells the user at what point of the weight a goal becomes high enough that the goal dominates the other goals.
5. *Save present data* is the option exercised in order to preserve for the future whatever new criteria, alternatives, or relations one has recently created in a data file.

File Management

If option *1* is exercised, then the file management menu will appear on the screen. It requires the user to either access an existing file or create a new file. Accessing or creating involves typing the name of a master file and a data subfile. The illustrative example here involves a master file called *das1*, which is the second demonstration file in the set of files on the program disk. The specific data file is called *SHRTPROB* which stands for short problems, and is used to provide a short illustration of how the program deals with the five methodological problems mentioned above. The names of master files and data files are limited to eight characters.

Data Management

The three displays in Table 1.2 were accessed or created by exercising the data management option on the main menu. Doing so causes the data management menu to appear on the screen. That sub-menu also has five options that one could exercise covering:

1. changing the **total budget**, where one is allocating scarce resources
2. changing the **alternatives**, their minimum allocations, or their previous actual allocations
3. changing the **criteria**, their measurement units, or their relative weights
4. changing the **scores** of the alternatives on the criteria
5. changing the **method** for dealing with multi-dimensional criteria from raw score analysis to percentaging analysis, or back.

Table 1.2 The input data

A. THE ALTERNATIVES OR POLICIES

	Budgets	
Alternative	Minimum	Actual
1 POLICY 1	0.00	0.00
2 POLICY 2	0.00	0.00

B. THE CRITERIA OR GOALS

Criterion	Meas. Unit	Weight
1 CRIMES SOLVED	CRIMES/CAP	2.00
2 DOLLAR COST	$1,000	−1.00
3 CIVIL CASES PROC.	100'S	1.00

C. THE RELATIONS BETWEEN THE ALTERNATIVES AND THE
CRITERIA

	ALTERNATIVE / CRITERIA SCORING	
	CRIMES S	CIVIL CA
POLICY 1	100.00	0.00
POLICY 2	60.00	12.00

The alternatives for this problem are labeled *Policy 1* and *Policy 2*. They involve no minimum or actual allocations, since this is initially not an allocation problem, but rather one designed to choose the best policy. The data file contains three criteria, but only two are activated, namely crimes solved and civil cases processed. The measurement units are 100 crimes *per capita* (for crimes solved), and civil cases counted in units of 100 (for civil cases processed). Crimes solved *per capita* is considered twice as important as civil cases processed. Policy 1 is predicted as solving 100 units of crime, but it processes no civil cases. Policy 2 processes 12 units of civil cases, but it solves only 60 units of crime. The variety of typefaces shown in Tables 1.1 and 1.2 is one small aspect of the variety which the program provides. Any display which appears on the screen can be easily printed by just hitting the *Print-Screen* and the *Shift* buttons.[2]

Weights and relation scores tend to come from four sources:

1. **Authority**. For example, the US Supreme Court (relying on William Blackstone) has said that it is ten times as bad to convict an innocent person as it is to acquit a guilty person.
2. **Statistical or observational analysis**. For example, if operating under a 10 to 1 tradeoff on conviction rates produces twice as

much respect for the legal system as a 5 to 1 tradeoff, then that observation might lead one to conclude that avoiding conviction errors should be considered twice as important as avoiding acquittal errors, assuming respect for the law is the higher goal that one is seeking.

3. **Deduction.** For example, if we know that conviction errors are ten times as bad as acquittal errors, then we can deduce that wrongly holding a defendant in jail is less than ten times as bad as wrongly releasing a defendant since holding is less severe than convicting.

4. **Sensitivity analysis.** For example, if we are trying to decide on the relative weight of conviction errors versus acquittal errors, it might be quite helpful to determine at what point the tradeoff makes a difference in the bottom-line conclusion as to what legal policy to adopt. Thus if the issue is whether five-person juries can be allowed, there would be no need to argue that the tradeoff should be 10 to 1 or 5 to 1 if the sensitivity analysis shows that the five-person juries have an unacceptably greater conviction rate than six person juries even if the tradeoff is 2 to 1.

THE TRANSFORMED DATA AND THE INITIAL CONCLUSION

Transformed Data

Table 1.3A transforms the raw scores of Table 1.2C into weighted raw scores. It does so by multiplying by two the raw scores in the crimes column to reflect that crime units are considered twice as important as civil case units in this context. Doing so is the simplest meaningful way of dealing with multi-dimensional criteria. We are in effect saying that one crime unit gives twice as much satisfaction as one civil unit. Therefore, in terms of satisfaction, two civil units equal one crime unit. If we have one crime unit and one civil unit, then we have the equivalent of either three civil units in terms of satisfaction, or one and a half crime units.

Primary Analysis

Table 1.3B shows the combined raw scores for each policy taking the weighting into consideration. It indicates that for Policy 1, 100 crime units plus 0 civil units is equal to the satisfaction of 200 civil units.

Table 1.3   Transforming the input data into an initial conclusion

A. THE TRANSFORMED DATA REFLECTING THE RELATIVE WEIGHTS OF THE GOALS		
	WEIGHTED	
	CRIMES S	CIVIL CA
POLICY 1	200.00	0.00
POLICY 2	120.00	12.00
B. THE INITIAL CONCLUSION AS TO WHICH POLICY IS BEST		
	Combined	
Alternative	Rawscores	%
1 POLICY 1	200.00	60.24
2 POLICY 2	132.00	39.76

Table 1.3B also shows that 60 crime units and 12 civil units is equal to the satisfaction of 132 civil units. The second column of Table 1.3A converts the combined raw scores of 200 and 132 into percentages by calculating 200/332 or 60.24% and 132/332 or 39.76%.

The main alternative way in which the program deals with multi-dimensionality is by converting the raw scores of Table 1.2C into weighted part/whole percentages in Table 1.3A instead of weighted raw scores. The unweighted part/whole percentages for the crimes column would be 100/160 or 62.50% and 60/160 or 37.50%. The unweighted part/whole percentages for the civil column would be 0/12 or 0% and 12/12 or 100%. It is easier, however, to work with weighted raw scores in this problem because crimes solved and civil cases processed have enough concreteness that one can meaningfully say that one extra crime unit is twice as satisfying or N times as satisfying as one extra civil unit. Weighted part/whole percentages are easier to work with where the criteria are more abstract, such as the criterion of respect for the law as measured on a 1–5 scale.

Table 1.3 indicates that Policy 1 is initially the better policy since 200 satisfaction units is more than 132 satisfaction units. Table 1.3 also indicates that Policy 1 is the better policy by 68 satisfaction units, since 200 minus 132 is 68. If both criteria had equal weights of 1.00 apiece, then the combined raw scores would be 100 and 72 for the two policies. Those figures are arrived at by simply adding across the raw scores in Table 1.2C. Under those circumstances, Policy 1 would still be the winner, but by 28 points rather than 68 points.[3]

Table 1.4   The tie-causing values of the relation scores and weights

	THRESHOLD ANALYSIS POLICY 1 VS POLICY 2	
	CRIMES S	CIVIL CA
POLICY 1	72.00	−28.00
POLICY 2	88.00	40.00
Weight	0.300	3.333

SENSITIVITY ANALYSIS

Threshold Analysis

Table 1.4 shows a form of sensitivity analysis as to what it would take to make the second place alternative into the first place alternative. More specifically, it shows what it would take to make up the 28-point gap if the criteria were weighted equally. A separate analysis could show what it would take to make up the 68-point gap when crimes solved are given twice the weight of civil cases processed.

Each threshold analysis gives as many answers as there are relations in the raw data matrix of Table 1.2C, plus as many criteria as there are which could receive relative weights. There are thus six answers or tie-causing values in Table 1.4. Those answers involve noting there would be a tie between Policy 1 and Policy 2:

1. If Policy 1 were to solve **only 72 crimes rather than 100 crimes**.
2. If Policy 1 were to process **minus 28 civil cases**, but that is impossible.
3. If Policy 2 could improve to the point where it is **solving 88 crimes rather than 60**. That could also be interpreted as meaning that if Policy 2 could improve to solving at least 89 crimes, then Policy 2 would be the winner.
4. Likewise, **40 is the tie-causing value or threshold value** of the relation between Policy 2 and civil cases processed. That means if Policy 2 could move up from 12 civil cases to 40, there would be a tie.
5. If the weight of crimes solved were to be lowered to **0.30 rather**

than 2.00. That is especially important because the weights are generally the most subjective aspects of this kind of evaluation analysis. That figure tells us that so long as crimes have a weight greater than 0.30, Policy 1 will be the winner.

6. If the weight of civil cases processed were to move up from **1.00 to 3.33**. The threshold weight of 3.33 or 3⅓ is the reciprocal of the threshold weight of 0.30 or 3/10. One can check these threshold values by reinserting them into the weights of Table 1.2B or the relation scores of Table 1.2C. For example, if civil cases had a weight of 3.33, then the 12 civil cases for Policy 2 would be multiplied by 3.33 to equal the equivalent of 40 criminal cases. Policy 2 would then have 100 overall satisfaction units equal to the 100 overall satisfaction units of Policy 1.

The above analysis is referred to as a "threshold analysis" because it informs the user of the threshold value of each input item, above which one alternative is best, and below which another alternative is best. Threshold analysis is more useful than the what–if analysis associated with spreadsheet programs, whereby one can change a cell item and see the effect of the change on the row total, the column total, and the grand total. Where there are only six input items, what–if analysis can be time-consuming because each of the six items could reasonably take five or more values. It is better to see for all items simultaneously at what points a change would make a difference.

Other Sensitivity Analysis

Although what–if analysis is not as useful as threshold analysis for dealing with quantitative inputs, it can be a useful form of sensitivity analysis for qualitative inputs. For example, the P/G% program can quickly show the user what the effects are of (1) adding, subtracting, consolidating, or subdividing alternatives, (2) specifying a maximum or minimum characteristic of one or more alternatives, (3) adding, subtracting, consolidating, or subdividing goals, (4) specifying a maximum or minimum degree of achievement on one or more goals, and (5) changing the relations between alternatives and goals to provide for more refinement or less refinement, or alternative units of measurement.

The P/G% program also provides for other forms of sensitivity analysis, including:

1. An **insensitivity range** shows how far down and up each input can go without affecting which alternative is the winner.
2. A **multiple threshold change** is an amount that when added or subtracted to a combination of inputs will generate a tie.
3. A **change slope** indicates by how much the gap changes between two compared alternatives if an input increases by one unit.
4. A **best scenario** shows the overall score of an alternative if all the inputs were changed to favor the alternative as much as possible. A worst scenario is the opposite.
5. A **convergence value** shows the weight that will cause a criterion totally to dominate the allocation of resources among the alternatives, as described below in discussing allocation analysis.
6. A **threshold curve** shows all the combinations for two inputs that will generate a tie. A **threshold band** does so for three inputs. A threshold **pair of bands** does so for four inputs.

All these forms of sensitivity analysis inform the user of the effects of changes in the inputs on the conclusion. Sensitivity analysis can be especially helpful in dealing with missing information. It does not tell the user the exact values for the missing information. Instead, it tells the user the values that make a difference in changing the conclusion. Thus, one need not be concerned with whether an input item is a 20 or 70 if both values result in the same alternative being the first choice.[4]

ALLOCATION AND CONSTRAINT ANALYSIS

Allocation Analysis

Tables 1.3B and 1.4 consider this evaluation problem to involve determining (1) which policy is best, (2) the rank orders of the policies, or (3) the relative desirability of the policies. Table 1.5A and 1.5B consider this evaluation problem to involve determining how to allocate $1,000 or 1,000 monetary units between the two policies or budget categories. Table 1.5A does the allocating without minimum constraints per policy. It allocates the $1,000 to each policy in proportion to the allocation percentages shown in the right-hand column of Tables 1.3B and 1.5A. The allocation percentages convert into $602 and $398 for each policy.

Table 1.5   Allocating scarce resources to the policy categories

A. WITHOUT MINIMUM CONSTRAINTS PER POLICY		
Total Resources = 1000.00		
Alternative	Alloc.	P/W %
1 POLICY 1	602.41	60.24
2 POLICY 2	397.59	39.76
B. WITH MINIMUM CONSTRAINTS PER POLICY		
Total Resources = 1000.00		
Alternative	Alloc.	P/W %
1 POLICY 1	520.48	60.24
2 POLICY 2	479.52	39.76
C. WITH THE FIRST CRITERION AT THE CONVERGENCE WEIGHT OF ONE		
Total Resources = 1000.00		
Alternative	Alloc.	P/W %
1 POLICY 1	581.40	58.14
2 POLICY 2	418.60	41.86

Any allocation problem involves a huge number of alternatives. One can, for example, allocate $1,000 to Policy 1 and $0 to Policy 2; $999 to Policy 1 and $1 to Policy 2; and soon down to $0 to Policy 1 and $1,000 to Policy 2. The number of alternatives becomes astronomical if we allocate to three or more alternatives and if we increase the amount allocated to $1,000,000.

By allocating in proportion to those weighted raw scores, we are in effect saying that the ratio between the raw scores bears a similarity to the ratio between elasticity coefficients, non-linear regression coefficients, or marginal percentage rates of return. One can show that allocating in proportion to such quantities is in conformity with classical calculus optimization.

The allocation of 60% to Policy 1 and 40% to Policy 2 is based on calculating that 200/332 is 60% and 132/332 is 40%. An alternative way to conceive the allocation problem is to recognize that if the allocation were based only on crimes solved, then Policy 1 would receive 100/160 or 62.5% of the scarce resources, and Policy 2 would receive 60/160 or 37.5%. Likewise if the allocation were based only on civil cases processed, then Policy 1 would receive 0/12 or 0% of the scarce resources, and Policy 2 would receive 12/12 or 100%. The next logical step would be to calculate the weighted average of those two allocations. That means Policy 1 would receive twice 62.5% divided by 3, or 42%. Policy 2 would then receive twice 37.5% plus

100% divided by 3, or 58%. That approach is more in conformity with classical calculus optimization, although it is slightly more difficult to apply. The differences between the two approaches tend to be small in terms of the resulting allocation percentages.

Constraint Analysis

Table 1.5B does the allocating with a minimum constraint of $400 per policy. Table 1.5B takes those equity minimums into consideration before optimizing by giving $400 to each policy off the top of the $1,000, thereby leaving a $200 residue to be allocated in accordance with the criteria of crimes solved and civil cases processed. Thus Policy 1 gets $400 plus 60% of the $200 residue (which is an extra $120) for a total of $520. Policy 2 gets $400 plus 40% of the $200 residue (which is an extra $80) for a total of $480. That method of considering minimum constraints guarantees that they will be considered, but it produces undesirable results in light of the criteria which the problem is seeking to optimize or maximize.

A better approach is post-optimizing (rather than pre-optimizing) constraint analysis. It involves optimizing in light of the allocation percentages in the right-hand column of Tables 1.3B and 1.5B, ignoring the minimum constraints, and then making adjustments if the minimum constraints are not satisfied. That approach results in $520 to Policy 1 and $480 to Policy 2. Those allocations do satisfy the minimum requirements of $400 apiece, and therefore there is no need for adjustments. Adjusting for minimums after optimizing will always produce results closer to the optimum (or the same results) as adjusting for minimums before optimizing, while at the same time satisfying the minimums.

Convergence Sensitivity

The concept of threshold analysis applies especially to a problem where it is relevant to talk about what it would take to make the second-place alternative into the first-place alternative. That idea is not so applicable in an allocation problem where every alternative, policy, or budget category tends to receive something, even if we are allocating only in the light of efficiency criteria. In an allocation problem, the key counterpart of threshold analysis is convergence analysis. It involves asking "what does the weight of crimes to civil cases have to become in order for the crimes criterion to totally dominate the allocation?" Totally dominating in this context means giving crimes a high enough weight so the allocation percentages are within five percentage points of 100/160 or 62% and 60/160 or 38% to Policy 1 and Policy 2, respectively. Those would be the allocations if crimes solved were the only criterion. To find the convergence weight, one starts with a weight of one and moves upward until the allocation percentages are within plus or minus five percentage points of those maximum allocations.

In this problem, convergence is reached at a weight of one for crimes solved because at that weight, the allocation percentages are 58% and 42% as is shown in Table 1.5C, and those percentages are within five percentage points of 62% and 38%. The 58% comes from adding 100 to 0 and dividing by 172. The 42% comes from adding 60 to 12 and dividing by 172. The 172 comes from adding 100 to 72. The 100 and the 60 are multiplied by a weight of one, as are the 0 and 12. The weight of one may seem like a low figure for reaching convergence which is virtually the equivalent of a weight of infinity. That, however, is part of the nature of diminishing returns whereby increasing the weights of criteria often has only slight marginal incremental effects. That is useful information since one need not argue whether the weight of crimes solved to civil cases should be 1, 2, 5, or higher if a weight of 1 gives virtually the equivalent of a weight of infinity in this substantive context with the numbers being what they are.[5]

SOME CONCLUSIONS

The P/G% software deals with the five methodological problems by implementing the following principles:

1. **Multi-dimensional criteria** are handled by working with weighted raw scores where the criteria have enough concreteness to make such weighting meaningful. Otherwise part/whole percentaging is used to convert the criteria into dimensionless numbers with weights assigned to the criteria, rather than the units of measurement.
2. **Missing information** is handled by changing questions that ask for the exact value of an input item to questions that ask whether the input item is above or below a threshold value. Threshold values

are at a point where a higher or lower score will affect the alternative that is considered best.

3. **Multiple alternatives** that are so many one cannot determine the effects of all of them can be handled by working with intervals, or by working with budget categories rather than allocation alternatives.

4. **Minimum and maximum constraints** are best handled by optimizing without taking the constraints into consideration, and then making adjustments if the optimizing solution does not satisfy all the constraints.

5. **Simplicity** is promoted by having a user-friendly computer program that requires virtually no technical knowledge in order to use the program or to interpret the results, even though the program is based on principles of classical calculus optimization.

A copy of the P/G% floppy disk, Program Manual, and Datafiles Manual can be obtained for experimental use from Stuart Nagel, 361 Lincoln Hall, University of Illinois, Urbana, Illinois 61801, 217–359–8. There is no charge to cover the cost of reproducing the program and the documentation to buyers of this present book on *Decision-Aiding Software*. The floppy disk includes both the program and almost 100 data files containing tentative alternatives, criteria, and relations for evaluation problems in such fields as government structures, economic policy, urban planning, social problems, political science, criminal procedure, judicial administration, health care, and personal decision-making. Users are encouraged to communicate their experiences to Stuart Nagel so we can further improve the software and the documentation.[6]

Appendix: Distinguishing P/G% From Alternative Approaches

A leading alternative to part/whole percentaging is the **analytic hierarchy process** (AHP).[7] It emphasizes paired comparisons in norming the raw scores and obtaining weights. One of its major defects is that it seeks to reduce relations to a 1–9 scale, regardless how precisely the goals might be capable of being measured. The P/G% method allows each goal to be measured differently in recognition of the fact that some goals can be measured more precisely, as well as the fact that the goals tend to be measured on different dimensions. If one alternative receives a part/whole percentage (p/w%) of 70% and another alternative receives a p/w% of 30% that logically means the first alternative has 70% of the total on the goal, and the second alternative has 30%. In the AHP system, however, a seven means "demonstrated importance" of one alternative over another and a three means "weak importance". The AHP method is not capable of working with goals like delay, crime, or even cost which are inherently negative goals in the sense that receiving low scores is desirable. Some negative goals can be easily converted to positive goals by calculating a complement such as the percent of the labor force that is unemployed. Many negative goals, however, need to be retained as negative goals in order for the results to make sense and in order for the user to feel comfortable with the analysis. The AHP method makes no distinctions between goals and policies. It distinguishes only between higher and lower levels in a hierarchy of concepts. That is generally too abstract for most users. The method is also far more complicated than necessary. When the method encounters inconsistencies in the weighting of goals or the scoring of relations, it applies arbitrary rules for dealing with the inconsistencies, rather than calling them to the attention of the user and asking for a reweighting or a rescoring designed to eliminate or lessen the inconsistencies.

Another alternative is Ward Edwards's **multi-attribute utility theory** (MAUT).[8] It emphasizes a form of interpolation for norming the raw scores. Its main defect is converting the raw scores into percentages through a method of interpolation which is highly arbitrary. The method talks in terms of an ambiguous "plausible maximum" and a "plausible minimum" on each goal between which the interpolation occurs. The plausible maximum on a goal is not the maximum score actually received by the alternatives. Nor is it the conceptual maximum allowed by the measurement scale of the goal. Rather, it is a figure likely to be short of the conceptual maximum, but somewhere greater than the actual maximum received. The same is true of the plausible minimum. Where those unnecessarily subjective maximums and minimums are perceived to be, however, determines the interpolated percentages and thus the outcome of the analysis. Other defects in the

16

MAUT method include the fact that its emphasis on linear interpolation does not take diminishing returns into consideration. The converted percentages do not involve allocating a total quantity of 100% to the policies the way part/whole percentaging does. The MAUT percentages are also not analogous to working with elasticity coefficients the way part/whole percentages are. Like the Saaty AHP method, the Edwards MAUT method is much more complicated than part/whole percentaging.

Another alternative is offered by X. T. Bui called the **electre** method which is widely used in Europe.[9] This method is based on the idea that no matter how many goals there are, and no matter how many different dimensions they are measured on, if one policy scores the highest on every goal, then it is the winner. This method tries to define winners who do not score the highest on every goal, but in some sense come closer to doing so than the other policies. One cannot simply count how many goals each policy scores the highest on, since the goals are weighted differently. If one looks to the rank order of each policy on each goal, that ignores useful information about the distance between each policy on each goal. The electre method emphasizes rank order in an unduly complicated system of paired comparisons.

Another set of alternatives can be grouped under the heading of **multi-objective programming**. These seek to deal with multi-criteria decision-making by developing models analogous to those in operations research and management science that are associated with mathematical programming or the mathematics of maximizing and minimizing objective functions through systems of reiterative guessing rather than classical calculus optimization. Multi-objective programming does have the advantage over linear, non-linear, dynamic, integer, and goal programming of being capable of considering more than one objective function or goal simultaneously. The methods of multi-objective programming are, however, often unbelievably complicated. It involves such techniques as scalarizing functions, the contracting cone method, the Wierzbicki method, the Zionts–Wallenius method, the Geoffrion–Dyer–Feinberg method, compromise programming, prospect ranking vectors, utility decomposition models, multi-criterion simplex methods, etc. Any reasonable multi-objective programming problem can be handled by Policy/Goal Percentaging. The variables are the alternatives. The objective functions are the goals. The coefficients within each equation are the relation scores. The values of the objective functions are the weights. For linear multi-objective programming, one allocates everything in P/G% to the one best alternative, and then makes adjustments to satisfy the constraints. For non-linear multi-objective programming, one allocates in P/G% to each alternative in proportion to the sum of their weighted raw scores or weighted part/whole percentages and then makes constraint-satisfying adjustments.

The P/G% approach differs from other decision aiding approaches by virtue of being able to deal meaningfully with all of the following decision-making situations: (1) multi-dimensional goals; (2) choosing the one best alternative; (3) choosing the best combination of alternatives; (4) making choices where risks and probabilities are involved; (5) making choices where doing too much or too little is undesirable; (6) allocating scarce resources, even where there are millions of alternative ways of allocating a given budget to a set of budget categories; (7) situations with multiple missing information; (8) situations involving public policy, law, business, medicine, or personal decision-making; (9) situations where all the goals are measured on the same dimension; (10) situations involving prediction as well as prescription; and (11) minimum or maximum constraints on the alternatives, goals, or other constraints.

The approach also differs from other approaches by virtue of having the following additional characteristics:

1. P/G% can easily go from alternatives, goals, and relations to drawing a conclusion.
2. It has been translated into a highly user-friendly microcomputer program.
3. It is based on mathematical justifications that relate to classical calculus optimization, especially if one views the part/whole percentages as proxies for non-linear regression coefficients.
4. It comes with lots of illustrative applications and years of relevant experience.
5. It is analogous to mathematical programming procedures such as linear, non-linear, integer, goal and multi-objective programming, but without the complexity and unrealistic assumptions.
6. The program can systematically compare optimum choices or allocations with actual choices or allocations in order to bring the optimum closer to the actual and vice versa.

There are other alternatives for handling multi-dimensional tradeoffs besides policy/goal percentaging, the Saaty AHP method, and the Edwards MAUT method, but the others are probably not as well known. They all have in common a system of (1) converting raw scores into relative numbers that can be added and subtracted, (2) weighting the relative importance of the goals, and (3) aggregating the converted scores (which show the relations between the policies and the goals) along with the weights of the goals in order to produce total scores for each policy. The conversion stage in the process seems to be the most controversial. It is hoped that this chapter will aid in simplifying the controversy of how to handle multi-dimensional tradeoffs in policy analysis and program evaluation.

Notes and References

1. On relations between evaluation research and microcomputers, see the symposium on that subject in the June 1986 issue of the *Evaluation Review*. Also see S. Nagel, "Microcomputers and Public Policy Analysis", *Public Productivity Review*, 9: 130–42 (1985). On the methodological problems perspective to evaluation, see S. Nagel, "Problems in Doing Systematic Problem Analysis," in S. Nagel, *Public Policy Analysis and Management* (Greenwich, Conn.: JAI Press, 1988).

2. On multi-criteria decision-making methods and software in general, see Milan Zeleny, *Multi-Criteria Decision-Making* (New York: McGraw-Hill, 1982). On Policy/Goal percentaging, see S. Nagel, "P/G% Analysis: An Evaluation Aiding Program", *Evaluation Review*, 9: 209–14 (1985) and S. Nagel, *Evaluation Analysis with Microcomputers* (Greenwich, Conn.: JAI Press, 1988).

3. On dealing with the problem of multiple dimensions on multiple goals, see A. Easton *Complex Managerial Decisions Involving Multiple Objectives* (New York: Wiley, 1973) and S. Nagel, "Nonmonetary Variables in Benefit–Cost Evaluation", *Evaluation Review*, 7: 37–64 (1983); S. Nagel, "Part/Whole Percentaging as a Useful Method in Policy/Program Evaluation", *Evaluation and Program Evaluation*, 8: 63–8 (1985); and S. Nagel, "Economic Transformations of Nonmonetary Benefits in Program Evaluation", *New Directions for Program Evaluation*, 26: 63–8 (1985).

4. On dealing with missing information through sensitivity analysis, see M. Thompson, *Decision Analysis for Program Evaluation* (Cambridge, MA: Ballinger, 1982); S. Nagel, "Dealing with Unknown Variables in Policy/Program Evaluation," *Evaluation and Program Planning*, 6: 107–20 (1983); and "New Varieties of Sensitivity Analysis," *Evaluation Review*, 9: 772–9 (1986).

5. On dealing with multiple alternatives of allocation analysis, see C. McMillan, *Mathematical Programming: An Introduction to the Design and Application of Optimal Decision Machines* (New York: Wiley, 1970) and S. Nagel, "Optimally Allocating Federal Money to Cities", *Public Budgeting and Finance*, 5: 39–50 (1985).

6. For further details concerning the methodological problems briefly referred to in this article and the relevance of microcomputers to overcoming them, see Nagel, *Evaluation Analysis with Microcomputers*.

7. See Thomas Saaty, *The Analytic Hierarchy Process: Planning, Priority Setting, Resource Allocation* (New York: McGraw-Hill, 1980).

8. See Ward Edwards and Robert Newman, *Multi-Attribute Evaluation* (Beverly Hills, Calif.: Sage, 1982).

9. See X. T. Bui, *Evaluation Planning with Basic* (Berkeley, CA: Sybex, 1981).

Part II
Skills the Software Enhances

2 Choosing Among Alternatives

The purpose of this chapter is to show how spreadsheets can be used systematically to process a set of goals to be achieved, alternatives for achieving them, and relations between goals and alternatives in order to choose or explain the best alternative, combination, allocation, or predictive decision-rule.

In the context of spreadsheet analysis, the goals are on the columns, alternatives are on the rows, relations are in the cells, overall scores for each alternative are in a column at the far right, and a capability exists for determining what it would take to bring a second-place or other-place alternative up to first place.

Spreadsheets are especially capable of being developed through appropriate macros for dealing with the key analytic problems in systematic decision making. Those problems include:

1. **Multiple dimensions on multiple goals**, such as trying to obtain overall scores for alternatives when the goals are measured in dollars, miles, hours, tons, 1–5 scales, and other measurement units.
2. **Multiple missing information**, such as trying to decide between two or more alternatives where one does not know the benefits, the costs, or the probabilities of success for some of the input items.
3. **Multiple alternatives that are too many to determine the effects of each one**, such as an allocation problem which allows for over a million ways of allocating $1,000 to ten different budget categories.
4. **Multiple and possibly conflicting constraints**, such as when one must have a minimum amount of food, shelter, and recreation expense per month, but the sum of the minimums adds to more than one's total income.
5. **The need for simplicity in** drawing and presenting conclusions in spite of all that multiplicity.

This chapter will illustrate spreadsheets applied to choosing among alternatives in three situations. One is a generic example with no

Table 2.1   The raw data for a generic example

	Apps Disk Create Edit Locate Frames Words Numbers Graph Print 7:24 pm			

[BEST-CHOICE] (Library)
[GENERIC EXAMPLE]

	A	B	C	D	E
1		INITIAL DATA			
2		*ALTERNATIVE/CRITERIA			
3				CRITERION #1	CRITERION #2
4				GOAL A	GOAL B
5		Measurement		FRANCS	0–10 SCALE
6		Weights		−1	2
7					
8	Y	Alternative #1	CHOICE 1	120.00	6.00
9	X	Alternative #2	CHOICE 2	30.00	2.00
10					
11					
12					

BEST-CHOICE
BEST-CHOICE   Doc: 1/1   CAPS

---

specific subject matter, but useful for seeing the big picture. The second involves deciding whether or not to get married in light of the criteria of companionship and privacy. The third example involves a litigation dispute in which each side is trying to decide whether to go to trial or accept a settlement offer, and a third party mediator is trying to get both sides to agree to a mutually beneficial settlement.

A GENERIC EXAMPLE

The Raw Data

Table 2.1 shows what a spreadsheet looks like when it is being used to choose among alternatives by way of the Best Choice software. In this simple example there are two alternatives to choose among. They are labelled *Choice 1* and *Choice 2*. There are two criteria for deciding among the choices, although there could be a lot more than two choices or criteria. The criteria are labeled *Goal A* and *Goal B*.

Goal A in this example happens to be measured in francs, but it could be measured in hours, miles, dollars, or whatever seems appropriate to the subject matter. Goal B is measured on a 0–10 scale. Goal A is given a negative weight because it is like a golf score or a cost where having a low score is desirable. Goal B is given a positive weight because it is like a benefit or a basketball score where having a high score is desirable. It is given a weight of 2 to show that it is approximately twice as important as Goal A.

Choice 1 receives a score of 120 franc units on Goal A, whereas Choice 2 receives a score of only 30 franc units in our hypothetical data. On Goal B, Choice 1 receives a score of 6, and Choice 2 receives a score of 2. The sources of alternatives, goals, and relation scores include consulting authority, past experience, reasoning by analogy, experimental guesses, or other sources. All weights and relation scores are subject to possible changes as part of the what–if analysis which helps determine the effects of different weights and scores. The *Y* or Yes next to the alternatives and the criteria show the alternatives and criteria that are being actively considered.

Intermediate Analysis and Tentative Conclusion

Table 2.2 shows the raw data converted into part/whole percentages in order to be able to determine an overall score for each alternative in spite of the fact that each goal is measured so differently. The part/whole percentages for the first column are calculated by adding 120 francs to 30 francs to obtain the whole, which is 150 francs. Each part is then divided by the whole, meaning 120 divided by 150, which equals 80%, and 30 divided by 150, which equals 20%. Likewise, the percentages for the second column are calculated by adding 6 and 2 to obtain 8 as a whole. The part/whole percentages are then 6 divided by 8 or 75%, and 2 divided by 8 or 25%. We are in effect saying that within the whole of Goal B, Choice 1 is worth 75% of the whole, and Choice 2 is worth 25%.

Table 2.3 shows the part/whole percentages converted into weighted part/whole percentages. That simply involves multiplying column 1 of Table 2.2 by −1 to yield −80% and −20%. It also involves multiplying column 2 of Table 2.2A by the weight of 2 which yields 150% and 50%. We are in effect saying that the percentages shown for Goal A should be subtracted because Goal A is a cost or a negative goal. We are likewise saying that the percentages for Goal B should be doubled because it was previously decided that Goal B is twice as important as Goal A.

Table 2.4 shows the sums of the weighted part/whole percentages for each alternative. For alternative 1, that means adding −80% to

Table 2.2   Converting the raw data into part/whole percentages

	GOAL A FRANCS −1	GOAL B 0–10 SCALE 2
CHOICE 1	80.00%	75.00%
CHOICE 2	20.00%	25.00%
	100.00%	100.00%

Table 2.3   Weighting the part/whole percentages

	GOAL A FRANCS −1	GOAL B 0–10 SCALE 2
CHOICE 1	−80.00%	150.00%
CHOICE 2	−20.00%	50.00%
	−100.00%	200.00%

Table 2.4   Summing across each alternative

	SUMS
CHOICE 1	70.00%
CHOICE 2	30.00%
	100.00%

150% and obtaining 70%. For Alternative 2, that means adding −20% to 50% and obtaining 30%. Those sums indicate that Alternative 1 is more desirable than Alternative 2 given that:

1. Alternative 1 scores 120 on Goal A, and Alternative 2 scores 30.
2. Alternative 1 scores 6 on Goal B, and Alternative 2 scores 2.
3. Goal A is a negative goal, and Goal B is a positive goal.
4. Goal B is twice as important as Goal A.

One could also very roughly interpret the 70% and 30% as meaning that if this were an allocation problem instead of a problem of choosing which alternative is best, then one should allocate 70% of

Table 2.5 The tie-causing values for each weight and relation score

	GOAL A FRANCS −1.667	GOAL B 0–10 SCALE 1.200
CHOICE 1	ERR	3.71
CHOICE 2	0.00	3.23

the scarce resources to Alternative 1 and 30% to Alternative 2. That is only a rough interpretation, however, since there is a separate option specifically designed to calculate allocation percentages. It deals with negative goals, negative scores, and other aspects of the raw data in a way that is especially designed to do meaningful allocations.

What–if Analysis

Table 2.5 shows what it would take to bring a second-place or other-place alternative up to first place. This is sometimes referred to as **what–if** analysis, because it shows what would happen to the tentative conclusion if there were changes in the weights, relation scores, criteria, alternatives, measurement units, or other inputs. It is also referred to as **sensitivity analysis**, because it shows how sensitive (or not so sensitive) the tentative conclusion is to changes in those inputs. Each cell and weight in Table 2.5 is a **tie-causing or breakeven** value. Another name for this kind of analysis is **threshold analysis** because each of those tie-causing values is at a threshold above which one alternative wins and below which another alternative wins.

Reading from left to right and from the bottom row up, the tie-causing values can be interpreted as follows:

1. The zero in the lower righthand corner says that if Choice 2 were to drop from 30 to zero, then there would be a tie in the two sums of Table 2.4. That may be an impossible change, although it may be partly possible.
2. The lower righthand corner shows that if Alternative 2 could rise from 2.00 to 3.23 on Goal B, then there would be a tie between the two alternatives. Thus, if Alternative 2 could rise slightly higher than 3.23, then Alternative 2 would move from being in second place to being in first place.

3. The *ERR* for error shows that there is no score which Choice 1 could have on Goal A that would be high enough to move the second-place alternative into first place, given that Goal B is twice as important as Goal A, and given how well Choice 1 does on Goal B.

4. The *3.71* shows that if Choice 1 were to drop from 6.00 to 3.71, then Choice 1 would be tied with Choice 2. If Choice 1 were to drop slightly more than that amount, then it would move into second place.

5. The *−1.667* is the tie-causing or threshold weight of Goal A. It means that if the importance of Goal A could increase from −1.000 to −1.667, then there would then be a tie since Alternative 2 does better on Goal A.

6. The *1.200* in the upper righthand corner shows that if the relative weight of Goal B were to drop from 2 to 1.2, then there would be a tie. One could test the accuracy of that tie-causing value by inserting the 1.2 of Table 2.5 in place of the 2 in Table 2.1, and ask for or calculate a new set of summation scores. The new set would be 50% for Alternative 1 and 50% for Alternative 2.

The threshold analysis of Table 2.5 is especially useful for resolving disputes over the subjectivity of weights or relation scores and over missing information. For example, suppose one person were arguing that Goal B deserves a weight of 2, and another person were arguing for a weight of 3. There would be no need for them to argue further since a weight of either 2 or 3 is above the 1.2 tie-causing value. That means with either weight, Alternative 1 would still be the winner. The threshold analysis can also be helpful in planning strategies for how to make a second-place alternative into first place.

CHOOSING BETWEEN STAYING SINGLE AND GETTING MARRIED

Drawing a Tentative Conclusion

Table 2.6 applies the methodology to a simple personal example. The example is simple in that (1) there are only two alternatives and two goals, (2) both goals are measured on the same 0–10 scale, (3) both goals are tentatively given equal weight, (4) there is no missing information on the relations, and (5) there are no constraints. The

Table 2.6   Deciding whether to get married

Apps Disk Create Edit Locate Frames Words Numbers Graph Print 7:45 pm							
[BEST-CHOICE]							(Library)
[DECIDING WHETHER TO GET MARRIED]							
	D	E	F	G	H	I	J
3			CRITERION #1	CRITERION #2			
4			Companionship	Privacy			
5			0–10 SCALE	0–10 SCALE	Sum of		
6			1	1	Raw Scores		
7							
8	Get Married		7	3	10		
9							
10			(9)	(5)			
11							
12	Stay Single		4	8	12		
13							
14			(2)	(6)			
15							
16	Weights		1	1			
17							
18			(1.67)	(.60)			BEST-CHOICE
					BEST-CHOICE	Doc:	1/1

Notes:

1. The numbers not in parentheses are raw scores on a 0–10 scale for companionship and a 0–10 scale for privacy.
2. The initial weights are 1.00 for both goals.
3. The numbers in parentheses are the threshold values which will cause getting married to be of equal satisfaction with staying single. They each involve adding or subtracting 2 from the raw scores since 2 is the threshold difference when summing the raw scores for both alternatives.
4. Since it may be difficult to improve on the companionship and privacy of getting married by 2 points, and it may be difficult to recalculate companionship and privacy on staying single by 2 points, the program reduces to whether the weight of companionship is more than the weight of privacy or is only as much.
5. "Getting married" in this context could refer to a specific person or just to the abstract idea.

basic alternatives are to get married or to stay single. The basic goals are companionship and privacy.

On a 0–10 scale, getting married scores a 7 on companionship, but only a 3 on privacy in the eyes of the relevant decision-maker. On the other hand, staying single scores only 4 on companionship, but an 8 on privacy. If one gives equal weight to companionship and privacy, then the sum of 7 plus 3 on getting married adds to 10. The sum of 4 plus 8 on staying single adds to 12. Thus, staying single outscores getting married in the initial results by 2 points.

What–if Analysis

There would be a tie if getting married could move up from a 7 to a 9 on companionship, or from a 3 to a 5 on privacy. Likewise, there would be a tie if staying single were considered to be worth only a 2 on companionship rather than a 4, or only worth a 6 on privacy rather than an 8.

The threshold analysis says that if companionship is given a weight of 1.67, then there will be a tie. It also says that if privacy is given a weight of 0.60 when companionship has a weight of 1, then there will be a tie. Thus, if companionship is only as valuable as privacy, then the decision-maker should stay single. On the other hand, if companionship is worth at least twice as much as privacy (rounding to the nearest whole number), then he or she is better off getting married in view of the goals to be achieved, the alternatives available, and the relations between the alternatives and the goals.

Implications and Consequences

Even in this simple example, one can see that the computer program can be helpful in various ways such as (1) organizing one's ideas in terms of alternatives, goals, and relations, (2) scoring the relations so as to provide consistency on each goal, (3) enabling one to see quickly the summation score for each alternative, (4) revealing the threshold value for each relation and each weight, and (5) enabling the user to make changes in the relations and weights to see how sensitive the initial conclusion is to input changes.

The above example is a true example, not a hypothetical one. When I was traveling to Switzerland in 1986, my mother met me at O'Hare Airport to wish me well. She asked what I was carrying. I told her that it was a computer which could aid in making decisions. She asked if it could help her decide whether to get remarried since she had been a widow for a while. I told her it might be helpful. We then found an outlet, and she proceeded to indicate what she considered to be the relevant criteria and the scores of the alternatives on the criteria. Staying single came out ahead in the initial analysis. The threshold analysis, however, showed that if companionship were considered as more important than privacy, then she should get married given the relative scores of getting married versus staying single on those two criteria. She did get married to the person she had in mind about a year later, and they have been living happily ever since then.

INTERACTIVE BUSINESS DECISION-MAKING

A Litigation Example

Tables 2.7 and 2.8 illustrate what is involved in a super-optimum settlement. The plaintiff demands $700,000 as a minimum in order to settle. The defendant offers $350,000 as a maximum in order to settle. The object of a super-optimum settlement is to provide the

Table 2.7 Settle versus trial from the plaintiff's perspective

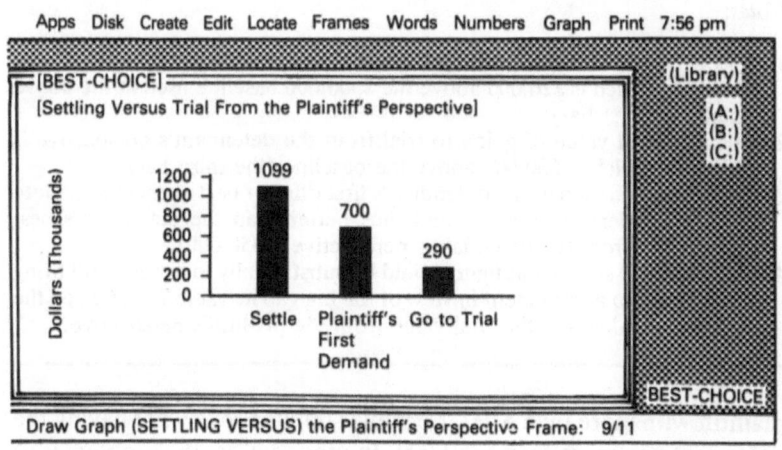

Notes:

1. The expected value of settling from the plaintiff's perspective is $1,099,000, as described in the text (the first bar).
2. The middle bar shows that the plaintiff's first demand or best expectation was $700,000.
3. The expected value of going to trial from the plaintiff's perspective is only $290,000, as described in the text (the third bar).

Table 2.8   Settle versus trial from the defendant's perspective

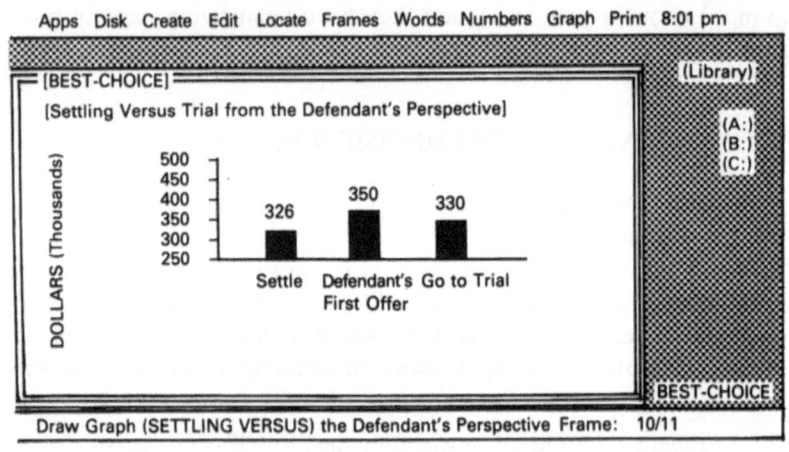

Notes:

1. The expected value of settling from the defendant's perspective is only $326,000, which is $26,000 above the $300,000 baseline used in the above graph (the first bar).
2. The expected value of going to trial from the defendant's perspective is $330,000, which is $30,000 above the baseline (the third bar).
3. The second bar shows the defendant's first offer or best expectation. Note that the settlement is lower and thus better than the defendant's best expectation from the defendant's perspective ($350,000).
4. The $326,000 settlement figure could be substantially lower and still bring the plaintiff to a settlement in view of the big gap in Table 2.7 between the settlement value and the trial value from the plaintiff's perspective.

plaintiff with more than $700,000 while simultaneously not having the defendant pay more than $350,000. In other words, the problem is to find a number that is simultaneously bigger than $700,000 and smaller than $350,000, which are roughly the best expectations of the plaintiff and defendant respectively.

Such a settlement can be arrived at by considering additional settlement criteria beyond the exchange of money. In almost every damages case, the defendant is an insurance company, a manufacturer, a transportation company, or some other kind of company that can offer something of considerable value to the plaintiff, but having relatively low cost to the defendant. In this case, it was possible for the defendant to consider offering electronic equipment, insurance claims, and insurance annuities to the plaintiffs and their insurance companies. That combination of equipment, claims, and annuities had an estimated cost value of only $325,000 to the defendants as indicated by Table 2.8. That combination however, had an estimated purchase value of $1,099,000 to the plaintiffs.

Benefits of Computer-aided Mediation

Such a solution could conceivably be developed without computer-aided mediation. The computer-aided mediation, however, greatly facilitates being able to deal with four or more criteria simultaneously from both the defendant's perspective and the plaintiff's perspective. It also facilitates making calculations concerning the expected value of going to trial. From the plaintiff's perspective, the expected value of going to trial is only $290,000 as shown in Table 2.7, which is far less than the special settlement value of $1,099,000, or the traditional settlement value of something between $350,000 and $700,000. Likewise from the defendant's perspective, the expected value of going to trial is $330,000 which could cost the defendant more than the $326,000 settlement.

The computer-aided mediation is also helpful for arriving at a predicted damages figure and a predicted probability that liability will be established. Those predictions are based on various factual elements, diverse estimates, and previous experience. The predicted damages figure in this case was $756,250. The predicted victory probability in this case was 0.37. Thus the predicted or expected damages discounted by the probability of winning was approximately $300,000, which was roughly the cash settlement value of this case. That cash settlement can be considered as a fall-back settlement if the super-optimum settlement cannot be achieved.

OTHER ASPECTS AND SOME CONCLUSIONS

Comparing the Examples

This chapter has presented three examples of how Framework spreadsheets can be used to choose among alternatives. Each example is different on dealing with the problem of multiple dimensions on multiple goals:

1. The generic example involves adding francs and 0–10 scores thereby requiring part/whole percentaging to convert those units into dimensionless numbers.
2. The getting-married example solves the multi-dimensionality problem by measuring all the goals on 1–5 scales, although one still needs to weight the goals for their relative importance.
3. The litigation example involves all the goals being measured in dollars. That eliminates the multi-dimensionality and weighting problems since a dollar increase in income is as valuable as a dollar decrease in expense.

Each example is different on dealing with the problem of missing information:

1. The key missing item in the generic example is probably the relative weight of Goal B to Goal A. That problem, however, can be resolved by just reaching agreement that Goal B is more important than Goal A.
2. The getting-marrried example involves a concrete application of the above principle such that if companionship is more important than privacy, then the decision-maker should get married but not if privacy is as important as companionship, given the relation scores.
3. The key missing information item in the litigation example is how big a settlement does the plaintiff have to receive to make settling more attractive than going to trial, or how low an offer can the defendant make in order to make settling more attractive than going to trial from the defendant's perspective?

Other points to note with the three examples are:

1. The threshold analysis facilitates being a more effective advocate because it shows what one needs to bring a second-place or other-place alternative up to first place.
2. Although allocation analysis was not discussed in detail, one can see from the generic example how part/whole percentaging can be converted into allocation percentages.
3. The generic and getting-married examples involve a single decision-maker or group. The litigation example involves two decision-makers or groups interacting with each other to determine whether each side should settle or go to trial. The litigation

example can also involve a third party seeking a solution in which each side receives something that is of substantial value to it, but gives something that is not of substantial value.

Broader Considerations

Some miscellaneous points about the software in general, as contrasted to these three specific examples, include:

1. The software seeks to capture the essence of what good decision-makers **implicitly do** when choosing among alternatives, although they may not explicitly do so.
2. The best way to weight goals is probably to determine which goal is the *least important* and give it a weight of 1. Then decide how many times more important each other goal is relative to that anchor point.
3. The software can deal with a set of alternatives arranged from **low input to high input** where doing too much or too little is undesirable. That means the summation scores will rise for each successive alternative and then drop when they reach a peak.
4. The software can deal with benefits and costs that need to be **discounted or multiplied** for the probability of their occurring. In such a situation, the weights consider both importance and probability.
5. Multiple missing information can be considered by working with weights and relations scores at both their **best and worst values**.
6. The software **stimulates creativity** in developing alternatives, criteria, and ways of measuring the criteria.
7. The software can be used for **making** decisions, **predicting** decisions, **influencing** decisions, or **teaching** decision-making, among other uses.

Numerous other examples could be given since the idea of choosing among alternatives occurs in all fields of knowledge. For example:

1. In the realm of **physics**, one could talk about choosing among alternative energy sources such as nuclear, oil, coal, synthetic fuels, and solar energy.
2. In the realm of **business**, one could analyze alternative investments, the quantity to produce, or the price to charge.

3. In **social work**, one could decide whether to take away or leave an allegedly abused child with its family.
4. In **the arts**, one could make comparisons among authors, composers, or painters.
5. In **public policy**, one could discuss whether a public function is best handled by private enterprise, government subsidies, regulation, or government ownership.
6. Besides getting married, applicable **personal problems** could include big purchases, job decisions, vacations, education decisions, and health matters.
7. One can also easily develop applications in medicine, engineering, law enforcement, agriculture, teaching, labor, and other human activities.

Notes and References

1. For further information on decision-aiding software in general, see Benjamin Radcliff, "Multi-Criteria Decision Making: A Survey of Software", *Social Science Microcomputer Review* (Spring 1986) and Charles Spezzano, "Decision Support Software", *Popular Computing* (October 1985). For further information on the Best Choice decision-aiding program described in this article, see S. Nagel, "A Microcomputer Program for Evaluation Analysis", *Evaluation and Program Planning* (1987): 159–68. The Best Choice software can be obtained by writing to S. Nagel at 361 Lincoln Hall, University of Illinois, Urbana, Illinois 61801 or calling 217–359–8541. There is no charge to buyers of this present book on *Decision-Aiding Software*.

3 Allocating Scarce Resources

The purpose of this chapter is to describe a method of allocating scarce resources across budget categories in a way that is both rational and feasible. It is rational because it allocates in proportion to proxies for elasticity coefficients in accordance with classical calculus optimization. It is, however, feasible in the sense that the proxies are of such a nature that they are easily obtained and can be easily worked with.

This chapter is partly inspired by the kind of concern expressed by V. O. Key, Jr in his article on "The Lack of a Budgetary Theory". In that article he defines public budgeting as "the allocation of expenditures among different purposes so as to achieve the greatest return". He laments the fact that in dealing with budgeting, public administration has emphasized the preparation of forms for requesting funds, rather than the more important question of "On what basis shall it be decided to allocate x dollars to activity A instead of activity B?"[1]

The illustrative example involves two budget categories. One is money for the police, and the other is money for the courts. There are two allocation criteria. One is crime reduction, and the other is fair procedure. The scoring of the alternatives on the criteria is relative scoring, which means noting the budget category that does better and roughly how much better. Those basic concepts as to the budget categories and the allocation criteria are shown in Table 3.1A.

Before proceeding with the illustrative example, one might note the following general points:

1. This presentation is designed to emphasize the budgeting methodology, not any particular software. The methodology is facilitated by using spreadsheet analysis for multi-criteria decision making, but any brand of spreadsheet-related software can be used.[2]
2. The example is broadly applicable with generic budgeting characteristics. It is not meant to be a factual case study of any specific government agency or activity.[3]
3. The methodology is simple in the sense of being easy to understand and apply. It is not, however, simplistic in the sense of

Table 3.1   Using P/G% to allocate resources to budget categories

---

1A. THE ALTERNATIVE BUDGET CATEGORIES AND THE ALLOCATION CRITERIA

Alternative	Criterion	Meas. Unit	Weight
1 POLICE	1 CRIME REDUCTION	RELATIVE X	1.00
2 COURTS	2 FAIR PROCEDURE	RELATIVE X	2.00

1B. THE RELATIVE SCORING OF THE ALTERNATIVES ON THE CRITERIA

	ALTERNATIVE / CRITERIA SCORING	
	CRIME RE	FAIR PRO
POLICE	2.00	1.00
COURTS	1.00	3.00

1C. ALLOCATION PERCENTAGES IN LIGHT OF EACH CRITERION

	PART / WHOLE %	
	CRIME RE	FAIR PRO
POLICE	66.67	25.00
COURTS	33.33	75.00

1D. WEIGHTED ALLOCATION PERCENTAGES
(With One Criterion Considered Twice as Important)

	WEIGHTED PART / WHOLE %	
	CRIME RE	FAIR PRO
POLICE	66.67	50.00
COURTS	33.33	150.00

1E. AVERAGING THE WEIGHTED ALLOCATION PERCENTAGES

Alternative	Combined W P/W	%
1 POLICE	116.67	38.89
2 COURTS	183.33	61.11

1F. APPLYING THE AVERAGE ALLOCATION PERCENTAGES TO THE TOTAL RESOURCES

Total Resources = 500.00

Alternative	Alloc.
1 POLICE	194.44
2 COURTS	305.56

---

oversimplifying by leaving out important considerations. Although simple, the methodology is based on classical calculus optimization and mathematical programming.[4]

4. The presentation emphasizes allocation on the basis of goals to be achieved, budget categories available for achieving them, and rough relations between goals and budget categories in order to

arrive at a tentative set of allocation percentages which can then be subject to various forms of what–if analysis.[5]

5. The ideas are innovative, but they are being increasingly adopted in the literature of evaluation research, social science micro-computing, legal decision-making, and related fields.[6]

SCORING THE ALTERNATIVES

To score the alternatives on **crime reduction**, one asks which budget category is **less effective on crime reduction**. Nearly everyone would say the courts are less effective than the police in reducing crime.

1. The courts, however, do reduce crime by sentencing convicted criminals. That does have some deterrence effect on the general public, although it may not have much deterrent effect on the specific defendant.
2. Proof that the police are somewhat effective in reducing crime are studies that show highway speeding is reduced by the presence of more visible police cars. The Kansas experiment which found virtually no change in the crime rate of a neighborhood in which the police were temporarily removed is not inconsistent since would-be criminals were not notified that the police were being removed.
3. After giving the less effective category a score of 1, one asks how much more effective is the next category. People might disagree as to how much more effective a 10% increase in police expenditures might be relative to a 10% increase in court expenditures, but perhaps they might generally say twice as effective. Therefore, give the police a score of 2 on crime reduction.

To score the alternatives on **fair procedure** one asks which budget category is **less effective**. Nearly everyone would say the police are less effective than the courts in separating out the innocent from the guilty which is the essence of fair procedure.

1. The police, however, do some separation of the innocent from the guilty when they decide who should be given warnings and who should be arrested.
2. Proof that the courts are somewhat effective in separating the innocent from the guilty is the fact that there are so few cases of

convicted people who are subsequently found to have been innocent. There are many cases of people who have not been found
guilty who subsequently do commit crimes, although that does not
necessarily indicate that they were previously guilty. The concept
of fair procedure, however, places more weight on freeing the
innocent than on convicting the guilty anyhow.
3. After giving the less effective category a score of 1, one asks how
   much more effective would a 10% expenditure increase be for the
   courts in comparison to a 10% expenditure increase for the police.
   Most people would probably say that there is a bigger gap regarding the effectiveness of the courts on fair procedure than there is
   regarding the effectiveness of the police on crime reduction. The
   courts are supposed to be a more substantial part of the crime
   reduction system than the police are in the guilt determination
   system. Therefore we tentatively give the courts a score of 3 on
   fair procedure.

   In technical terms, the 2–1 on crime reduction, and the 1–3 on fair
procedure are substitutes or proxies for non-linear elasticity coefficients or regression equation exponents. The relative scores of
police and courts on crime reduction and fair procedure are shown in
Table 3.1B. Also, technically speaking, one should not talk in terms
of how much more effective the police are than the courts on crime
reduction – rather, one should talk in terms of how much more
effective an extra dollar or $100 to the police would be in reducing
crime than an extra dollar or $100 to the courts would be. Likewise, it
is the general effect of incremental dollars to the police and courts on
fair procedure that we are interested in, not incremental quantities of
police or judges. These relative scores can be obtained by averaging
the general opinions of knowledgeable insiders, subject to the kind of
sensitivity analysis that will be discussed later.

WEIGHTING THE GOALS

The criteria of crime reduction and fair procedure need to be
weighted in terms of their relative importance. To do the weighting,
one asks between those two criteria which criterion is less important
to the purposes for which the money is being allocated. More people
associated with the legal system would say crime reduction is less
important than fair procedure. They would thereby implicitly agree

with William Blackstone in direction, although not necessarily in magnitude, that it is ten times better to acquit the innocent than it is to convict the guilty, or it is ten times worse to convict the innocent than it is to acquit the guilty.

After giving the less important criterion a weight of 1, one asks how much more important or desired is the next criterion. Ten to one would be too high in this context since were are not talking about convicting or acquitting a specific defendant, but rather about crime reduction and fair procedure which are only analogous concepts. For the sake of simplicity and illustrative purposes, we can tentatively say fair procedure is about twice as important as crime reduction to whoever has the responsibility for allocating the $500 budget that needs to be allocated. The far right of Table 3.1A shows those relative weights.

DOING THE ALLOCATING WITH SEPARATE ALLOCATION PERCENTAGES

Table 3.1C shows that if the $500 were to be allocated to the police and the courts on the basis of only crime reduction, and the police do twice as well on that criterion as the courts do, then it would be logical to allocate ⅔ or 67% of the budget to the police and ⅓ or 33% to the courts. The reason one does not allocate all of the budget to the police is because of the occurence of diminishing returns, whereby additional funds allocated to a budget category produce increased returns but at a diminishing rate. That means that each additional dollar allocated to the police may produce an additional crime reduction, but each reduction gets smaller as the easy crime gets reduced and the crime that is more difficult to deal with remains. The first dollar allocated to the courts will not produce as much reduction as the first dollar allocated to the police. The 499th dollar, however, will do more good if allocated as the first dollar to the courts than as the 499th dollar to the police.

If one does not allocate all to the police in crime reduction, then how much does one allocate? One can prove by classical calculus optimization that the budget will produce a maximum crime reduction if it is allocated to the police and the courts in proportion to those relative scores or proxies for elasticity coefficients.

Table 3.1C also shows that if the $500 were to be allocated to the police and the courts on the basis of only fair procedure, and the courts do three times as well on that criterion as the police do, then it would be logical to allocate ¼ or 25% of the budget to the police and ¾ or 75% to the courts. This is true for the same reasons that we would not allocate all of the $500 to the police if we were considering only crime reduction. For effectiveness, efficiency, and equity, we would generally allocate only a proportionate allocation. This assumes for the moment that there are no political, legal, or other constraints that require certain minimum or maximum allocations to the police or to the courts. If there were, then adjustments would have to be made for those considerations after first allocating optimally without considering the constraints.

DOING THE ALLOCATING WITH WEIGHTED ALLOCATION PERCENTAGES

Table 3.1D is the same as Table 3.1C except the allocation percentages associated with fair procedure have been doubled to take into consideration that fair procedure is tentatively considered twice as important as crime reduction. Thus, the 25% and 75% allocation percentages to the police and courts under fair procedure become 50% and 150%.

Table 3.1E adds the allocation percentages across the row that pertains to the police budget category, meaning 67% plus 50% equals 117%. Table 3.1E also adds the allocation percentages across the row that pertains to the courts budget category, meaning 33% plus 150% equals 183%. Those are the **combined or aggregate allocation percentages**. They cannot be used directly for allocation percentages since one cannot allocate more than 100%. They need to be divided by the sum of the weights which is 1 plus 2, or 3. If we divide 117% by 3, we get 39%. If we divide 183% by 3, we get 61%. Those two percentages represent the weighted average of the allocation percentages. That means they average the separate allocation percentages from Table 3.1C, taking into consideration the relative importance of each set of percentages.

Table 3.1F applies the 39% and the 61% to the $500 in total resources to be allocated. Doing so means multiplying $500 by 0.388 and 0.611. The results are $194 to the police and $306 to the courts. That assumes that only crime reduction and fair procedure are the allocation criteria, with weights and relative scores like those shown in Tables 3.1A and 3.1B. If we add another goal like providing employment, doing so would probably increase the allocation to the police compared to the courts. If we had a constraint that said neither the police nor the courts could receive less than 70% of what they received last year nor more than 150%, then the police probably would receive a larger portion of the $500.

POST-OPTIMIZING ANALYSIS IN SYSTEMATIC ALLOCATION

Table 3.2 shows some forms of analysis that can occur after one has arrived at the initial allocations shown in Table 3.1F. Table 3.2A compares the past allocation amounts for police and courts of $300 and $100 with the recommended amounts of $194 and $306. One would expect the recommended amounts to be about 125% higher than the past amounts since the past total resources were only $400, and the present total resources are $500. The differences or residuals between the actual and the recommended are, however, too big to be explained by an increase in the total resources. If that were the only explanation then the police would receive $375 and the courts would receive $125.

Explanations for why the police may be over-allocated and the courts may be under-allocated are:

1. People doing the allocating may consider crime reduction to be as important, or maybe even more important, than fair procedure.
2. People doing the allocating may perceive that fair procedure can be bought more cheaply than it can be. They may thus provide only a small allocation to the public defender's office within the courts, thinking that the public defender can adequately represent all potentially innocent defendants on such a small budget.
3. There may be other goals operating in the minds of the decision-makers that we have not included such as the employment goal mentioned, whereby the police are viewed in some cities as providing important employment opportunities but not so much the courts.

Table 3.2B shows what it would take to bring the police allocation up to the level of the court allocation if the two allocation criteria had equal weights. The table shows the threshold value for each relation score and each weight. At that value, there would be a tied allocation

Table 3.2   Post-optimizing analysis in P/G% allocation

2A. COMPARING THE PAST ALLOCATION AMOUNTS WITH THE RECOMMENDED AMOUNTS
Total Resources = 500.00

Alternative	Actual	Alloc.	Resid
1 POLICE	300.00	194.44	105.56
2 COURTS	100.00	305.56	−205.56

2B. BRINGING THE POLICE ALLOCATION UP TO THE COURT ALLOCATION (With the Criteria Having Equal Weight)
THRESHOLD ANALYSIS

	POLICE	COURTS	Weight
CRIME REDUCTION	3.00	0.67	1.500
FAIR PROCEDURE	1.50	2.00	0.667

2C. BRINGING THE POLICE ALLOCATION UP TO THE COURT ALLOCATION (With Fair Procedure Having Twice the Weight of Crime Reduction)
THRESHOLD ANALYSIS

	POLICE	COURTS	Weight
CRIME REDUCTION	??	0.00	3.000
FAIR PROCEDURE	2.14	1.40	0.667

2D. THE WEIGHT AT WHICH EACH CRITERION REACHES A MAXIMUM INFLUENCE
CONVERGENCE ANALYSIS

	Weight	
CRIME REDUCTION	8.00	
FAIR PROCEDURE	8.00	Stopping difference set at 5.0 percentage points

---

of 50% apiece between the two budget categories. That means that the six threshold figures are as follows:

1. If the police were to score 3 to 1 on crime reduction, rather than 2 to 1.
2. If the courts were to score 0.67 to 2 on crime reduction, rather than 1 to 2.
3. If the police were to score 1.5 to 3 on fair procedure, rather than 1 to 3.
4. If the courts were to score 2 to 1 on fair procedure, rather than 3 to 1.
5. If the weight of crime reduction to fair procedure were to go up to 1.5 to 1, instead of 1 to 1.

6. If the weight of fair procedure to crime reduction were to go down to 0.67 to 1, instead of 1 to 1.

One can substitute any of those changes in Table 3.1A or 3.1B and then apply the procedures of Table 3.1C through 3.1F. The result will be $250 to the police, and $250 to the courts.

Table 3.2C shows the threshold values under the more realistic situation of having some criteria more important than others. That situation makes the threshold values less obvious than when the criteria have equal weight. Nevertheless, all the threshold values are still tie-causing values. For example, if the courts were to score zero on crime reduction, then the police would get 100% of the budget on the crime-reduction criterion. Adding 100% to 50% instead of 67% to 50% in Table 3.1B would now give a combined score of 150%. That would exactly equal adding 0% to 150% on the courts row. The pair of question marks shows that no matter how high the police score is on crime reduction, there will not be an equal allocation if the courts give three times the effectiveness on fair procedure, and if fair procedure is twice as important as crime reduction.

If one were to allocate only on the basis of crime reduction, then the allocation percentages would be 67% and 33% as is shown in Table 3.1C. That is the equivalent of giving crime reduction a weight of infinity so that it totally overwhelms fair procedure. Table 3.2D shows that with a weight of only 8 for crime reduction, the allocation percentages will be within five percentage points of 67% and 33%. With a weight higher than 8 for crime reduction there is very little incremental gain toward the maximum figures of 67% and 33% in view of diminishing returns. Likewise, with a weight of only 8 for fair procedure, the allocation percentages will be within 5 percentage points of the 25% and 75% shown in Table 3.1C. Thus there is no need to argue whether fair procedure should receive a weight of 8 to 1 or 10 to 1 compared to crime reduction, since anything above 8 to 1 produces approximately the same allocation and is roughly the equivalent of a weight of infinity.

SOME CONCLUSIONS

From this analysis, one can conclude that one can rationally and feasibly allocate to budget categories by answering the following series of questions:

1. What are the **budget categories** to which we want to allocate, and what are the **goals** that we are seeking to achieve?
2. On the first goal, which budget category has the **lowest marginal rate of return for an extra dollar or monetary unit**? Give it a score of 1 on the first goal.
3. On the first goal, how do the other budget categories **compare with that lowest MRR budget category**? Is the second budget category twice as effective in putting one monetary unit to use in achieving the goal or three times as effective? If three times as effective, give it a score of 3, and do likewise with the other budget categories.
4. Do likewise with the second goal, and **however many goals there are**.
5. Looking across the goals rather than down the budget categories on a single goal, answer the question as to which goal is the **least important** to whoever the decision-makers are. Give that goal as a weight of 1.
6. How do the other goals **compare with that base goal**? If another goal is four times as important, give it a score of 4. An alternative approach would be to give all the goals a weight of 1, and then have the computer program indicate for each goal what its convergence weight or critical weight is. Above that weight, little is to be gained in view of diminishing returns.
7. **Convert the raw scores on the first goal into part/whole percentages.** Allocate in proportion to those part/whole percentages, or simply use those part/whole percentages as allocation percentages. Do likewise with the second goal, and so on through all the goals.
8. Give each budget category a **weighted average allocation** by averaging across the separate allocations taking the weights of the goals into consideration.

There are variations and other aspects of these basic procedures such as variations to take into consideration (1) missing information, (2) minimums or maximums on the budget categories, (3) minimums or maximums on the goals, (4) conflicting constraints such as minimums that add up to more than the total budget, and (5) situations where one is seeking to minimize costs while meeting a minimum satisfaction level, as contrasted to seeking to maximize benefits while meeting a maximum budget constraint.

One might also note that the development of a rational and feasible system for budget allocation is in conformity with the ideas of

V. O. Key concerning the need for a budgetary theory, as expressed in his 1940 article[7] in the following ways:

1. He admired the work of economists in developing allocation theory, which he considered highly rational for allocating in accordance with marginal rates of return or elasticity coefficients as is done here.

2. He felt the work of economists was not sufficient for public budgeting because their examples tended to be almost exclusively from the private sector, where everything is measured in dollars and where information on cause and effect relations is more readily available. The proposed method is especially applicable to the public sector where the goals are non-monetary (like crime reduction and fair procedure), and where precise information is not so available.

3. V. O. Key was a pioneer in the application of quantitative analysis in political science. His book, *A Primer of Statistics for Political Scientists* was probably the first book written on statistical analysis for political scientists.[8]

4. V. O. Key was also a pioneer in the application of political science to important policy problems, such as public policy toward electoral reform as manifested in his classic book on *Politics, Parties, and Pressure Groups*.[9]

5. V. O. Key was thus an unusual political scientist who bridged mainstream political science on voting behavior and mainstream public administration on budgeting. He also bridged both quantitative behavioralism and a strong reform orientation in the tradition of Charles Merriam, Harold Lasswell, and the Chicago Political Science Department.

It is hoped that this short chapter will make it clear that it is possible to be rational and feasible simultaneously in allocating a budget or other scarce resources. Normally to achieve rationality, one has to sacrifice feasibility or simplicity, and vice versa. That does not have to be so. With the above procedures and their variations, one can develop and apply a theory of rational and feasible budget allocation in the spirit of V. O. Key's call for a budgetary theory.[10]

Notes and References

1. V. O. Key, Jr., "The Lack of a Budgetary Theory," *American Political Science Review*, 34: 1137–44 (1940).
2. On multi-criteria decision-making, see Ching-Lai Hwang and Kwangsun Yoon, *Multiple Attribute Decision Making: Methods and Applications* (Frankfort: Springer-Verlag, 1981); and Milan Zeleny, *Multi-Criteria Decision Making* (New York: McGraw-Hill, 1982). On spreadsheet analysis applied to decision making, see Owen Carroll, *Decision Power with Supersheets* (Homewood, Ill.: Dow Jones-Irwin, 1986); and Jack Holt, *Cases and Applications in Lotus 1–2–3* (Homewood, Ill.: Irwin, 1988).
3. On general aspects of budgeting, especially the effective and efficient allocating of scarce resources, see Lee Friedman, *Microeconomic Policy Analysis* (New York: McGraw-Hill, 1984); and Irene Rubin (ed.), *New Directions in Budget Theory* (Albany: State University of New York Press, 1988). For more specific examples in the field of public administration, see S. Nagel, (ed.), *Public Administration and Decision-Aiding Software* (Westport, Conn.: Greenwood Press, 1989).
4. For further details on the P/G% Decision-Aiding Software which is partly an MCDM spreadsheet-based budget allocation system, see S. Nagel, *Evaluation Analysis with Microcomputers* (Greenwich, Conn.: JAl Press, 1988). For other related decision-aiding packages, see S. Nagel (ed.), *Decision Analysis and Decision-Aiding Software* (New York: Wiley, 1989).
5. On systematic decision-making via goals, means, and relations between goals and means, see S. Nagel, *Public Policy: Goals, Means, and Methods* (New York: St. Martin's Press, 1984); and S. Nagel, *Policy Studies: Integration and Evaluation* (Westport, Conn.: Praeger, 1988). Both books emphasize the importance of what–if analysis, especially in Chapter 13 of the first book and Chapter 9 of the second one.
6. For other applications of the P/G% Decision-Aiding Software, see the forthcoming symposium issue on "Decision-Aiding Software and Public Administration" of the *International Journal of Public Administration*, and the forthcoming symposium issue on "Law, Decision-Making, and Microcomputers" of the *Legal Studies Forum*.
7. See note 1 above.
8. V. O. Key, *A Primer of Statistics for Political Scientists* (New York: Crowell, 1954).
9. V. O. Key, *Politics, Parties, and Pressure Groups* (New York: Crowell, 1953).
10. For further details concerning this approach to rational and feasible budget allocation, see Philip Kotler, *Marketing Decision Making: A Model Building Approach* (New York: Holt, 1971); S. Nagel, B. Malis, and M. Mills, "Using Percentaging Analysis for More Productive Budgeting," 44 *Public Productivity Review* 65–92 (1987); S. Nagel, "Optimally Allocating Federal Money to Cities," *Public Budgeting and Finance*, 5: 39–50 (1985); and "Finding an Optimum Mix in Allocating Scarce Resources" in S. Nagel, *Policy Evaluation: Making Optimum*

Decisions (New York: Praeger, 1982). All the procedures described in this chapter can be made even more accurate and simple by using multi-criteria decision-making software such as the P/G% or Best Choice program which is described in S. Nagel, "Evaluation Analysis with Microcomputers," *Public Productivity Review*, 42: 67–80 (1987).

4 Explaining and Predicting Behavior

The purpose of this chapter is mainly to discuss how one can determine the motives, goals, or values of past decision-makers from knowing what decisions they have reached and their likely perceptions of the relevant facts. One may also be able to deduce their perceptions from knowing their decisions and goals.

The chapter is divided into three parts. The first part deals with the decision-making of Chief Justice John Marshall in deciding the case of *Marbury* v. *Madison* (1803). That case established the principle that US courts could declare unconstitutional acts of legislatures or administrators. The second part deals with the decision-making of President Franklin Roosevelt in deciding to go ahead with the development of the atomic bomb. The Marbury case involves deducing goals from decisions on specific issues and likely perceptions. The atomic bomb case involves deducing goals and the process whereby the decision was reached, knowing that the perceptions of the benefits, probability of success, and the costs were highly unclear.

The third part of the chapter deals with general principles partly suggested by the examples in the first two parts. Those general principles lead to a conclusion that it is possible to deduce values and perceptions in past decisions. One must, however, be alert to the possibility of alternative motives and perceptions, which might also be consistent with the decisions reached and other aspects of the decision-making situation.

This chapter has important theoretical significance. It deals with the deduction of values and perceptions in past decisions, regardless of the subject matter or the source of the decisions. The analysis applies equally well to decisions that are legislative, executive, judicial, administrative, or voting. One example that is used is the judicial decision of *Marbury* v. *Madison*. Another example is the executive decision to go ahead with the Manhattan Project. The general discussion in the third part of the chapter cuts across all decisions. The chapter is thus relevant to all fields of political science, including a concern for decision-making at the international, national, regional, state, or local levels on any subject matter.

APPLYING A SPREADSHEET PERSPECTIVE
TO DEDUCING MOTIVES

One of the most useful innovations associated with the advent of microcomputers is the development of spreadsheet analysis, especially by way of Lotus 1–2–3. A spreadsheet is simply a table with columns and rows. Lotus 1–2–3 is brand-name software which enables one to easily enter data into a spreadsheet table and manipulate the data. The manipulation can produce a variety of insights, especially as to what might happen to the conclusions if some of the input data were changed.

One especially useful purpose of spreadsheet analysis is to aid in making decisions. In that regard, a spreadsheet can be used to process a set of (1) goals to be achieved on the columns, (2) available alternatives for achieving them on the rows, (3) relations between goals and alternatives in the cells, (4) overall scores for each alternative at the far right, and (5) a capability for determining what it would take to bring a second-place or other-place alternative up to first place.

A variation on that decision-making use is to work backwards from the decisions reached to the hypothesized goals of the decision-maker or decision-makers. This assumes we know the alternatives that were available. It also assumes we know how the decision-makers probably would have perceived the relations between the hypothesized goals and the alternatives if those really were their goals. Another variation on this is to work backwards from the decisions reached to the hypothesized perceived relations, rather than to the goals. People are, however, usually more interested in deducing goals or motives than deducing perceptions, especially social scientists.

For example, if we know the decision-makers have chosen Alternative 1 over Alternative 2, we might hypothesize the reason was because the decision-makers were seeking Goal A and Goal B. To test that hypothesis, we ask how the decision-makers would be likely to score Alternatives 1 and 2 on Goals A and B if those were the true goals of the decision-makers. If Alternative 1 receives high scores on both goals and Alternative 2 receives low scores on both goals, this is partial confirmation that those were the goals of the decision-makers.

This kind of testing, however, is only a partial confirmation because it is somewhat like a blood test for paternity. If the baby and the alleged father have very different blood types, then the alleged father is not likely to be the real father. If they have the same blood type, then the alleged father may or may not be the real father. Likewise, if Alternative 2 scores higher than Alternative 1 on both goals, then it is not likely that the decision-makers who chose Alternative 1 were pursuing those goals. If, however, Alternative 1 scores higher on both goals, then the decision-makers may or may not be pursuing those goals because other goals might also be consistent with the decision, just as other men might be the father when the blood types match.

This kind of testing can be greatly facilitated with modern spreadsheet software because one can easily try out lots of different goals and different perceptions to see how well alternative explanations hold up in comparison to the hypothesized goals and the assumed perceptions. The advent of "what–if" analysis in social science has been beneficial in that regard. That includes related concepts like breakeven, threshold, and critical value analysis. The reader should bear in mind the broadness of these perspectives.

DEDUCING GOALS IN *MARBURY* v. *MADISON*

Table 4.1 applies a spreadsheet or matrix perspective to analyzing the case of *Marbury* v. *Madison*. Each row represents a separate issue in the case or a sub-decision involved in arriving at the overall decision. Each column represents a likely goal of the decision-maker. The cells in the matrix show how a yes answer on each issue relates to each goal. The column at the far right shows how many overall points each yes answer would receive by summing the points per goal. The far right also shows the decision-maker's actual decisions on each issue. If the goals have been properly determined and weighted, then all the issues on which a no answer was reached should each have less total points than the issues on which a yes answer was reached. The data has been analyzed using the Policy/Goal Percentaging software. It processes goals to be achieved, policies for achieving them, and relations between goals and policies in order to arrive at a best policy, decision, or combination.

The Issues and the Goals

More specifically, the separate issues in the *Marbury* case were:

Table 4.1   Briefing by analyzing multiple issues: the *Marbury* case

A. THE ISSUES AND OUTCOMES		B. THE GOALS, SCALES, AND WEIGHTS		
Alternative	Previous Outcome	Criterion	Meas. Unit	Weight
1 DISQUALIFY ONESELF	NO	1 ATTACK JEFFERSON	1–3 SCALE	3.00
2 NO JURIS/W. MERITS	YES	2 AVOID NONCOMPLY.		2.00
3 UPHOLD/S. NOT APPLY	NO	3 JR ESTABLISH.		4.00
4 UPHOLD/CONST. ALLOW	NO	4 LEGAL CONSISTENT.		1.00
5 APPT. CONTINUITY	YES			
6 JUDICIAL SUPREMACY	YES			
7 JR JUDICIAL ONLY	NO			
8 JP IS PUB. MINISTER	NO			
9 CONG. CHANGE JURIS.	NO			
10 GRANT APPOINTMENT	NO			

C. HOW SAYING YES ON EACH ISSUE SCORES ON THE GOALS

	ATTACK J	AVOID NO	JR ESTAB	LEGAL CO
DISQUALIFY ONESELF	1.00	3.00	1.00	3.00
NO JURIS/W. MERITS	3.00	2.00	2.00	1.00
UPHOLD/S. NOT APPLY	1.00	3.00	2.00	3.00
UPHOLD/CONST. ALLOW	2.00	2.00	2.00	2.00
APPT. CONTINUITY	2.00	2.00	2.00	3.00
JUDICIAL SUPREMACY	2.00	2.00	3.00	2.00
JR JUDICIAL ONLY	2.00	2.00	2.00	2.00
JP IS PUB. MINISTER	2.00	2.00	2.00	1.00
CONG. CHANGE JURIS.	2.00	2.00	1.00	1.00
GRANT APPOINTMENT	3.00	1.00	1.00	2.00

D. TOTAL SCORES OF SAYING YES ON EACH GOAL

Alternative	Combined Rawscores	Previous Outcome
1 DISQUALIFY ONESELF	16.00	NO
2 NO JURIS/W. MERITS	22.00	YES
3 UPHOLD/S. NOT APPLY	20.00	NO
4 UPHOLD/CONST. ALLOW	20.00	NO
5 APPT. CONTINUITY	21.00	YES
6 JUDICIAL SUPREMACY	24.00	YES
7 JR JUDICIAL ONLY	20.00	NO
8 JP IS PUB. MINISTER	19.00	NO
9 CONG. CHANGE JURIS.	15.00	NO
10 GRANT APPOINTMENT	17.00	NO

1. Should John Marshall disqualify himself in view of his not delivering the commission to William Marbury while Marshall was Secretary of State, which commission Marbury is now seeking?
2. Should John Marshall find that the court has no jurisdiction to hear the case, but still discuss whether Marbury deserves the commission?

3. Should he uphold the statute which authorizes the Supreme Court to issue writs of *mandamus* in cases warranted by the law by saying that the statute does not apply in this case since hearing the case is not warranted by Article III of the Constitution?
4. Should he uphold the statute by saying that the Constitution requires the Supreme Court to grant original jurisdiction in cases involving diplomats or states as a party, but Congress can add to that list so long as Congress does not decrease the list?
5. Is an appointment to a non-political office by a previous President binding on the subsequent President?
6. Should the Supreme Court have the final word on what the Constitution means?
7. Should the Supreme Court exercise judicial review only in matters involving the judicial process?
8. Is a justice of the peace a public minister who can seek the original jurisdiction of the US Supreme Court?
9. Can Congress by ordinary statute change the jurisdiction of the Supreme Court?
10. Should Marbury be granted his appointment by the Supreme Court?

The criteria that John Marshall may have had in mind in answering yes or no to these 10 questions or issues include:

1. Attack Jefferson in view of the fact that he is the leader of the Jeffersonian party, and Marshall is one of the leaders of the Federalists, and Marbury is a federalist appointee.
2. Avoid issuing a court order that will result in non-compliance and embarrass the Supreme Court.
3. Establish the principle that the Supreme Court and other courts have the power to review the constitutionality of acts of Congress and the President.
4. Be legally consistent with prior precedents and procedures.

Those four criteria or goals are weighted 3, 2, 4, and 1 respectively to show their possible relative importance in John Marshall's hierarchy of values in this case. A good proof that those weights make sense is the fact that they are the only set of weights which will explain all the *NO* and *YES* entries in the prior outcome column of Table 4.1A.

Relating Yes Answers to the Goals and Overall Scores

Table 4.1C shows how each decision of the 10 decisions scores on each of the four criteria. The scoring is on a 1–3 scale where 3 = conducive to the criterion, 2 = neither conducive nor adverse, and 1 = adverse to the criteria. For example, disqualifying oneself would be adverse to providing John Marshall with the opportunity to attack Jefferson or to establish judicial review. It would, however, avoid non-compliance and be legally consistent with accepted judicial practice under those disqualifying circumstances.

Table 4.1D shows the total scores for each of the 10 decisions. These total scores involve adding the weighted relation scores across each decision. For example, disqualifying oneself receives a 16 which equals $(1\times3)+(3\times2)+(1\times4)+(3\times1)$. The computer quickly calculates an overall weighted relation score for each alternative decision. Any decision which receives 21 or more points is answered yes, and any decision which receives 20 or less points is answered no. That perfect consistency gives support to the idea that we have captured the essence of John Marshall's goals, his relative weights, and his perceptions of how the alternative decisions relate to the goals.[1]

DEDUCING THE REASONING IN THE MANHATTAN PROJECT DECISION

The Nature of the Problem

The concrete example is President Roosevelt's 1941 decision on whether to develop an atomic bomb. The basic alternatives were either to develop an atomic bomb or not to develop an atomic bomb. Three criteria were especially important. One was the quantity of lives that would be saved if the atomic bomb were successfully developed before the war would be over anyhow. A second criterion was the probability that an atomic bomb could be successfully developed before the end of the war. The third criterion was the cost of developing an atomic bomb as of 1941.

Information was almost totally missing on all three criteria. On the first criterion as to the quantity of lives that would be saved if the atomic bomb were successfully developed, there were conflicting opinions. One opinion was that the Japanese would fight to the last person and that there would be a tremendous loss of both American and Japanese lives in order to occupy the Japanese islands. That opinion tended to argue that an atomic bomb would make little difference in American lives saved while conquering Japan. The only way that a large number of American lives could be saved is if millions of Japanese lives were taken by way of numerous atomic bombs. On the other hand, the more optimistic opinion was that one or two atomic bombs could be so devastating that Japan might surrender without requiring an invasion of the home islands. That opinion turned out to be more accurate as of 1945, but the prevailing opinion as of 1941 was that the Japanese would be unlikely to surrender without an invasion.

On the second criterion of the probability of success, opinions also differed greatly. The prevailing opinion was probably that it would take many years to develop an atomic bomb since it was such a revolutionary concept in warfare, physics, and in human thinking. Research on atomic energy had barely begun as of 1941. That meant starting almost completely from scratch with basic research, as well as applied research. The more skeptical opinion had a double argument. First, the idea of an atomic bomb might be an impossible idea. Second, even if it were possible, there was not enough time to develop it before the war would be over anyhow. Those who argued in favor of a higher probability of success may have been partly motivated by wishful thinking and also by a feeling that something had to be done along these lines for fear that Nazi Germany might develop an atomic bomb first.

On the third criterion of cost, there may have been even less information than on the other criteria. The cost could range so high as to cripple the defense effort and the domestic economy. On the other hand, the cost could actually be low since once the research and development for something like this is completed, the production costs are not likely to be very high given the big bang one can then get from relatively few dollars. A big question on cost, though, is how many billions of dollars would it take to complete the research and development. The important point is there was virtually no reliable information on the quantity of lives likely to be saved, the probability of timely success, and the annual or total cost.

In spite of that unclear situation, the literature describing the decision-making process indicates that President Roosevelt was not the least bit paralyzed by indecision. He was not in a brain-racking quandary, and he never indicated any serious second thoughts as to the decision he reached. The literature is scant, but one can read between the lines that President Roosevelt may have used a best–worst analysis in reaching his decision.

Such an analysis involves saying that although we cannot determine the benefits, the probability of success, or the costs, we can more easily know the range of possibilities. This is true not only with the atomic bomb subject matter, but with any subject matter. It is, for example, obviously easier to say the worst probability is zero and the best probability is 1.00 than it is to say what the exact probability is.

Scoring the Alternatives on the Criteria

Applying that approach to the atomic bomb problem, Table 4.2 seeks to reconstruct what may have been in President Roosevelt's mind. On the quantity of lives saved, Table 4.2B shows that the best occurrence would be about 500,000 lives that might otherwise be lost. The worst occurence is to save only about 60,000 lives. Those figures are hypothetical since we do not have any exact records as to President Roosevelt's calculations. Whatever figures we use, however, can be helpful in illustrating how best–worst analysis operates.

In a go/no–go decision like this, the no–go alternative has no benefits and no costs. In other words, if the atomic bomb is not developed, then that alternative can result in no lives saved due to the use of the atomic bomb. This emphasizes that the lives saved in this context are American lives. The non-development of the atomic bomb would have saved some Japanese lives which were lost at Hiroshima and Nagasaki, but still more Japanese may have been lost to conventional bombing and warfare if the war had been prolonged. Likewise, if the atomic bomb is not developed, then there can be no costs incurred as part of the development. If non-development results in a net gain of nothing, then the question can be thought of as determining whether the development of the atomic bomb will produce a positive net gain with the benefits exceeding the costs, or a negative net gain with the costs exceeding the benefits.

The best probability of success is given as 0.70. The worst probability of success is given as only 0.10. In theory, the probability could go as high as 1.00, but that is obviously an unrealistic best in

Table 4.2 Best–worst analysis: deciding whether to develop the atomic bomb as of 1941

A. THE ALTERNATIVES AND THE EVALUATIVE CRITERIA

Alternative	Criterion	Meas. Unit	Weight
1 DEVELOP ATOM BOMB	1 WORST Q SAVED	1000 LIVES	0.10
2 DO NOT DEVELOP	2 BEST Q SAVED	1000 LIVES	0.70
	3 WORST $ COST	$1 BILLION	1.00
	4 BEST $ COST	$1 BILLION	1.00

B. HOW THE ALTERNATIVES SCORE ON THE CRITERIA

	BEST Q	WORST Q	BEST $	WORST $
DEVELOP ATOM BOMB	500.00	60.00	10.00	100.00
DO NOT DEVELOP	0.00	0.00	0.00	0.00

C. THE OVERALL SCORES OF EACH ALTERNATIVE

	BEST Q	BEST $	WORST Q	WORST $	MIDPT. Q	MIDPT. $
DEVELOP ATOM BOMB	350.00	10.00	6.00	100.00	178.00	55.50
DO NOT DEVELOP	0.00	0.00	0.00	0.00	0.00	0.00

Notes:

1. The basic criteria are benefits to be received and costs to be incurred in this and in most go/no–go decisions or conflicting choice decisions.
2. The benefits here are the quantity of lives saved measured in 1000 of lives. The costs are the billions of dollars which the development might cost.
3. The weights of the benefits and costs reflect the idea that the worst scenario provides for a 0.10 probability that the atomic bomb development will be successful before the war would be over. The best scenario provides for a 0.70 probability.
4. The best scenario provides for a saving of 500,000 lives if the atom bomb succeeds before the war would otherwise be over, and a worst scenario of only 60,000 lives saved.
5. The best scenario provides for a cost of only $10 billion, and the worst scenario provides for a cost of $100 billion.
6. The midpoint (*MIDPT.*) refers to the average between the best and the worst.
7. The issue boils down to which is better to save approximately 112,000 lives or to save $5.5 billion. President Roosevelt chose the lives saved over the dollars saved, and ordered the atomic bomb developed. He might have decided otherwise if there were fewer lives involved and more dollars.

this context. Likewise, a zero probability is obviously an unrealistic worst in this context. The best cost is $10 billion a year, whereas the worst cost with this hypothetical data is $100 billion a year.

How does one aggregate that information? The most logical thing is to calculate the overall score for each alternative using the best scores and the worst scores on lives saved, probability, and cost. That is what is shown in Table 4.1C. At its best, developing the atomic bomb will save 350,000 lives. That is calculated by discounting the 500,000 lives by the high 0.70 probability of success. At its best, the cost will be $10 billion. The cost does not depend on whether the bomb works or not, whereas the lives saved due to the bomb does require that it be successful. At its worst, developing the atomic bomb has an expected value of only 6,000 lives saved. That is calculated by discounting the 60,000 lives by the low 0.10 probability of success. At its worst, the cost will be $100 billion, as mentioned above.

Deciding With Best, Worst, and Midpoint Scores

With that aggregated information, how does one reach a decision? There are basically three approaches. They involve looking at either the best scores, the worst scores, or the midpoints between the best and worst scores. If we look at the best scores, the problem becomes one of deciding which is better between (1) saving 350,000 lives or (2) saving $10 billion. In view of the fact that these are the best scores, one could rephrase the problem as being one of deciding between (1) saving as many as 350,000 lives, or (2) saving only $10 billion. Since President Roosevelt decided to go ahead with the atomic bomb, his reaction would have been favorable to the development alternative presented in its best possible light, although not necessarily more favorable than the non-development alternative at its best.

If we look at the worst scores, the problem becomes one of deciding which is better between (1) only saving 6,000 lives or (2) saving as much as $100 billion. If President Roosevelt considered development to be the best alternative even with the worst possible scores for that alternative, then he surely would have decided in favor of going ahead. In other words, if an alternative is the better alternative both at its best and at its worst, then it is clearly the better alternative.

The time to look at the midpoints between the best and the worst overall scores is if developing the atomic bomb is the better alternative at its best, but not the better alternative at its worst, or vice versa. The midpoints take both the best and the worst into consideration. They represent averages between the possible best and worst. In this case, the problem then becomes one of deciding which is better between (1) saving about 178,000 lives or (2) saving $55.5 billion. The 178,000 lives is the midpoint between 350,000 and 6,000. The $55.5 billion is the midpoint between $10 billion and $100 billion.

One might ask why not obtain one overall score for each alternative. The overall score for not developing the atomic bomb is zero, as mentioned above. There is no meaningful overall score for developing the atomic bomb in the sense of subtracting costs from benefits. The costs are measured in billions of dollars, and the benefits are measured in thousands of lives. Creating one overall score might require (1) converting lives into dollars, (2) converting dollars into lives, or (3) converting both lives and dollars into a common unit. There is unlikely to be agreement on how to make such a conversion. Another alternative would be to transform both sets of scores into part/whole percentages or some other dimensionless numbers. That would not be meaningful here. All the development scores would be transformed into 100% because each one is both the part and the total in their respective columns. Part/whole percentages also lose some information and imagery that is preserved by working with the raw scores in a paired comparison manner as has been done here.

In general, the best decision-making approach in this context is to work with the midpoints between the best and the worst overall benefits and between the best and the worst overall costs. That gives both perspectives equal weight on the assumption that the truth usually tends to be somewhere between the best and the worst possible outcomes. One would, however, choose the alternative that does better on the worst scores if the alternative that does worse does unacceptably worse. For example, if $100 billion is a totally impossible loss, then the development alternative might have to be rejected. An analogous example would be with two possible investments where one is likely to be far more profitable than the other, but the more profitable investment involves a high risk of losing one's right arm. Under those circumstances, one might readily choose the less profitable investment. The atomic bomb example would be more analogous if it involved choosing between two or more weapons systems, rather than just a go/no–go decision. It was, however, basically a go/no–go decision.

Likewise, one would pick the alternative that does better on the best scores even if it does poorly on the worst scores but not unacceptably poorly, where the other alternative does not satisfy a minimum degree of benefits. For example, if at least 20,000 lives must be saved to justify any development, then that would rule out an alternative weapons system which cannot save that many lives no matter how well it does when one looks to the worst scores. Along related lines, one can ignore the best scores of an alternative if the benefits are beyond the maximum needed. For example, any investment that would provide an individual with $1 million per year might be no more valuable than $50,000 per year since $50,000 a year should be enough to cover virtually everything that one might need.

Consistency With Other Values or Perceptions

As for how President Roosevelt aggregated the best and worst overall scores for each alternative, all we know is that his decision was to develop the atomic bomb. That decision would be consistent with any one of the following aggregations:

1. The development alternative won on the best scenario, and won on the worst scenario.
2. The development alternative won on the best scenario, lost on the worst scenario, but won on the midpoints scenario.
3. The development alternative won only on the best scenario, and lost on both the worst and the midpoints scenario, but President Roosevelt gave extra weight to the best scenario because:

   (1) he felt an obligation to save a lot of lives and this was the only weapons system that could satisfy that obligation, or
   (2) he worried that if he rejected the development alternative and it would have worked, then his regret would have been overwhelming, but not so if he tried the development alternative and it failed, or
   (3) his personality was highly optimistic, such that he felt the best outcomes were much more likely to occur than the worst outcomes.

4. The development alternative lost in the best scenario, but won on the worst and midpoint scenarios.

5. The development alternative won on the worst scenario, lost on the best, but won on the midpoints.
6. The development alternative won only on the worst scenario, and lost on the other two, but President Roosevelt gave extra weight to the worst scenario because:

   (1) he felt an obligation not to spend wastefully and the competing alternative would violate that obligation, or
   (2) he worried that if he accepted the competing alternative and it failed, then his regret would have been overwhelming, but not so if he accepted the development alternative (points 6(1) and 6(2) assume a competing alternative, not just a no–go decision), or
   (3) his personality could have been highly pessimistic, at least on this issue, such that he felt the worst outcomes were more likely to occur than the best outcomes.

GENERAL PRINCIPLES IN DEDUCING MOTIVES AND PERCEPTIONS FROM DECISIONS

An optimum decision-making model takes the basic syllogistic form of (1) Y is good, (2) X causes Y, and (3) therefore adopt X. An alternative form is (1) it is optimum to maximize benefits minus costs (B–C), (2) X will maximize B–C, and (3) therefore adopt X. The first premise can be symbolized V for value judgement; the second premises can be symbolized P for perception or R for reality; and the conclusion can be symbolized D for decision.

Such models have many uses. The most common use is for making decisions. Another use is for influencing decisions. The second use recognizes that if we want decision-makers to adopt X, we should influence their perceptions of what X causes and encourage them to have a favorable attitude toward what X causes. Another use is for predicting decisions. That use recognizes that if we know that the values or perceptions of a decision-maker have changed in the first or second premise, we may be able to predict how the decision-maker is likely to change his or her decisions. Another use is for measuring decisional propensities. That use recognizes that asking decision-makers what their decisional propensities are is likely to lead to answers that they think will make them look good. To avoid that, one can ask about their values and perceptions and then deduce from those more reliable answers what their decisional propensities are likely to be.

One Goal and One Choice

The key question in this analysis is, "What can we deduce about V, P, and/or R by knowing D with or without additional information?". If we merely know that X was adopted, we cannot know that Y is valued even if we know that X causes Y. This is because X may also cause Z which the decision-maker may be seeking. The judicial system presumes that a decision-maker intends to cause Y when he or she does X if it is common knowledge that X causes Y. That presumption, however, is rebuttable if the decision-maker has a satisfactory alternative explanation. Likewise, if X is adopted, we cannot know the decision-maker perceives X causes Y, even if it does so. If virtually everyone knows that X causes Y, then from that inductive generalization, we can deduce the decision-maker also knows that X causes Y, but that is not a deduction from the decision to do X.

One might, however, think that if we know the decision plus one of the premises, we should be able to deduce the other premise. That is also not necessarily so. For example, if we know the decision-maker adopted X, and he or she perceives that X causes Y, this does not necessarily mean that Y is being sought as a goal since the decision-maker may also perceive that X causes Z which is what he or she may be really after. The decision-maker may even adopt X and recognize that X causes Y, and yet consider Y to be undesirable. That would be so if he or she recognizes that the amount of Z which X causes is enough to offset the undesirable Y.

On the other hand, if we know the decision-maker adopted X, and he or she positively values Y, one might then think we could deduce that the decision-maker must perceive that X causes Y. That, however, does not necessarily follow since the decision-maker might think there is an inverse relation between X and Y, but X is still adopted because it produces the Z effect which he or she may also desire. Thus, knowing the D conclusions and the P or V premise does not necessarily enable us to deduce the other premise.

A key reason why one cannot easily work backwards from decisions and perceptions to motives or goals sought (or backwards from decisions and goals sought to perceptions) is because the second premise is an asymmetrical causal statement, rather than a symmetrical equality statement. If for example the syllogism were (1) Y is good, (2) X equals Y, and (3) therefore adopt X, then the situation would be different. With that kind of syllogism, we can deduce the first premise if we know the second and the third. However, we cannot deduce the second premise if we know the first and third. This is especially so when we are just working with abstract symbols, rather than real facts.

Multiple Goals and/or Choices

Further to underline the need for careful thinking in optimizing models, one might note that if (1) Y is good and (2) X causes Y, it does not necessarily follow that X should be adopted. This is so because X may also cause Z which may be more bad than Y is good. In other words, one should adopt X only if it has no offsetting adverse side effects. The one-goal syllogism in effect assumes there are no relevant goals other than Y.

One can extend the above analysis to deal with multiple goals and multiple policies. Doing so involves a basic syllogism like (1) Y_1 and Y_2 are good, (2) X_1 and X_2 have relations with Y_1 and Y_2 respectively, and (3) therefore adopt X_1 rather than X_2 because X_1 generates a greater sum of Y_1 and Y_2 than X_2 does. We could also talk about a weighted sum, like a weighted average where each goal is given a relative weight to consider its measurement units and its normative value. With a syllogism like that, knowing which X has been adopted tells us little about the perceived relations of the second premise or the normative values of the first premise for the same reasons that apply to the simpler syllogism which involves only one goal and one policy. Even with many decisions, one cannot inductively or deductively arrive at the motives of a decision-maker, although one may be able to generalize statements about patterns of behavior which one cannot do with only one decision.

Although one may not be able to deduce specific goals or perceptions from decisions, one can deduce highly general goals and perceptions from decisions. For example, if the Supreme Court allows segregation in 1896 and disallows it in 1954, we can conclude that the Court found the benefits minus the costs of segregation to be positive in 1896 and to be negative in 1954. That does not tell us what the Court considered the benefits or the costs to be, unless the Court explicitly says what they are and we accept their statements. Merely saying the net benefits shifted is true by definition, since all decisions seek to maximize benefits minus costs or net satisfaction, and net satisfaction is what decisions seek to maximize. Thinking in terms of benefits minus costs of the decision-makers can, however, help stimulate more systematic evaluation of the decisions.[2]

SOME CONCLUSIONS

There are many uses for optimizing models or for P/G% spreadsheet matrices such as making, influencing, predicting, and measuring decisions. An additional use is deducing motives and perceptions from decisions and other aspects of decision-making situations. One would think that use would be easier in a situation involving only abstract symbols which thereby clarify the decision-making situation and eliminate muddying facts. On the contrary, deducing motives and reconstructing decision-making is easier when a real factual situation is involved. Under those circumstances, one can eliminate alternative explanations that make no factual sense in light of what we know about the situation, even though those alternative explanations could be consistent with abstract symbolic logic.

Deducing motives from decisions and likely perceptions is very much like determining causation in social science. X is considered to cause Y if (1) X and Y vary together, (2) X precedes Y in time, and (3) there is no third variable Z which when held constant will cause the covariation between X and Y to disappear or substantially lessen. A typical way of determining causation in social science is to develop a causal model in which some variables are hypothesized to be the cause or a cause of other variables, while other relations are non-causal covariations or are non-relations. Parts of the model are then tested for the influence of Z variables.

When one or more Z variables are held constant, the relation between X and Y may not substantially lessen. We therefore tentatively accept the relation as being a causal relation until a new explanation or Z variable is adequately offered for the covariation. Likewise, in determining motives, if a Y goal or V value does explain an X or D choice and a P perception, it makes sense to accept the Y goal as at least one of the decision-maker's true goals until an alternative explanation is adequately offered. Adequately offering an alternative explanation means showing it to be as consistent or more consistent with the X or D choice and the P perception than the original explanation.

Deducing motives has been a fascinating concern for people in history, psychology, law, and other fields. Historians do it by compiling lots of circumstantial evidence. Psychologists do it by working with theories of human behavior including theories that relate to sex, power, and biological needs. Lawyers do it partly by operating with a variety of rebuttable presumptions. Policy analysts can also do it by in effect reversing the policy evaluation process. The normal order is to go from values and facts to decisions or policy recommendations. Motivational analysis works backwards from policies to hypothesized values. Working backwards, however, requires special caution where asymmetrical reasoning is involved, as previously mentioned.

The main benefit of determining motives and reconstructing past reasoning processes may be to obtain a better understanding of how people who are acknowledged to be good decision-makers reach their decisions. That includes a highly revered Supreme Court Chief Justice like John Marshall and President like Franklin Roosevelt. The essence of expert systems software is the idea of emulating what experts do in a given field of analysis, rather than trying to impose an abstract model on future decision-makers that may wrongfully bear no relation to how experts actually decide. Thus, seeking deduced values and perceptions in past decisions is consistent with an expert systems approach to developing principles of effective and efficient decision-making.

In that regard, it is hoped that this chapter will contribute to the development of principles of decision-making, including the idea of weighted goals and summation scores which we attributed to John Marshall, or the idea of best–worst analysis which we attributed to Franklin Roosevelt. It is also hoped that this chapter will contribute to the development of principles that relate to deducing values and perceptions in past policy decisions.[3]

Appendix : MCDM and Social Science Prediction

Multi-criteria decision-making and P/G% can be used for prediction or explanation, as well as for prescription or evaluation.

Using the approach for prediction involves six key elements or steps:

1. Listing the **cases, casetypes, or other units of analysis** which are to be analyzed.
2. Listing the **tentative criteria** to aid in explaining why some cases were decided one way and other cases were decided differently. That listing might also involve indicating the relative importance of each criteria.
3. Listing how each case **scores on each of those predictive criteria**. That listing can use whatever measurement units seem comfortable, such as a yes–no dichotomy, a 1–5 scale, years, dollars, apples, etc.
4. **Summing the scores for each case across the criteria** in order to give each case an overall score. Doing so might involve transforming the raw scores into dimensionless part/whole percentages.
5. **Relating the set of summation scores for the cases to the actual or presumed outcomes** of those past cases or casetypes. One can thereby develop a decision-rule indicating the summation scores that are associated with certain kinds of outcomes.
6. Doing a **sensitivity analysis** whereby one determines how the decision-rule, the presence of inconsistencies, or an action strategy might be affected by changes in the cases, criteria, weights, relations, measurement units, or other inputs.

To eliminate inconsistencies in applying the initial predictive decision-rule, use one or more of the following changes in the inputs or procedures for arriving at a new decision-rule.

1. **Changing the cases or casetypes** by adding or subtracting, consolidating or subdividing, or specifying a maximum or minimum on a characteristic of a casetype.
2. **Changing the predictive criteria** by adding or subtracting, consolidating or subdividing, or specifying a maximum or minimum on a predictive criterion. Changing the relative weights of the predictive criterion may be especially important.
3. **Changing the relations between cases and criteria** to more refined or less refined measurement, to alternative units of measurement, or to different scoring for some of the relations.
4. **Changing the drawing of the conclusion as to the predictive decision-rule** by (1) expanding or contracting the indeterminate area, (2) changing the upper or lower cutoff, (3) predicting degrees rather than a dichotomy or vice versa, (4) predicting degrees with a non-linear, rather than a linear

equation or a different kind of non-linear equation, and (5) recognizing a constraint such that if it is present, all cases will be decided positively, or all cases will be decided negatively, regardless how they score on the predictive criteria.

Multiple regression as compared to P/G% may be (1) too complicated, (2) too imperfect in its predictive power, (3) too invalid in its attempt to describe empirical realities, (4) too irrelevant for predicting what is essentially a kinked or threshold relationship rather than a smooth line or curve, (5) too incomplete in expressing unweighted summation relations, (6) too demanding of large samples, (7) too inflexible in not allowing one to change the predictive weights, and (8) too cumbersome for doing a lot of recoding.

An important point is that the P/G% approach would not be very feasible without the interactive flexibility of microcomputer programming. Microcomputers allow the users quickly to change the various inputs, and to see what effects the changes have on reducing inconsistencies. The P/G% program is especially helpful in indicating the changes in various inputs that will eliminate inconsistencies by way of its special sensitivity analysis features. That interactive flexibility is an important sense in which microcomputers can aid in improving social science prediction.

Notes and References

1. For further details on deducing goals in *Marbury* v. *Madison*, see Charles Warren, *The Supreme Court in United States History* (Boston, Mass.: Little Brown, 1935); Charles G. Haines, *The Role of the Supreme Court in American Government and Politics 1789–1835* (Berkeley, CA: University of California Press, 1944); and Robert Carr, *The Supreme Court and Judicial Review* (New York: Rinehart, 1942): 57–74. On deducing goals in judicial decisions in general, see Glendon Schubert, *Quantitative Analysis of Judicial Behavior* (Riverside, N.J.: Free Press, 1942): 173–268.
2. For further details on the Roosevelt decision to proceed with the development of the atomic bomb, see H. Smyth, *Atomic Energy for Military Purposes: The Official Report on the Development of the Atomic Bomb* (Princeton, N.J.: Princeton University Press, 1947); Arthur Compton, *Atomic Quest* (New York: Oxford University Press, 1956); and R. Clark, *The Birth of the Bomb* (New York: Horizon, 1961). On decision-making under conditions of uncertainty including best–worst analysis, see Edward Quade, *Analysis for Public Decisions* (Amsterdam: North-Holland, 1983): 33–42; and Samuel Richmond, *Operations Research for Management Decisions* (New York: Ronald, 1967): 487–92.
3. On the determination of motives in history, see Jacques Barzun and Henry Graff, *The Modern Researcher* (New York: Harcourt, Brace, 1957): 115–130. On determining motives in psychology, see Peter Lindsay and Donald Norman, *Human Information Processing* (New York: Academic Press, 1972): 592–639; and Gardner Lindzey (ed.), *Handbook*

of Social Psychology: Theory and Method (Reading, Mass.: Addison-Wesley, 1954): 57–258. On determining motives in law, see Wayne LaFave and Austin Scott, *Handbook on Criminal Law* (St Paul: West, 1972): 191–218.

5 Teaching With Microcomputers

A number of articles have been written ʻon how useful micro-computers can be for teaching social science research methods, which generally means statistical analysis. Microcomputers are useful for that purpose because students can quickly obtain output from ar-chived data or inputted data and then experiment with changing the inputs and the procedures to gain insights as to the effects and meaning of various aspects of statistical analysiṣ. That can be done while the instructor lectures, explains, and discusses what is or should be happening. Microcomputers can also be used by students for organizing data, drafting reports, retrieving information, and inter-acting with other people. It is the purpose of this chapter to describe a way in which microcomputers can be used to teach public policy substance, rather than methods or office practice, especially where the substance involves controversial issues.[1]

FOUR IMPORTANT ELEMENTS

The essence of the substantive microcomputer approach is ideally to work with the following procedures:

1. All class sessions organized in terms of controversial issues
2. All students having access to shared microcomputers in each class session
3. All microcomputers having access to data files for each contro-versial issue
4. All data files having access to software that is capable of process-ing the data so as to maximize the learning experience.

On the first point, arranging for a variety of controversial issues can easily be done given the nature of public policy subject matter. Doing so may be a desirable approach to teaching, regardless whether one is using microcomputers. There are now textbooks for many courses organized in terms of controversial issues such as Leslie Lipson, *The Great Issues of Politics: An Introduction to Political*

Science[2] Herbert Levine, *Political Issues Debated: An Introduction to Politics*,[3] and George McKenna and Stanley Feingold (eds.), *Taking Sides: Clashing Views on Controversial Political Issues*.[4] Any course that deals with constitutional law or other court cases inherently deals with controversial issues, as manifested in the majority, concurring, and dissenting opinions. Likewise, any substantive public policy course tends to be inherently organized in terms of controversial policy issues.

On the second point relating to hardware, if there is a shortage of microcomputers, then have three or five students per micro-computer. Each micro can be put on a round table where three or five students can each have access to the keyboard. That is not only less expensive than a one-on-one arrangement, but it may also provide more learning experience because the three or five students tend to help and reinforce each other. Arranging for hardware can be more easily done now by virtue of the availability of IBM PC portables at many universities for only approximately $1,000 with discounts. Thus, at a cost of only $10,000, one can obtain enough hardware to service large classes of 50 students apiece when they are seated five students to each large round table.

On the third point of arranging for the data files, a data file in this context means a matrix showing (1) alternatives to choose among on the rows, (2) criteria or goals on the columns, and (3) relations between alternatives and criteria in the cells. Such a matrix can facilitate debating, discussing, and choosing the best alternative, combination, or allocation. There are now almost 200 such data files available for issues that relate to political science, public policy, and law. They are available from Decision Aids, Inc., 1720 Parkhaven Drive, Champaign, Illinois 61820. There is no charge to buyers of this present book on *Decision-Aiding Software*. The data relate to such institutional issues as federalism, separation of powers, judicial review, party systems, democracy versus dictatorship, and socialism versus capitalism. The data files also relate to public policy contro-versies in the realm of agriculture, civil liberties, criminal justice, defense, economic regulation, education, energy, environmental pro-tection, foreign policy, health, housing, labor, minorities, women, poverty, technology, transportation, and zoning, which covers A to Z in policy controversies. The data files also relate to numerous Su-preme Court cases individually or in sets. Seeing the format of these data files and using them can stimulate instructors to develop more data files, including ones of special relevance to their courses.

On the fourth point of arranging for software that can process such data, the processing should include:

1. allowing changes in the alternatives, criteria, and relations in order to facilitate experimenting and creativity
2. showing what alternative, combination, or allocation is best in light of (1) the alternatives available, (2) the criteria and their relative weights, and (3) the relations between the alternatives and the criteria
3. showing what changes would be necessary to bring a second-place alternative up to first place.

For that kind of software, one can obtain a copy of the Policy/Goal Percentaging software from Decision Aids, Inc., along with the 200 data files. There is no charge to buyers of this present book on *Decision-Aiding Software*. That includes a Datafiles Manual, a Program Manual, and summarizing articles. The program is called Policy/Goal Percentaging (P/G%) because it relates policies or alternatives to goals or criteria, and it uses part/whole percentaging to deal with the criteria being measured in different ways. The software is capable of processing the alternatives, criteria, and relations for any substantive problem in order to indicate the best alternative, combination, or allocation in light of those alternatives, criteria, and relations. The software is also capable of flexibility in allowing additions, subtractions, and other changes in the alternatives, criteria, and relations. It can also indicate what changes are needed in order to bring the second-place alternative up to first place.[5]

BENEFITS AND OBJECTIVES

Microcomputers provide the following benefits for teaching purposes beyond what can be provided by good teaching materials and class sessions:

1. Microcomputers are useful for students to absorb information through **interactive questions and answers**
2. They are useful for **role playing** in order better to learn various skills and procedures
3. They can **stimulate creativity** on the part of students by allowing them easily to input new data, ideas, and methods in order to see their effects

4. They can be used **along with** lectures, discussion, textbooks, and other **traditional teaching devices**, rather than requiring a choice choosing between such devices and microcomputers
5. Relevant **hardware** is becoming less expensive and much more widely available
6. There is an increasing quantity of **software** being developed for a variety of courses in political science, policy studies, public administration, and related fields
7. Faculty and trainers are becoming more knowledgeable about the **potential** of microcomputers, and students are becoming more receptive to using them.

The use of microcomputers for teaching either methods or substance in undergraduate or graduate courses can have a significant impact on education. For example, at the 1984 annual meeting of the American Society for Public Administration (ASPA), I conducted an all-day workshop dealing with decision analysis in public administration. The participants asked questions and made comments during the day. In their evaluations, however, they complained about the lack of participation. At the 1985 ASPA annual meeting, I conducted the same all-day workshop, but this time with microcomputers and hands-on experience. There were virtually no questions or comments during the day. The participants were practically enthralled by the experience of working with the microcomputers. In their oral and written evaluations, the participants commented favorably on the feeling of participation that working with the microcomputers gave them, even though the oral participation was substantially less.

In the context of teaching public policy analysis or political science, there are five major learning objectives in using microcomputers to facilitate role playing. The first objective is to enable the students to process a set of policy goals to be achieved, available alternatives for achieving them, and relations between goals and alternatives in order to choose the best alternative, combination, or allocation. The second objective is to enable the students to deal with such policy analysis problems as (1) multiple dimensions on multiple goals, (2) multiple missing information, (3) multiple alternatives that are too many to determine the effects of each one, (4) multiple and possibly conflicting constraints, and (5) the need for simplicity in spite of all that multiplicity.

The third objective is to enable the students to handle sensitivity analysis whereby one determines how the bottom-line conclusion in a policy analysis is likely to change as a result of changes in the goals, alternatives, relations, weights, constraints, and especially the various ways of handling the analytic problems mentioned in the second objective. As a fourth objective, the courses can enable the students to work with microcomputers which can facilitate a fast and meaningful handling of the inputs and procedures. A final objective is to enable the students to report the results of the above policy analysis activities in a way that is clear and helpful to governmental decision-makers and other political scientists.

SPECIFIC PROCEDURES

Further to stimulate involvement where there are five students per microcomputer, the students can be grouped in terms of their ideological or substantive interests. For example, with 25 students, the five sets might cover relatively strong liberals, mild liberals, neutrals, mild conservatives, and relatively strong conservatives. To facilitate interaction across such groups, students can be encouraged to suggest new alternatives, criteria, and relations for the other groups to try out. That kind of interaction facilitates innovative compromises that may be even better than the best expectations of either side, rather than just better than the worst expectations. Instead of dividing the students and the microcomputers into ideological groups, they can be divided in terms of their substantive interest. That can be especially useful if the groups are going frequently to create their own data files.

An important point is that the data files do not require precise quantitative data. One can do meaningful analyses when relations are expressed on 1–2 (or no–yes) scales, or 1–3 (or no–maybe–yes) scales, or more precise scales that relate to years, miles, dollars, percentages, or other measurement units. The software is capable of dealing with a variety of measurement units by such methods as converting them all to 1–5 scales or part/whole percentages. The software is also capable of showing that there is no need to argue over whether a relation is scored 60 or 80 because anything above 45 arrives at the same results. The software can handle missing information by determining critical values, above which the decision would go one way and below which another way. One then merely has to determine whether an item is above or below that threshold, rather than determine the item's exact score. The software can also handle problems where the number of alternatives is too great to determine the effects of each one, and where conflicting constraints are present.

An illustrative problem might be how to provide legal services for the poor, as part of a political science course on the judicial process. The class might go through the following steps when the class is creating a new data file rather than manipulating an existing one:

1. Start out with **some policies** and then **some goals**. For example, the alternative policies might be salaried government lawyers versus unpaid volunteers. The goals might be inexpensiveness, accessibility, political feasibility, and competency.
2. **Add to the policies and the goals** in light of the initial set.
3. **Consolidate policies and goals that heavily overlap,** as indicated by the fact that they are likely to have the same relation scores.
4. **Divide policies and goals** when one realizes that the initial wording may have been too gross.
5. **Insert relation scores using pluses and minuses.** Go down one column or goal at a time in order to promote consistency within each goal.
6. **Convert the pluses and minuses into numbers on 1–3 or 1–5 scales.** Revise the relation scores if one thinks that finer distinctions are sometimes necessary, such as a score of 2.5.
7. **Decide on tentative weights for the goals** by giving the least important goal a weight of 1, and expressing the weights of the other goals as multiples of the first goal. Do not weight the goals if they all seem about equally important, or if the weighting seems too difficult. The weighting can be postponed until after one sees the results, because one then often realizes that different weights will not change the results. The results may also help clarify how much difference there has to be in order to change the results.
8. **Sum across each policy in order to determine its overall score.** If the goals have different weights as multipliers, then sum the products across each policy. Each product involves the relation score multiplied by the weight of the goal to which it pertains.
9. **Observe the unweighted or weighted summation scores** to see if there is one outstanding policy, a scattered combination of outstanding policies, or an optimum level pattern where doing too little or too much is undesirable.

Relevant questions for exams and class might relate to the following:

1. What changes in the relative weights of the criteria (or changes in the scores of the alternatives on the criteria) are needed in order to make a certain second place alternative into first place? For example, given the data file on the Supreme Court case of *Ballew v. Georgia*, (1977) how much and why does the weight of avoiding a wrongful conviction have to rise from 1.00 relative to the weight of avoiding a wrongful acquittal in order for a 12-person jury to be optimum, a 6-person jury, or a single decision-maker?

2. What are the effects of adding or subtracting a criterion or alternative on the bottom-line solution as to which alternative is best? For example, given the data file on the effects of alternative means of resolving criminal cases, how and why would the initial allocation change between trials and plea bargains if expense is added as a criterion to delay reduction and respect for the law, or if diversion is added as an alternative means of resolving cases.

3. What changes in the alternatives, criteria, or relations are needed to have a predictive analysis conform to known reality as to how liberals, conservatives, or others tend to decide a certain controversial issue? For example, what criteria might be added and with what weights in order to understand why liberals are generally opposed to capital punishment and conservatives are generally in favor of capital punishment?

MISCELLANEOUS POINTERS FOR TEACHING SUBSTANCE WITH MICROCOMPUTERS

1. Provide each student with a copy of the program and the data files at the beginning of the semester or session. They can then work with the program and the data more easily outside of class.

2. Before the end of the semester each student should submit a short paper analyzing a data file which the student has created on a subject that is of particular interest to the student. The preparation of short memos is even more important in a methods course than a substance course in order to encourage the students to apply the methods.

3. The midterm and final exam can be given in the same classroom where the microcomputers are available. The students may need to take the exam in shifts so that each student will have a

microcomputer to use as an aid in developing the answers or analysis to each problem.

4. Questions should be asked in class that involve the use of the microcomputers in the answer.

5. At least in the beginning of the semester, the instructor should guide the students through the analysis of selected substantive problems by telling them collectively what they should type or hit on the keyboard.

6. The instructor should frequently arrange for different parts of the class to be experimenting with different alternatives, criteria, or relations. For example, the liberal, independent, and conservative groups in the class can each separately clarify their respective positions and observe where the relatively weak elements are in the diverse conclusions. This helps develop mutually satisfying compromises.

7. Give homework assignments in which the students are expected to create and manipulate data files. The data files can then be examined and discussed in class.

8. The students can be encouraged to experiment with the data files that are being discussed while the class is being conducted and raise questions and make comments concerning their experiences. It is a sign of interest if all the computers are working while the instructor is talking, assuming the computers are working class-related activities.

9. At the beginning of each class session, announce about two or three data files that will be discussed. Doing so (1) prepares the students for the day's activities, (2) keeps the class more on schedule, (3) informs the students what will be covered at the beginning of the next class period in light of what is left over, and (4) encourages more processing of the data files, rather than traditional lecturing.

10. The students learn better in class if they have a combination of (1) working with microcomputers at their seats and (2) observing the microcomputer display on a monitor or a projector which is under the control of the instructor. The use of a projector can, however, be a distraction from the more useful experience involved in working with the microcomputers.

11. Datafiles should occasionally be developed with the class by collectively working out the alternatives, criteria, relations, and analysis. An exciting but risky way to do that is to do it spontaneously without having worked out those inputs in advance.

That way the students get the benefits of participating in the development of new knowledge, rather than just absorbing what has been developed.

12. In discussing data files, it is helpful to have the monitor projector show the display which relates the alternatives to the criteria so the students can see the big picture, rather than focus too closely on just the alternatives or just the criteria.

13. If pressed for time in discussing a data file, go quickly to the initial bottom-line analysis and to the threshold or break-even analysis, rather than dwell on the preliminary inputs.

14. There is no need to give a term paper assignment in order to provide the students with experience in using microcomputers for analyzing public policy or political science problems. They will be getting plenty of that in the classroom if microcomputers are used to teach public policy or political science substance.

15. Learning experience can be enhanced by grouping the students in terms of their subject matter interests. Those interests can be determined at the beginning of the semester. Each group of students can be seated behind the same microcomputer to facilitate their working together. The class can sometimes work on problems where each group applies general principles to its specific subject matter.

16. Working with decision matrices enables the students to understand better (1) how to make decisions, (2) how to explain decisions that other people make, (3) how to influence other people's decision, and (4) especially what the goals, alternatives, relations, and conclusions might be for any given substantive problem.

SOME CONCLUSIONS

The P/G% approach represents a synthesis between inductive and deductive reasoning and between empiricism and rationalism in the following ways:

1. **The relations between policies and goals tend to be based on experience**, although generally not statistical correlation analysis.

2. **The overall analysis is deductive** with a prescriptive conclusion being deduced from premises that relate to goals, alternatives, and relations.

3. The goals and alternatives are often based on surveying decision-makers or their writings, which is a form of **empirical analysis**.
4. The relations, goals, and alternatives may sometimes be deduced from **other propositions about related relations, goals, and alternatives**.
5. Perhaps most important is the emphasis that P/G% places on sensitivity analysis. That kind of analysis does not tell us what the truth is. It may, however, tell us there is no difference on the bottom-line of what policy to adopt whether the truth is a 64 or an 83 with regard to a controversial relation or goal weight. In other words, we need empiricism to tell us what the reasonable ranges are for the input scores, but deduction tells us **at what point within those ranges a score crosses a threshold of changing the results**.

By way of its emphasis on sensitivity analysis, the P/G% micro-computer approach to teaching methods or substance stimulates a student to be constantly thinking about such matters as adding, subtracting, or otherwise changing (1) the alternatives, (2) the minimums and maximums on the alternatives, (3) the goals, (4) the measurement units for the goals, (5) the weights of the goals, (6) minimums and maximums on the goals, (7) the relations, (8) the budget to be allocated if there is one, and (9) any other inputs that are subject to change. That kind of stimulation is conducive to creativity as well as careful reasoning. Perhaps colleges need to do more with regard to encouraging creativity and careful reasoning. If the P/G% approach does have that effect, then it is indeed a useful method for teaching political science and public policy.

The investment of time and money in order to receive the benefits of teaching with microcomputers is low compared to the benefits obtainable. To paraphrase a policy analyst of the 1800s, researchers and teachers have nothing to lose but their less efficient research and teaching methods. They should unite in sharing experience and software for the good of the public policy profession and the improvement of public policy decisions.[6]

Notes and References

1. On Using Microcomputers as a teaching tool, see Kenneth Kraemer, "Curriculum Recommendations for Computers in Public Management

Education" (Washington, D.C.: NASPAA, 1984); Herbert F. Weisberg, "Microcomputers in Political Science", *News for Teachers of Political Science*, 1 (Summer 1983); Fiona Chen, "Teaching Computer Application in Public Administration", Eastern Washington University, School of Public Affairs (1984); and S. Nagel, "Microcomputers and Public Policy Analysis", in Don Calista (ed.), *Microcomputers and Public Productivity* (Special issue of the *Public Productivity Review*, 1985).

2. Englewood Cliffs, N.J. Prentice-Hall, 6th edn (1981).
3. Englewood Cliffs, N.J. Prentice-Hall (1982).
4. Guilford, Conn.: Dushkin, 2nd edn (1981).
5. On the P/G% software, see Benjamin Radcliff, "Comparing Multiple Criteria Decision-Making Programs", *Social Science Microcomputer Review*, 4 (1986); S. Nagel, "P/G% Analysis: A Decision-Aiding Program", *Social Science Microcomputer Review*, 3: 243 (1985); and S. Nagel, *Microcomputers, Evaluation Problems, and Policy Analysis* (Beverly Hills, Calif.: Sage, 1986).
6. Background material exists on teaching from a perspective of societal goals to be achieved, policy alternatives for achieving them, and relations between goals and alternatives in order to choose the best alternative, combination, or allocation. See, for example, the opening chapter to S. Nagel, *Public Policy: Goals, Means and Methods* (New York: St Martin's Press, 1984) and the Instructor's Manual which accompanies that book. Also see S. Nagel, "Using Microcomputers and P/G% for Teaching Policy Analysis and Public Policy", in Peter Bergerson and Brian Nedwek (eds), *Teaching Public Administration* (Program in Public Policy Analysis and Administration: St Louis University, 1985).

Part III
Obstacles the Software Helps Overcome

6 Multiple Dimensions on Multiple Goals

The Rand McNally *Places Rated Almanac* (1985) seeks to score 329 cities on nine different criteria.[1] It tries to handle the multi-dimensionality problem by giving a rank order from 1 to 329 to each city on each criterion and then adding the nine rank orders in order to give each city a total score. In 1985, Pittsburgh received the highest total score.

It is the purpose of this chapter to discuss three important aspects of that evaluation. First, the use of ranks to provide a common measurement unit, rather than dimensionless measures such as 1–5 scales or part/whole percentages. Second, the need to consider diminishing returns in relating raw scores to satisfaction. Third, the controversy between multiplying raw or transformed scores and adding them in order to obtain aggregate scores for each city or alternative.

The *Places Rated Almanac* ranked on nine criteria the 329 most populated metropolitan areas in the United States. The nine criteria are climate/terrain, housing, healthcare/environment, crime, transportation, education, the arts, recreation, and economics. Each city was scored on various objective indicators, such as percent of unemployment. The cities are then ranked from 1 to 329 on each indicator or each group of indicators. The criteria were considered equally important. The overall score for each city was determined by adding its nine ranks. Pittsburgh was the city with the lowest overall score and thus the best rank.

THE NEED FOR A COMMON MEASUREMENT UNIT

Ranks and 1–5 Scales

Converting all the raw scores into ranks distorts relations because the distance between a rank of 1 and 2 is the same as the distance between a rank of 2 and 3. In reality the gap between the raw scores of the first and second place cities may be much larger than the gap between the raw scores of the cities in 99th and 100th place. Part/

whole percentaging takes that into consideration by using the exact raw scores to arrive at part/whole percentages.

Another alternative to converting all the raw scores into money, ranks, or part/whole percentages is to convert them into scores on 1–5 scales. On such a scale, a 5 could mean highly conducive to the criterion; a 4 means mildly conducive; a 3 means neither conducive nor adverse; a 2 means mildly adverse; and a 1 means highly adverse. Unlike a system of ranks, there are more nearly equal psychological intervals between the 1–2 interval and the 4–5 interval in using a Likert scale. The Likert 1–5 scores can be added across the criteria for each city to give meaningful and simple results.

One can also average the nine Likert scores to get an average score between 1 and 5 for each city. That kind of overall score is meaningful in itself, unlike the overall scores that come from either adding ranks, multiplying them, or adding their logarithms. The Likert scale also lends itself to weighting the criteria. If a criterion, for example, receives a weight of 2 (meaning it is twice as important as the criteria that receive a weight of 1), then the Likert scale scores can be multiplied by 2 to equal 10, 8, 6, 4, and 2 before doing the adding. One might argue that the Likert scale is subjective, but so is ranking or any scoring method. It is easier to put cities into five scale scores than into 329 ranks. Ranks also make cities that are far apart on a criterion look close together if they have adjacent ranks. Ranks also make cities that are only a little apart look farther apart because the ranks do not enable one to show that kind of closeness. The psychometric literature shows that rating scales come closer to having equal interval properties than ordinal or ranking scales.[2]

The big disadvantage of converting all the raw scores into 1–5 scales is that doing so often needlessly loses valuable information. Suppose, for example, one of the criteria is distance, and it is capable of being measured in miles. It would then be wasteful to convert that information into a 1–5 scale. Doing so in effect converts a mileage odometer into a ruler that just measures very long, long, between long and short, short, and very short. Social science and decision science try to make vague measurement more precise, not precise measurement more vague. The Analytical Hierarchy Process (AHP) of Thomas Saaty converts all measurement into a 1–9 scale.[3] His 1–9 scale is in effect a 1–5 scale since he uses only adjectives or adverbs to refer to the odd numbers.

Part/Whole Percentages

Part/whole percentages are generally a more meaningful common measurement unit than either ranks or 1–5 scales. Part/whole percentages preserve the ratios between the raw scores which ranks lose. For example, suppose City A receives a score of 6 on popularity and City B receives a score of 2. City A would then get a rank of 1, and City B a rank of 2, which is only a 2 to 1 ratio. City A, however, would receive a part/whole percentage of 6/8 or 75%, and City B a percentage of 2/8 or 25%. The ratio of the percentages is 3 to 1, just like the raw scores.

The percentages are normed in the sense that they can go only from 0 to 100, and they add to 100. Converting the raw score to 1–5 scales might mean that a popularity score of 6 would be the equivalent of a 4 (mildly favorable) on a 1–5 scale, and a popularity score of 2 would be the equivalent of a 2 (mildly unfavorable) on a 1–5 scale. That transformation loses the ratio and the precision, although generally not as much as ranks do. One should also note that part/whole percentages can work with ranks, 1–5 scales, and other measurement units as raw scores.

THE NEED TO CONSIDER DIMINISHING RETURNS

There is also a need to consider diminishing returns when making comparisons across criteria and cities in order to determine which is the best city. "Diminishing returns" in this context refers to the fact that as a score worsens on crime, pollution, or other negative social indicators, satisfaction goes down but at a diminishing rate. Thus if the crime rate goes up one unit from 0 to 1, there would be a bigger drop in satisfaction than if the crime rate goes up one unit from 99 to 100. Likewise, as a score improves on compliance with the law, cleanliness of the air, or other positive social indicators, satisfaction goes up but at a diminishing rate. When compliance goes up one unit from 0 to 1, there will be a bigger increase in satisfaction than when compliance goes from 99 to 100.

Adding, Multiplying, Logging and 1–5 Scales

Suppose, for example, we have a competition between two cities on two equally important criteria and we ignore diminishing returns by simply adding across the criteria. We then get the following counter-intuitive tie:

	Criterion 1		Citerion 2		Overall Score
City A	1	+	100	=	101
City B	2	+	99	=	101

That tie runs contrary to intuitive common sense because it treats the distance between ranks 1–2 and ranks 99–100 as if they were equal. We know that moving from second place to first place is generally a greater achievement than moving from 100th place to 99th place in anybody's league, although entering the top 100 may be important. That defect in working with ranks can be at least partly remedied by changing the analysis without finding a different common measurement unit across the criteria. One approach is to multiply, rather than add the criteria. Doing so generates the following results:

	Criterion 1		Criterion 2		Overall Score
City A	1	×	100	=	100
City B	2	×	99	=	198

Those results are also counter-intuitive, although maybe not so much as the first set of results. The second set seems to go too far in the opposite extreme by saying that City A is almost twice as good as City B in terms of their overall scores. That in effect wipes out the importance of Criterion 2. Note that getting a low overall score is good like getting a low rank, and getting a high overall score is bad. A better way to deal with diminishing returns might be to add the logarithms of the ranks or other common measurement units. Doing so recognizes the well-established finding (going back at least to Daniel Bernouilli in 1730) that diminishing returns tend to follow a logarithmic pattern. Adding the logarithms (as determined by a pocket calculator) give the following more meaningful results:

| | Criterion 1 | | Criterion 2 | | Overall Score |
	Rank	Log	Rank	Log	
City A	1	0.00	100	2.00	2.00
City B	2	0.30	99	1.99	2.29

That system makes City A the winner, but by an amount that is more meaningful, since City A is not twice as good as City B.

A good system should have both accuracy and simplicity. The adding system lacks accuracy. It also lacks simplicity to have to rank 329 cities on nine different criteria. The multiplying system has accuracy in getting the cities in the right order, but not by the right intervals. It is also more complicated to have to multiply nine numbers for 329 cities than to add them. The logarithmic method has accuracy. It also has some simplicity by virtue of its emphasis on adding, but it also lacks simplicity since it requires a calculator and the average person does not understand logarithms. One, however, does not need to understand logs to be able to use them, just as people use electric lights and calculators without fully understanding how they work.

A 1–5 scale is an improvement over adding ranks, multiplying ranks, or taking the logarithms of ranks. It not only provides accuracy by having equal psychological intervals. It is also simple to use. Using a 1–5 scale, however, does not solve the diminishing returns problem. For example, assume that all the numbers on the scale are truly positive numbers, like 5 stars for doing super great, down to 1 star for not doing anything at all. There is probably a bigger incremental gain in going from a 1 to a 2 than there is in going from a 4 to a 5. Going from a 1 to a 2 is a 100% increase, whereas going from a 4 to a 5 is only a 25% increase.

Converting the 1–5, 0–10, or 0–100 scores to part/whole percentages does help. For example, suppose there are two criteria and two alternatives. The scores on the first criterion are 1 and 2, and the scores on the second criterion are 5 and 4. If we just add the scores, we have a tie at 6 apiece for each alternative. If we work with the part/whole percentages, then Alternative 1 gets a 1/3 or 33% on the first criterion and a 5/9 or 56% on the second criterion, for an overall total of 89%. Alternative 2 gets a 2/3 or 67% on the first criterion and

4/9 or 44% on the second criterion, for an overall total of 111%. That makes Alternative 2 rightfully the winner since 2 is 100% more than 1 on the first criterion, but 5 is only 25% more than 4 on the second criterion. An article in *Money* magazine (in 1987) which scored cities on multiple criterion on a 0–100 scale failed to consider these diminishing returns in working with 0–100 scales.[4]

Part/whole Percentages

Part/whole percentaging is meaningful in preserving information, as mentioned above. How though does part/whole percentaging deal with diminishing returns? First, part/whole percentaging treats the relation between the raw scores and satisfaction as having a diminishing returns relation. It does so by operating under the rule that the scarce resources to be allocated to the alternatives or the budget categories should not all be allocated to the category with the highest raw score. Suppose two alternatives on only one criterion receive scores of 6 and 12 respectively. Then all the budget should be allocated to the first alternative if the 6 is interpreted as being like a linear regression coefficient. On the other hand, the first alternative should get 67% of the budget, and the second should get 33% if the 6 is interpreted as being like a non-linear elasticity coefficient.

Second, one can translate raw scores into part/whole percentages using a non-linear rather than a linear translation. For example, suppose we have three alternative ways of disposing of criminal cases, namely through trials, diversion out of the system, and plea bargains. They score 2, 4, and 6 on the respect criterion. Those raw scores translate into 17% 33%, and 50% as part/whole percentages – that is, a linear translation because the increment between 17% and 33% is the same as the increment between 33% and 50%. A diminishing returns translation would involve a smaller utility increment when going from a raw score of 4 to 6 than when going from a raw score of 2 to 4. Such a translation can be easily obtained by working with the logarithms of 2, 4, and 6 in accordance with the findings of mathematicians like Bernouilli and psychologists like Wundt and Weber. The logarithms of those three numbers are 0.30, 0.60, and 0.78. Those numbers add to 1.68. The three part/whole percentages are thus 18% (or 0.30/1.68), 36%, and 46%. The increment between 18% and 36% is 18 percentage points, but notice the increment between 36% and 46% is only 10 percentage points. We thereby satisfy the principle of diminishing returns while still completely working within part/whole percentaging. There are other translations that would satisfy diminishing returns, such as taking the square root of each of the raw scores, but taking the logarithms has the most scientific respectability.

Third, kinked relations are dealt with in part/whole percentaging by way of constraints. For example, a constraint might specify that no alternative is acceptable unless it scores a minimum of 3 on a 1–10 scale on a criterion, but not more than an 8. That is the equivalent of a relation (between satisfaction and the criterion) that is not a continuous straight line. If the criterion scores were plotted on a horizontal axis, and satisfaction on the vertical axis, then the curve would be a horizontal straight line from a score of 1 to 3, a positive diagonal straight or curved line from 3 to 8, and then another horizontal line at zero satisfaction from 8 to 10. Another example would be a constraint that specifies that no allocation is acceptable unless it provides for a minimum of \$50 per alternative budget category and not more than \$90. If the dollars allocated to each alternative were plotted on a horizontal axis, and satisfaction on the vertical axis, then the curve would also be a horizontal straight line from \$0 to \$50, a positive sloping curve from \$50 to \$90, and then a horizontal line at zero satisfaction. From \$89 to \$90, the satisfaction curve drops vertically to show that above \$90 there is no satisfaction to the decision-maker because allocating over \$90 to that alternative is an illegal or unacceptable over-allocation.

Diminishing returns can be ignored where we are just trying to choose the best alternative on one criterion. This assumes diminishing marginal returns that taper off, rather than diminishing absolute returns that drop down. Diminishing marginal returns, however, cannot be ignored in an allocation problem. Thus in the example given, trials comes out the winner on respect with diversion second and pleas third, regardless whether we consider diminishing returns. If however, we are allocating cases to those disposition alternatives, then ignoring the diminishing returns would result in allocating 17%, 33%, and 50% to those alternatives. Considering diminishing returns would result in allocating 18%, 36%, and 46%. Likewise, if there are many criteria such as the nine criteria in evaluating the cities, the failure to consider diminishing returns could cause a city like Pittsburgh that gets almost no first places on the nine criteria to look good by being consistently high but not highest. When other cities have multiple first places, they are under-rewarded. When they have a rank of 100 rather than 99, they are over-penalized. This further illustrates the need for a meaningful system of multi-criteria decision-making such as part/whole percentaging.

MULTIPLYING RAW SCORES VERSUS ADDING PERCENTAGES

Multiplying Raw Scores

The idea of multiplying raw scores, the ranks, or other transformed scores for the cities was suggested by Geoffrey Loftus.[5] Multiplication with exponential weights (as contrasted to addition with multiplier weights) also has a respectable mathematical tradition, as reflected by such sources as P. W. Bridgeman.[6]

Multiplying the raw scores for a city (or other alternative being evaluated) provides the benefit of an aggregate score that is insensitive to the measurement dimensions used on the raw scores, such as whether they are days or months. For example, suppose we have two alternatives A and B, with two criteria of days saved and popularity. Alternative A saves 30 days and receives a popularity score of 5 on a 1–5 scale. Alternative B saves 60 days and receives a popularity score of 2. Note below that Alternative A receives an aggregate score relative to Alternative B of 1.33 to 1, regardless whether time-saving is measured in days saved or months saved:

	Days Saved		Popularity		Product	Ratio
City A	30	×	5	=	150	1.25
City B	60	×	2	=	120	1.00
	Months Saved		Popularity		Product	Ratio
City A	1	×	5	=	5	1.25
City B	2	×	2	=	4	1.00

If the raw scores were added, then the results would be influenced by whether days or months were used as a time measurement unit. The aggregate scores with days saved would be 35 versus 62, which would cause Alternative B to be the winner, rather than Alternative

A. The added aggregate scores with months saved would be 6 versus 4, with A the winner.

Further supporting the idea of multiplying is the fact that each criterion can be weighted by an exponent. Thus, if popularity is twice as important as days-saved, the aggregate scores for each alternative can be calculated by the formula, D^1P^2 = Weighted Product. In order to show diminishing returns, the lowest weight could be set at 0.01 or 0.10. One would then be working with decimal exponents that show diminishing returns such as $(d)^{0.10}(P)^{0.20}$. An exponent can be negative to show that a goal like crime is to be minimized rather than maximized.

Adding Part/whole Percentages

As a better alternative to either multiplying or adding raw scores, one can add part/whole percentages. Doing so produces the following dimensionless results:

	Days or months saved (P/W%)		Popularity (P/W%)	Sum	Allocation %
City A	33	+	71 =	104	52
City B	67	+	29 =	96	48

Note that the part/whole percentages are not influenced by whether days or months are used as a time measurement unit. Part/whole percentages can also be weighted. For example, if popularity is twice as important as time saving, then the popularity percentages would be multiplied by 2, yielding 142% and 58%. Adding those weighted popularity percentages to the times saved percentages gives Alternative A an aggregate score of 175%, and Alternative B an aggregate score of 125%. Dividing by the sum of the weights gives allocation percentages of 58% and 42% that sum to 100%. Part/whole percentaging can handle diminishing returns by the methods previously indicated.

The reasons why part/whole percentaging is more desirable than multiplying for obtaining aggregate scores are:

1. The part/whole percentages are **easier to interpret** especially

when one has a lot of alternatives. No matter how many alternatives there are, the bottom-line or right-column percentages always add to 100%. With the multiplying approach, one would express each alternative as a ratio or multiple of the worst alternative, or as a percentage of the best alternative.

2. The part/whole percentages easily lend themselves to **allocating scarce resources**.

3. They are also based on the idea of **allocating to each alternative in proportion to how well it scores on each criterion** in accordance with classical calculus optimization.

4. The **arithmetic is simpler**, especially when one has a lot of criteria. It is obviously easier to add than multiply, and easier to multiply than to exponentiate.

5. There is more **flexibility and objectivity** in dealing with diminishing returns, including the use of logarithmic transformations.

6. The multiplying approach makes no sense **if an alternative scores zero on a criterion**. No matter how well an alternative scores on the criteria, it will receive an overall score of zero if it has a zero on any one criteria. Ignoring the zeros or converting them to 1 s or 0.01 s can arbitrarily influence the result as to which alternative is best.

7. The multiplying approach is especially complicated in **trying to solve for tie-causing values** where exponents are involved.

8. There is now a good software package for handling part/whole percentaging called **P/G%** (Policy/Goal Percentaging).

9. A literature is developing on the use of part/whole percentaging, stemming from such sources as S. Nagel,[7] Thomas Saaty,[8] and others.

10. The multiplying approach is very sensitive to **rounding and measurement errors** because it works with exponent weights and multiplication, whereas P/G% works with multiplier weights and addition.

11. The multiplying approach chooses the alternative that is best on **benefits** divided by costs looking for the highest $(B)(C)^{-1}$ figure. The P/G% approach chooses the alternative that is best on a form of benefits minus costs by looking for the highest %B − C% figure. The benefit–cost literature (such as Nagel[9]) shows that B − C makes more sense than B/C as a composite goal.

PITTSBURGH VERSUS SAN FRANCISCO

To clarify further how meaningless adding ranks is compared to adding part/whole percentages, it might be quite useful to work with the actual data in the Rand McNally *Places Rated Almanac*.[10] The data below shows how the winning city of Pittsburgh compares with the fourth-ranked city of San Francisco on the first two criteria of climate and housing. San Francisco ranked first on climate, whereas Pittsburgh ranked 87th. Pittsburgh, however, ranked 186th on housing, whereas San Francisco ranked 327th. The overall score of Pittsburgh on these two criteria is thus 273, and the overall score of San Francisco is 328. Pittsburgh is thus the better of the two cities if we just use these two criteria and if we simply add the ranks.

| | Ranks | | Combined raw scores |
	Climate/terrain	Housing	
Pittsburg	87.00	186.00	273.00
San Francisco	1.00	327.00	328.00

On the other hand, the data below shows how Pittsburgh compares with San Francisco using the same criteria and the same ranks, but converting the ranks to part/whole percentages before adding them. Doing that results in San Francisco being the winner by a large margin in view of its low overall score. Which approach makes more sense? Merely adding the untransformed ranks does not make sense. The reason is that adding the ranks treats the 86-point difference between 1 and 87 as less important than the 141-point difference between 186 and 327. That is like saying that the difference between being in first place and second place in the National Football League is less important than the difference between being in 186th place and 188th place. That does defy common sense. In reality people would consider Pittsburgh and San Francisco to be about equally bad on housing, but to consider San Francisco way better on climate.

| | Part/whole percentages | | Combined W P/W (%) |
	Climate (%)	Housing (%)	
Pittsburgh	98.86	36.26	135.12
San Francisco	1.14	63.74	64.88

The reason for starting with only the first two criteria and only two cities is so one can see more clearly how adding ranks distorts reality. One might, however, argue that perhaps the distortion washes out if we use all nine criteria for judging "first-place" Pittsburgh against "fourth-place" San Francisco. The data below shows how Pittsburgh and San Francisco rank on all nine criteria. If we simply sum those ranks, Pittsburgh squeaks by with an overall sum of 735, as contrasted to the 775 of San Francisco.

	Ranks				
	Climate/ terrain	Housing	Health/ environment	Crime	Transportation
Pittsburgh	87.00	186.00	14.00	78.00	76.00
San Francisco	1.00	327.00	10.00	318.00	4.00

	Education	The Arts	Recreation	Economics	Combined Raw scores
Pittsburgh	7.00	12.00	90.00	185.00	735.00
San Francisco	18.00	7.00	2.00	88.00	775.00

On the other hand, the data below shows how Pittsburgh compares with San Francisco on all nine criteria when we logically convert the ranks into part/whole percentages in order to consider diminishing returns in a simple and valid way. On climate, Pittsburgh receives a part/whole percentage of 87/88 or 99%, and San Francisco receives a percentage of 1/88 or 1%, and so on through the nine criteria. As a result, San Francisco comes out the clear winner with an overall score of 335%, as contrasted to the 565% of Pittsburgh. Which approach makes more sense?

	Part/whole percentages				
	Climate/ terrain (%)	Housing (%)	Health/ environment (%)	Crime (%)	Transportation (%)
Pittsburgh	98.86	36.26	58.33	19.70	95.00
San Francisco	1.14	63.74	41.67	80.30	5.00

	Education (%)	The Arts (%)	Recreation (%)	Economics (%)	Combined W P/W (%)
Pittsburgh	28.00	63.16	97.83	67.77	564.90
San Francisco	72.00	36.84	2.17	32.33	335.10

It makes no sense at all for Pittsburgh to be considered the winner over San Francisco. San Francisco wins very big over Pittsburgh on three of the nine criteria, namely climate, transportation, and recreation. San Francisco wins moderately on three other criteria, namely health/environment, the arts, and economics. Pittsburgh wins moderately on only three of the nine criteria, namely housing, crime, and education. Pittsburgh, however, picks up 141 big points over San Francisco on housing even though Pittsburgh is in 186th place. It is amazing that Pittsburgh could be considered the winner over San Francisco under these circumstances when it loses so big on six of the nine criteria, including the criterion of economics, which may be especially important. Actually, Pittsburgh does worse than numerous other cities when the more meaningful approach of working with part/whole percentages is used, rather than working with the raw unprocessed ranks.

BROADER CONSIDERATIONS

When evaluating alternative cities, projects, or other alternatives across a number of criteria, one needs to be sensitive to a number of measurement problems. Some of these problems have not been discussed in this brief chapter because they are not part of the main controversy concerning evaluating cities. Those undiscussed but important problems include the following:

1. **The evaluating criteria to include.** Here it has been assumed that the criteria of the *Places Rated Almanac* make sense. Those criteria in random order consist of climate/terrain, housing, healthcare/environment, crime, transportation, education, the arts, recreation, and economics. One could easily mention other important criteria such as civil liberties, freedom of speech, equal opportunity, and good government. The criteria chosen may be easier to measure but not necessarily the most important.
2. **The relative weights of the criteria.** Here it has been, perhaps unreasonably, assumed that all the criteria should be weighted equally.
3. **The alternatives to include.** Here it has been assumed that it makes sense to have the alternatives consist of the 329 most populated metropolitan areas in the United States. The rankings might be substantially changed if different sub-sets of those cities or other cities were included, especially if only the 50 largest cities were included.

4. **How the ratings are to be determined.** Here it is questionably assumed that the authors of the *Places Rated Almanac* chose a meaningful set of data sources for ranking the 329 cities on the nine criteria, and properly aggregated the many data sources to get nine ranks for each city.
5. **How to deal with negative goals and negative scores.** A negative goal is like a golf score where scoring low is desirable. One way to handle negative goals is to make all the scores like golf scores, which is what ranking does. The situation can get more complicated when there is a mix of negative and positive goals that cannot all be meaningfully changed to go in the same direction. A negative score is like a temperature scale where some of the scores can be below zero. That may be the case with ranks or 1–5 scales. One way to deal with that problem is to ignore it, but doing so may distort one's findings.

The problems discussed in this chapter take those criteria, weights, alternatives, and ratings as givens. The chapter then proceeds to discuss the meaningfulness of the choices that have been made concerning the following problems:

1. The need for a **common measurement unit**, since one cannot meaningfully add such measures as average annual temperature to average number of rooms per family. Ranks provide a dimensionless measure, but not as well as 1–5 scales, which in turn are not as meaningful as part/whole percentages.
2. The need to consider **diminishing returns**, since there is only a small psychological gap between 99th and 100th as contrasted to a big psychological gap between first and second. One can improve upon adding ranks by multiplying them, logging them, or converting them into 1–5 scales. Part/whole percentages work even better.
3. The need to decide whether **raw scores should be multiplied** or whether their **percentages should be added**. Multiplying raw scores is an improvement over adding them by providing a common measurement unit and considering diminishing returns. Part/whole percentages is a further improvement for a number of reasons but especially because such percentages reflect the idea of choosing the alternative that maximizes benefits minus costs, rather than benefits divided by costs.

This discussion is thus part of what could be a larger discussion of the analytic problems involved in systematic evaluation across multiple alternatives on multiple criteria. That larger discussion includes such problems as:

1. **How to deal with missing information.** Throughout this chapter we have assumed that we are somehow capable of scoring each city on each criterion. A broader concern for evaluation problems might discuss the importance of sensitivity analysis in determining how the overall ranks of the cities might change if some of the ratings were unknown or were expressed as ranges rather than scores, or if we did not know or pretend to know that the criteria are equally important. For example, what changes in the importance weights would make the second-place or other-place city into first place.

2. **How to deal with multiple and possibly conflicting constraints.** The *Places Rated Almanac* is subtitled "Your guide to finding the best places to live in America". The book ignores the fact that many people may be subjected to constraints such as the need to live within a certain geographical area for reasons of job or family. Some university professors may be confined to no more than 20 or so cities that have major universities. The constraints may be conflicting if a university professor has to move from Cambridge, Massachusetts because he just received a divorce from a Harvard wife that he has to get away from, but he cannot find a better job than the one he has teaching at MIT.

3. The *Places Rated Almanac* operates on the assumption that the user is faced with a **mutually exclusive choosing problem.** Nowhere does the book deal with the highly common evaluation problem of the best way to allocate people, money, time, or other scarce resources across places. Suppose the federal government, a large corporation, or any government or business wants to know how best it should allocate its people or money across various places with regard to certain activities. That is an especially interesting evaluation problem since it goes to the heart of the key societal problem of who does and should get what, when, and how.

This chapter has touched on only a small part of the many controversial issues when evaluating cities or other alternatives across multiple criteria. The issues discussed are, however, fundamental. It is thus hoped the chapter will whet the appetites of its readers toward probing further into both the issues discussed and those not discussed. From that probing should come more meaningful methods of systematic evaluation.

Notes and References

1. R. Boyer and D. Savageau, *Places Rated Almanac: Your Guide to Finding the Best Places to Live in America* (Chicago: Rand McNally, 1985).
2. For example, see G. Kenny, "The Metric Properties of Rating Scales Employed in Evaluation Research", *Evaluation Review*, 10: 397–408 (1986) and J. P. Guilford, *Psychometric Methods* (New York: McGraw-Hill, 1954).
3. Thomas Saaty, *Decision Making for Leaders* (Belmont, Calif.: Wadsworth, 1982).
4. "The Best Places to Live in America", *Money Magazine*: 34–44 (August 1987).
5. Geoffrey Loftus, "Say It Ain't Pittsburgh", *Psychology Today*, 19(6): 8–10 (1985).
6. P. W. Bridgeman, *Dimensional Analysis* (New York: McGraw-Hill, 1922).
7. S. Nagel, *Policy Analysis with Microcomputers* (Greenwich, Conn.: Greenwood Press, 1988).
8. Saaty, *Decision Making for Leaders*.
9. S. Nagel, *Public Policy: Goals, Means, and Methods* (New York: St Martin's Press, 1984): 35–41.
10. R. Boyer and D. Savageau, *Places Rated Almanac*.

7 Multiple Missing Information

The purpose of this chapter is to discuss the use of graphic procedures for dealing with multiple missing information through a review of an inexpensive but versatile graphic package called the Equation Plotter. For an example of multiple missing information, suppose one is faced with two alternatives. The first alternative scores $100 on benefits, but is unknown on costs. The second alternative score is unknown on benefits, but scores $60 on costs. Which alternative should be adopted?

	Benefits	–	Costs	=	Net Benefits
Alternative #1	$100	–	?	=	?
Alternative #2	?	–	$60	=	?

The basic idea of this graphing analysis is to convert questions that ask for exact cost or benefit figures into simpler questions that ask only whether the combination of the missing information is above or below a threshold, breakeven value, or critical score. The problem is easier to grasp if we start with only one unknown. For example, suppose the first alternative above scores $100 in benefits and $20 on costs, and the second alternative is unknown on benefits but scores $60 on costs. The first alternative would have a profit or net benefits of $80, which the second alternative would have to exceed in order to be the better alternative. The only way the second alternative can do that is if it scores higher than $140 on benefits. The $140 is thus the threshold value of the missing benefits for Alternative 2. The question as to the exact value of those benefits thus simplifies to asking whether the value of those benefits is likely to be more or less than $140.

	Benefits	–	Costs	=	Net Benefits
Alternative #1	$100	–	$20	=	$80
Alternative #2	?	–	$60	=	?

If there is more than one unknown in a decision-making problem or in interpreting other kinds of data, a combination of two unknowns can be dealt with by plotting a threshold curve or indifference curve instead of thinking in terms of a threshold point. With three unknowns, one can think in terms of a pair of threshold curves or a threshold band. With four unknowns, one can think in terms of a pair of threshold bands. These concepts become clearer when illustrated with concrete problems, such as the problem of nuclear energy versus solar energy discussed in this chapter. The concepts also become clearer with equation-plotting software. Such software is now readily available and will be illustrated in this chapter.

THE GENERAL NATURE OF THE EQUATION PLOTTER

There is now an equation plotter available for using graphics software to handle multiple missing information. It is called the Dugdale–Kibbey Equation Plotter and it was developed by Sharon Dugdale and David Kibbey of the Computer-Based Education Research Laboratory at the University of Illinois. The Equation Plotter is available from Sunburst Communications, 39 Washington Avenue, Pleasant-Ville, NY 10570 for $60. A spreadsheet-based equation plotter is available without charge to buyers of this present book on *Decision-Aiding Software* by writing to Decision Aids, Inc., 1720 Parkhaven Drive, Champaign, Illinois, 61820. This program is part of a larger package called "Green Globs and Graphing Equations", which is designed to provide high school students with a better understanding of what is involved in graphing equations. That understanding is especially promoted through a game in which the students seek to develop equations that when plotted will go across the screen without hitting any of the strategically or randomly placed green globs. The software is easily learned by students or by professionals. It is user-friendly in how it handles errors. It is available for IBM or Apple compatible computers. It requires only 256K, although with a graphics adaptor.

To illustrate the Equation Plotter, we can work with a go/no–go problem, and then later indicate how the procedures change with a problem that involves conflicting choices. A simple go/no–go problem is one in which we adopt a proposal if the benefits discounted by the probability of their occurring are greater than the costs. We reject the proposal if the benefits (B) discounted by the probability (P) are less than the costs (C). That means the threshold or breakeven equation is $PB = C$. Suppose at first that we do not know what the benefits are likely to be or the probability of success, but we do know that the costs are likely to be $50. We can later add that we do not know the costs either.

To use the Equation Plotter, one must first establish a grid. Doing so involves the following four steps:

1. Choose a square grid rather than a rectangular grid so that one's perceptions of where the missing values might be will not be influenced by one variable having more physical distance than another variable.
2. Decide whether the probabilities should be shown on the vertical or horizontal axis, and likewise with the benefits. Normally a dependent variable is shown on the vertical axis, and an independent variable is shown on the horizontal axis. Here we are not talking about probabilities as dependent on benefits, or benefits as dependent on probabilities. Rather, we are trying to show a curve or straight line that represents combinations of probabilities and benefits that exactly equal the $50 in cost. The combinations are thus breakeven combinations because any of those combinations yield no profits or losses, but rather an exact equality between the expected benefits and the costs. For plotting purposes, we do want one unknown to be on each side of the equation, but it makes no difference whether the P or B is on the left or right side. For consistency with prior usage, we choose to show the probabilities on the vertical axis (Y) and the benefits on the horizontal axis (X).
3. The computer then asks for a minimum and maximum value on the probabilities or Y axis. We type 0 and 1.00. We could provide for a narrower range if the realistic minimum were higher than 0, or the realistic maximum were lower than 1.00.
4. The computer then asks for a minimum and maximum value on the benefits. The minimum is $0 since there can be no negative benefits. The maximum we indicate as being $200 or 200 monetary units. This is only for graphing purposes. If we pick too high a maximum, then all the action in the graph may be in the lower left-hand corner and hard to read. If we pick too low a maximum, then the action may be outside the graph. In either case we would want to change the maximum in order to improve the readability. The maximum, however, has no influence on the bottom line of whether to adopt or reject the project. This is unlike the best-

worst approach to multiple missing information where the minimum and the maximum determine the midpoints or averages which do influence which alternative is best.

The above four steps are incorporated into Table 7.1, which shows a grid from the Dugdale–Kibbey Equation Plotter. The minimums and maximums can be easily changed. Any time one wants to change them in order to blow up a small portion of the graph or in order to see the graph in a larger context, one just types *Control-S*. The screen will then ask what new minimums and maximums are desired on the *Y* variable and the *X* variable. This is one advantage of the Dugdale–Kibbey Equation Plotter over other equation plotters which are less flexible in setting the minimums and maximums. The Equation Plotter also has the important advantage of allowing multiple curves and straight lines to be displayed simultaneously, rather than just one at a time. The curves and straight lines can also be quickly changed.

Table 7.1 is not completely generated by the Equation Plotter. The Plotter shows only the minimums and maximums. The other calibration needs to be added by the user. The Equation Plotter also labels the axes only as *Y* and *X*. The user needs to give the axes more specific names. Perhaps a future version of the Equation Plotter will allow for more calibration and for more labeling of the axes.

PLOTTING ONE CURVE AND TWO SETS OF QUADRANTS FOR TWO UNKNOWNS

The threshold equation where there are no profits and no losses is $PB = \$50$ since we know in this example that the cost is \$50. The plotting equation is thus $P = \$50/B$ or $Y = 50/X$, where P is treated as the Y variable and B as the X variable. In order to have the Equation Plotter plot that equation, we type the equation in response to the prompt which appears beneath the lower left-hand corner of the grid. After typing the equation, we hit *Enter* or *Return*, and a curve corresponding to the equation immediately appears on the grid. That is what is shown in Table 7.1.

Any point on that threshold or indifference curve is a breakeven point. That means that any combination of probability of success and amount of benefits represented by a point on that curve will yield no profits and no losses. If the combination of probability and benefits happens to be exactly on that curve, then there is a tie between the

Table 7.1 Microcomputer graphics and missing information

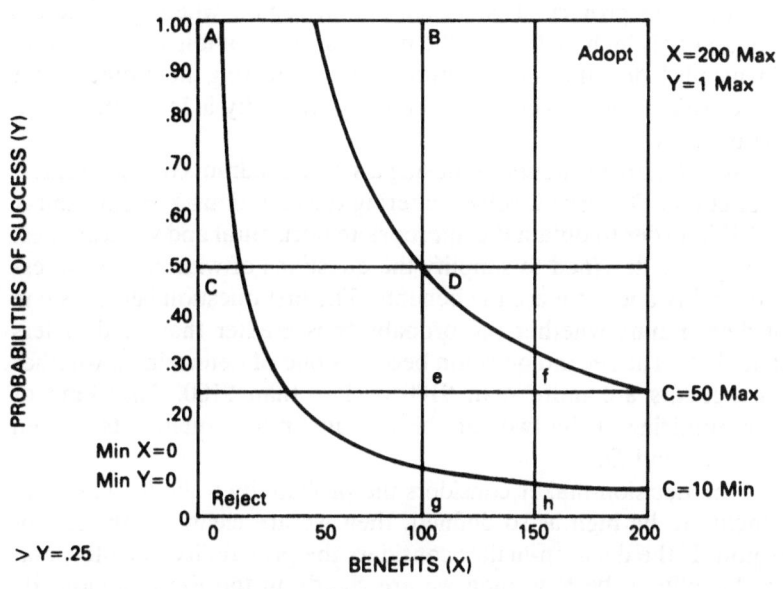

Notes:

1. This is a problem in deciding whether to adopt or reject a proposal in which one does not know the benefits, the probability of success, or the costs.
2. All one knows is that the benefits are from $0 to $200; the probability of success is from 0 to 1.00; and the costs are from $10 to $50.
3. The graph shows the probability of success on the vertical axis, and benefits on the horizontal axis. The *Adopt* region is thus in the upper right-hand corner, where the benefits are high and the probability of success is high. The *Reject* region is in the lower left-hand corner, where the benefits are low and the probability of success is low.
4. All points on the lower curve involve a combination of probability and benefits that exactly equal a cost of $10. All points on the upper curve involve a combination of probability and benefits that exactly equal a cost of $50. Both curves involve plotting the threshold or breakeven equation of $PB = C$, or $P = C/B$.
5. If the decision-makers perceive the combination of probability and benefits to be mainly above the upper curve, then the proposal should be adopted. If the decision-makers perceive the combination of probability and benefits to be mainly below the lower curve, then the proposal should be rejected.

two alternatives under consideration. Thus, any combination of *P* and *B* which is mainly above the curve should generally result in adopting the project. That is the *Adopt* region where the success probability is high and so are the benefits. Any combination of *P* and *B* which is below the curve should result in rejecting the project. That is the *Reject* region where the success probability is low, and so are the benefits.

Table 7.1 involves superimposing a set of quadrants on the indifference curve. Doing so involves entering the equations *Y = 0.50* and *X = 100* in order to obtain the appropriate horizontal and vertical lines. Doing so is designed to simplify the questions of what is the success probability and what are the benefits. The first question becomes one of determining whether the probability is greater than 0.50 or less than 0.50. The second question becomes one of determining whether the benefits are more than $100 or less than $100. That kind of dichotomizing of the two variables results in four quadrants labeled *A, B, C,* and *D*.

If the decision-maker considers the probability to be high and the benefits to be high as so defined, then we are clearly in the *Adopt* region. If the decision-maker considers the probability to be low and the benefits to be low, then we are clearly in the *Reject* region. If, however, the decision-maker perceives the probability to be high and the benefits to be low, then we are in quadrant *A* which is partly in the *Adopt* region and partly in the *Reject* region, although mainly in the *Reject* region. Likewise, if the decision-maker perceives the probability to be low and the benefits to be high, then we are in a similar position.

Suppose the decision-maker does perceive the combination of probability and benefits to be in quadrant *D*. The next step might logically be to superimpose a set of sub-quadrants on quadrant *D*. That is what is done in Table 7.1 by entering the equations *Y = 0.25* and *X = 150*. Doing so generates four sub-quadrants labeled *e, f, g,* and *h*. If the decision-maker considers the probability as being below 0.25, then the project should clearly be rejected. Likewise, if the decision-maker considers the probability to be above 0.25 and the benefits to be above 150, then the project should clearly be accepted as being in quadrant *f*, which is almost completely above the threshold curve.

Only if the decision-maker considers the probability as being between 0.25 and 0.50 and the benefits as being between 100 and 150 do we have a further problem. We can then superimpose a third set of quadrants on sub-quadrant *e*. That would be a rare occurrence since normally two sets of quadrants are enough to determine that the missing information is more likely to result in adopting or rejecting without having to go to a third set of quadrants. A third set, however, should be no more difficult to handle, although it may be easier to say whether a probability is more or less than 0.50 than whether it is more or less than 0.375 or 0.38.

PLOTTING TWO CURVES AND TWO SETS OF QUADRANTS FOR THREE UNKNOWNS

Table 7.1 adds a second indifference curve. The first indifference curve involved a cost of $50. Assume that $50 is the maximum the cost is likely to be. The second indifference curve involves a cost of $10, and assume that $10 is the minimum the cost is likely to be. The two indifference curves create an indifference band. Any combination of probability and benefits mainly above that indifference band is in the *Adopt* region, and below is in the *Reject* region. Any combination completely within the indifference band can be considered as indicating adoption if it is closer to the *Adopt* than the *Reject* region, and it would indicate rejection if it is closer to the *Reject* region.

If we suppose our decision-maker is in quadrant *D* on the first set of quadrants and in sub-quadrant *e* on the second set of quadrants, then the decision-maker should adopt the project since quadrant *e* is more in the *Adopt* than the *Reject* region. The combination is not in the *Reject* region at all. Thus, by adding a third unknown, we may make the problem easier to resolve, rather than more difficult. That is so in this case because if the second indifference curve is accurate with a lower cost than the first curve, then we now have a bigger *Adopt* region. A better way of putting it is that we now have a smaller *Reject* region and a bigger gray area.

PRESENTING THE VISUAL AID TO THE DECISION-MAKER

What we have presented so far is really the behind-the-scenes theory of the use of indifference curves for dealing with multiple missing information. When working with a decision-maker, the best way to proceed might be as follows:

1. Determine what components constitute the **benefits** in the decision to be reached. Also, determine what components constitute the **costs**. Here the benefit components are P and B, and the cost components are C.

2. Indicate to the decision-maker that the *threshold equation* here is $PB = C$. More generally, the B components equal the C components at the threshold. In a conflicting choice problem rather than a go/no–go decision, the general threshold equation would be the B minus C components of the first choice versus the B minus C components of the other choice. An example of a go/no–go threshold equation would be $PB = C$, $P_1 B = P_2 C$, and $PB_1 + B_2 = C$. The regions are called "Adopt" and "Reject". In the Adopt region, the benefits outweigh the costs, whereas the costs outweigh the benefits in the reject region. An example of a threshold equation for a conflicting choice problem would be $B_1 - C_1 = B_2 - C_2$ or $P_1 B_1 - C_1 = P_2 B_2 - C_2$. The regions are called "Adopt Alternative 1" and "Adopt Alternative 2". In the Alternative 1 region, the benefits minus the costs of Alternative 1 are greater than the benefits minus the costs of Alternative 2, whereas in the Alternative 2 region, the benefits minus the costs of Alternative 2 are greater.

3. Indicate the **two most important unknown variables**. Put one on the vertical axis of a grid and the other on the horizontal axis, as is shown in Table 7.1.

4. Instead of plotting the threshold equation, the next logical step in working with a decision-maker might be to **dichotomize each of the two most important unknown variables**. In this context the decision-maker is asked whether he or she perceives the success probability as being greater or less than 0.50. That means above or below the horizontal line. The decision-maker is also asked whether he or she perceives the benefits as being greater or less than $100. That means to the right or left of the vertical line.

When discussing the theory behind the indifference curve analysis, we start with an indifference curve and then we superimpose quadrants on it. When working with a decision-maker, we start with quadrants or a dichotomizing of the variables. We do not show the indifference curve until after the decision-maker has indicated where he or she perceives the combination of unknown variables to be in terms of the quadrants, rather than more precise measures. If the indifference curve were shown before those perceptions of the decision-maker were determined, then the perceptions might be unduly influenced by where the indifference curve is. Thus the decision-maker might have a tendency to say quadrant *b* if the decision-maker wants the project to be adopted, and to say quadrant *c* if he or she wants the project to be rejected. Holding back on showing the indifference curve decreases that kind of rationalizing or justifying of decisions already reached. These visual aids are designed mainly to enable decision-makers to reach meaningful decisions, rather than to rationalize questionable decisions.

If the decision-maker says either quadrant *b* or *c*, then the indifference curve can be shown and the matter settled. If the decision-maker says either quadrant *a* or *d*, then further probing needs to be done, but not to the point of ever asking the decision-maker for an exact probability or an exact amount of benefits. Suppose the decision-maker says quadrant *d*. Then divide that quadrant into sub-quadrants, as is shown in Table 7.1 by dichotomizing the low probabilities and dichotomizing the high benefits. If the decision-maker can position the combination as being in quadrant *f*, *g*, or *h*, then we can show Table 7.1 and consider the matter settled. Otherwise, we may need to divide sub-quadrant *e* into further quadrants.

Table 7.1 shows one set of quadrants superimposed on a maximum cost indifference curve and a minimum cost indifference curve. The purpose of showing this figure is to clarify how the analyst might communicate the meaning of the four quadrants to the decision-maker (DM):

1. If the DM perceives the combination as being in quadrant *b*, then **adopt the project**.
2. If the DM perceives the combination as being in quadrant *c*, then reject the project if the costs are likely to be **as high as $50**, but adopt the project if they are more likely to be **as low as $10**.
3. If the DM perceives the combination as being in quadrant *a* or *d*, then there is a need to clarify where in those quadrants. That is where developing a second set of quadrants can be especially helpful to determine whether the rough position is more in (or closer to) the "Adopt" region than the "Reject" region, or vice versa.

CONCLUSIONS

From this analysis one can conclude a set of important related ideas for dealing with multiple missing information through the use of indifference graphs. Those ideas include:

1. It is easier for people to say whether a probability or a score is **above or below a certain figure** than it is to say exactly what the probability or the score is.
2. The notion of being above or below a certain number or breakeven value applies if we have only **one unknown at a time**.
3. With two unknowns, we have to talk in terms of being above or below an indifference curve on which all points are **breakeven or threshold points**.
4. With three unknowns, we are talking about being above or below a pair of indifference curves or an indifference band, with the **top curve showing the third variable at its maximum and the bottom curve at its minimum**, or vice versa.
5. With four unknowns, we can talk in terms of two indifference bands as to whether the combination of unknowns is **mainly above or mainly below the pair of indifference bands**.
6. The **Equation Plotter** is excellent software for the above purposes, but one can do the same kind of curve drawing with Lotus 1–2–3 or other software that is capable of drawing curves to fit through a set of dots. This can be contrasted with regression analysis where the curve is smooth, rather than kinked, and generally does not go through all the dots.
7. An **indifference curve** in this context contains a set of points all of which provide equal satisfaction. The Y and X axis, however, do not show desired products. Instead they show alternative values for two unknown variables in the threshold equation in which the benefits and costs of one alternative are set equal to the benefits and cost of a second alternative.[1]

Notes and References

1. For further details on this analysis, see C. Moore, *Profitable Applications of the Break-Even System* (Englewood Cliffs, N.J.: Prentice-Hall, 1971);

S. Nagel, "Dealing with Unknown Variables in Policy/Program Evaluation", *Evaluation and Program Planning*, 6: 7–18 (1983); S. Nagel, "New Varieties of Sensitivity Analysis", *Evaluation Review*, 9: 772–9 (1986); and Samuel Richmond, *Operations Research for Management Decisions* (New York: Ronald Press, 1968): 108–12, 547–9.

8 Multiple and Possibly Conflicting Constraints

The purpose of this chapter is to discuss how to deal systematically with a variety of constraints in public policy analysis.

DEFINING AND CLASSIFYING CONSTRAINTS

Public policy analysis can be defined as processing a set of (1) governmental goals to be achieved, (2) alternatives for achieving them, and (3) relations between goals and alternatives in order to choose the best alternative or combination in light of the goals, alternatives, and relations. A constraint is a condition that must be met in order for a policy recommendation to be adopted regardless of the degree of other goal achievement.

There are a variety of constraints in public policy analysis. A basic classification is between quantitative and qualitative constraints. Quantitative constraints are generally measured in terms of the numerical degree to which they are met (or not met) on a ranking or an interval scale. Qualitative constraints tend to be discussed simply in terms of whether they are met or not met.

Examples of quantitative constraints include:

1. Minimum or maximum benefits or costs per person, place, group, activity, allocation object, or policy alternative. These are **equity constraints**.
2. Minimum or maximum levels of goal achievement per policy on one or more goals. These are **effectiveness constraints**.
3. A maximum overall cost level. This is a **budget constraint**.
4. A minimum overall benefits level. This is a **safety-net constraint**.
5. A minimum or maximum ratio between the benefits or costs of one alternative and another alternative, or between one goal and another goal. These are **ratio or balance constraints**.

Examples of qualitative constraints include:

1. **Political constraints** refer to the obstacles that public policies have

to overcome in order to be officially adopted. Those obstacles may include legislative approval, approval by the chief executive, and approval by the courts.

2. **Administrative constraints** refer to the obstacles that public policies have to overcome in the implementation process after they have been adopted in order to be considered successful.

3. **Ethical constraints** refer to prohibitions or mandates as to what is considered professionally proper for policy analysts, rather than what is considered to be a political or legal prerequisite. An example of an ethical constraint is the need to present all major viewpoints in an evaluation.

4. **Predictive constraints** refer to declarations or findings that a case or a given subject with a certain characteristic will lead to a victory for a certain side regardless what other variables are present.

5. There are also miscellaneous qualitative constraints that relate to the **specific subject matter of the policies under consideration**, such as approval by certain key interested groups or persons.

The same constraint can fit into more than one category. For example, an equity constraint might also be a political or legal constraint. A constraint can even sometimes be quantitative and sometimes qualitative. One should also note that any given policy problem can involve many types of constraints simultaneously. The above list can serve as a general checklist to help assure that all constraints have been satisfied in a public policy analysis.[1]

SEQUENCING BETWEEN OPTIMIZING GOALS AND SATISFYING CONSTRAINTS

There are basically two orders with regard to sequencing between optimizing goals and satisfying constraints. One can determine that all policies or budget categories satisfy the constraints first, and then make decisions as to how to optimize or maximize the goal variables. A second alternative is to choose among the discrete alternatives or allocate scarce resources to the budget categories in order to maximize the goal variables, and then make adjustments for any constraints that have not been adequately satisfied. Either approach satisfies the constraints, but one can show that optimizing the goals first and then satisfying the constraints will minimize the deviations between the optimum and actual scores.

For example, suppose we are seeking to allocate a $500 criminal-justice budget between police and courts. Suppose further the following facts:

1. There are two goals. One is crime reduction, and the other is fair procedure.
2. On crime reduction, the police do about twice as well as the courts. We thus give the police a score of 2, and the courts a score of 1 on that allocation criterion.
3. On fair procedure, the courts do about three times as well as the police. We thus give the police a score of 1 on fair procedure, and the courts a score of 3.
4. The overall score for the police would thus be 2 + 1 which adds to 3, and the overall score for the courts would be 1 + 3 which adds to 4.
5. If everything else were held constant, we would give the police 3/7 or 43% of the $500 and the courts 4/7 or 57%. We are thereby treating the sum of these scores as proxies for elasticity coefficients to which our scarce resources should be allocated proportionately. With a $500 budget, the police would get $214, and the courts would get $286. That is what is shown in Table 8.1A.

Suppose we now add a constraint that both the police and the courts should get 80% of what they were getting last year. At that time, there was a budget of $400 for these two items. The police received $300 last year, and 80% of that is $240. The courts received $100, and 80% is $80.

If we satisfy the constraints first and then optimize, we would go through the following steps with the above data:

1. Give $240 to the police and $80 to the courts off the top of the $500 budget, leaving $180 available to allocate in accordance with the criteria of crime reduction and fair procedure.
2. We then allocate 3/7 or 43% of the $180 to the police, which is $77. We also allocate 4/7 or 57% of the $180 to the courts which is $103.
3. The police thus get $240 from satisfying the constraints and $77 from the optimizing, which is a total of $317. The courts get $80 from satisfying the constraints and $103 from optimizing, which is a total of $183.
4. The sum of the two allocations add to $500 thereby satisfying the maximum budget constraint. The police get $317 which is more

Table 8.1   The proper order between optimizing and satisfying constraints

A. THE SOLUTION WITH NO CONSTRAINTS		
Total Resources = 500.00		
Alternative	Alloc.	P/W %
1 Police	214.29	42.86
2 Courts	285.71	57.14

B. SATISFYING THE CONSTRAINTS FIRST AND THEN OPTIMIZING		
Total Resources = 500.00		
Alternative	Alloc.	P/W %
1 Police	317.14	63.43
2 Courts	182.86	36.57

C. OPTIMIZING FIRST AND THEN SATISFYING THE CONSTRAINTS		
Total Resources = 500.00		
Alternative	Alloc.	P/W %
1 Police	240.00	48.00
2 Courts	260.00	52.00

Notes:

1. Table 8.1 shows that it is better (1) to optimize first and then make adjustments to satisfy the constraints than it is (2) to satisfy the constraints first and then optimize. The first alternative comes closer to the optimum allocation without constraints, although it does satisfy the constraints.
A. Table 8.1A shows the allocation solution with no constraints. It involves giving 43% to the police and 57% to the courts because the police have 3/7 of the total points available and the courts have 4/7.
B. Table 8.1B shows the allocation solution if the constraints are satisfied before optimizing. In this situation, the minimum constraints provide for giving each activity 80% of the allocation from the previous year. In that year, the police received $300, and the courts received $100. The minimums are thus $240 and $80 for a total of $320. There is $500 available, leaving $180 to allocate on the basis of efficiency after the $320 has been allocated. The police receive 3/7 or 43% of the $180, which adds $77 to the $240 for a total of $317. The courts receive 4/7 or 57% of the $180, which adds $103 to the $80 for a total of $183. Those allocations correspond to percentages of 63% and 37%.
C. Table 8.1C shows the allocation solution if we optimize first and then make adjustments to satisfy the constraints. The first step in that two-step process yields the same results as Table 8.1A. Those results, however, are $26 below the minimum for the police, and $26 above the minimum for the courts. We therefore, logically take $26 from the courts' allocation and give it to the police allocation. The result is an allocation of $260 to the police and $240 to the courts. Those allocations correspond to percentages of 48% and 52%. The 48% and 52% of Table 8.1C are obviously closer to the optimums of 43% and 57% of Table 8.1A than are the 63% and 37% of Table 8.1B.

than their minimum of $240, and the courts get $183 which is more than their minimum of $80, thereby satisfying both minimum constraints. That is what is shown in Table 8.1B.

If we optimize first and then satisfy the constraints, we would go through the following steps with the above data:

1. Give 3/7 or 43% of the $500 to the police, which is $215. Give 4/7 or 57% of the $500 to the courts, which is $285.
2. We then observe that the police would be getting $25 less than their minimum requirement of $240. The courts would be getting more than $25 above their minimum requirement of $80.
3. We therefore take $25 from the $285 initially given to the courts, leaving the courts with $260. That $25 is given to the police so the police now have $240.
4. The sum of the two allocations is $500, thereby satisfying the maximum budget constraint. The separate allocations satisfy the minimum constraints. That is what is shown in Table 8.1C.

This shows that the order of satisfying the constraints and optimizing goals can produce different results. The second approach of optimizing first is better when there is a difference. It is better because it comes closer to achieving the optimum while still satisfying the constraints. The optimum with no constraints would be $214 to the police and $286 to the courts. The first approach deviates from those figures by +$103 and −$103, since it allocates $317 and $183. The second approach deviates from those figures by only +$25 and −$25, since it allocates $240 to the police and $260 to the courts.

The reason why the first approach does not do as well is because some activities, places, or budget categories are not worth more than the minimum. That is all they get under the second approach. The first approach, however, automatically gives them the minimum initially, and then it allocates beyond the minimum if a budget category has a positive score on the goals to be achieved, regardless how low the positive score is. Any positive score entitles a relatively ineffective budget category to receive a proportionate share of the residue after the minimums have been taken out of the total budget to be allocated.

Tables 8.1A and 8.1B were generated by the microcomputer program called Policy/Goal Percentaging (P/G%). The program is called that because it relates policies to goals, and it uses part/whole percentaging for dealing with multi-dimensionality on the goals and for dealing with allocation problems. The program is useful for processing a set of (1) goals to be achieved, (2) alternatives for achieving them, and (3) relations between goals and alternatives in order to choose the best alternative, combination, or allocation. The program has an option for satisfying the constraints first and then optimizing, as is shown in Table 8.1B. There is, however, no automatic option yet for optimizing first and then satisfying the constraints. If the constraints are not satisfied by the optimizing, the adjustments needed may be better done by a human decision-maker working with a calculator than trying to program all the possible adjustments. The following steps are appropriate to follow for proper sequencing of the optimizing and the constraints-satisfying when using P/G%:

1. Find the optimum choice or optimum allocation, ignoring the constraints.
2. Observe which alternatives are excluded or under-included in the allocation contrary to the constraints.
3. Give those alternatives automatically whatever inclusion or allocation the constraints require.
4. Redo the optimizing with the remaining alternatives and the remaining resources. The alternatives from step 3 can be deactivated by toggling off their identification numbers. Likewise, the budget can be appropriately adjusted.

The above example could have been made more complicated by having more budget categories, more goals, differently weighted goals, and other variations. Such variations will be discussed later in this chapter. The important point is the need to optimize first and then satisfy the constraints, rather than vice versa.[2]

EQUITY CONSTRAINTS

Quantitative constraints can relate to equity, effectiveness, the total budget, a safety net, or a desired ratio. Equity constraints involve minimum benefits or maximum costs per person, place, group, allocation object, or policy alternative. The purpose of this section is not to discuss what constitutes a fair minimum or maximum for different subject matters or other substantive issues. Rather the purpose is to clarify the methodology of dealing with constraints. That includes further clarifying how one optimizes first and then makes adjustments for satisfying minimum benefits or maximum costs per alternative.

Suppose in the initial example that we add a third budget category to cover prisons and other correctional expenses. Suppose further that corrections are considered only half as effective in crime reduction as the courts are and only one-fourth as relevant to fair procedure as the police are, as is shown in Table 8.1. Suppose also that corrections are considered to need a minimum of $40. In light of that information, what is the optimum allocation, and how should the constraints be dealt with?

**Making Adjustments to Satisfy
the Constraints**

If there are *two* budget categories with one below its minimum and the other above its minimum, then calculate what it would take to bring the "below" category up to its minimum. Then take that amount from the allocation of the "above" category, as is done in moving from column 5a to column 7a on police and courts in Table 10.4. In this example, the police are $26 below their minimum, and the courts are $206 above their minimum. We logically take $26 from the courts allocation and give it to the policy allocation to satisfy the minimum constraints.

If there are *three* budget categories with one below its minimum and the other two above their minimums, then take the deficit from the allocations of the categories that have surpluses. Take from those categories in proportion to their relative effectiveness. Thus if one category is twice as effective as the other, then it should contribute less toward the deficit. More specifically, perform the following steps.

1. Note that the police are $45 short of their minimum in the three-way allocation shown in columns 5a and 6.
2. Determine the relative overall effectiveness of courts and corrections by dividing 4 by 4.75 which is 84%, and dividing 0.75 by 4.75 which is 16%.
3. Work with the complements of those two percentages in determining how much of the $45 is charged to the courts and how much to corrections. Ideally, the courts category should pay only

16% of the $45 which is $7.20, and corrections should pay 84% of the $45 which is $37.80.

4. That ideal or optimum way of covering the deficit will not work here because if we take $37.80 away from the $50 allocation of corrections, then corrections will only get $12.20 which is substantially below its minimum of $40.

5. Therefore, just take as much as possible from corrections which is only $10, and take the rest of the $45 from the courts category which is $35.

6. That makes the adjusted allocations in the three-way situation $240, $220, and $40 respectively. Those figures add to $500, and they come as close as possible to the optimum allocations while satisfying all the minimum constraints.

7. A simpler way to deal with the last column in Table 10.4 is to give police the $240 minimum which it would otherwise not be entitled to if it were not for the constraint. The remaining $260 is then divided between courts and corrections with courts receiving 4.00/4.75 or 84% of the remaining $260, which is $218. Corrections receives 0.75/4.75 or 16% of the remaining $260, which is $42.

If there are *four* budget categories with one below its minimum and the other three above their minimums, then the procedure is slightly different. Suppose the effectiveness percentages for apportioning the deficit are 60%, 20%, and 10%. Those three percentages add to 100%. We would not use them as multiplying coefficients in apportioning the deficit because doing so would place the heaviest burden on the most effective budget category. We therefore take the complements of those three numbers which are 40%, 80%, and 90%. Those three percentages add to 200%. We therefore divide each of them by 2 to obtain the multiplying coefficients of 20%, 40%, and 45%. If there were four budget categories involved, we would divide the complementary percentages by 3 so they would add to 100%. The general rule is that we divide the complementary percentages by $N-1$ where N is the number of budget categories having surpluses which are being taxed to cover an equity deficit in one or more of the other budget categories. The general rule also says that we apply those multiplying percentages only up to the point where a budget category with a surplus has its surplus wiped out and not beyond that point.

Perhaps a better way to adjust to satisfy the equity constraints with two, three, and four budget categories is as follows:

1. With two budget categories, suppose category A is below its minimum and category B is above its minimum. After allocating in proportion to their aggregate scores, then give category A its minimum. Give the rest of the total budget to category B.
2. With three budget categories, suppose A is below its minimum and B and C are above their minimums. Then give A its minimum. Divide the rest of the total budget between B and C in proportion to their aggregate scores.
3. With four or more budget categories, one can reason by analogy to the three-category situation. No matter how many budget categories are below their minimums in the initial optimizing, give them their minimums and then remove them from further allocating. The remainder of the total budget then gets divided proportionately among the other budget categories. This assumes that the sum of the minimums does not add up to more than the total budget. If that assumption is not true, then we have a budget constraint problem which is discussed later.

Variations and Implications

The same general rules would apply if we had a situation in which we were allocating tax burdens instead of allocating expenditure benefits. In that situation, the initial allocation might result in one person, place, or group being overly taxed by exceeding a maximum constraint. That person would be relieved of the excess by having it spread among the other budget categories in proportion to how well they score on whatever criteria are being used to allocate the tax burdens.

If these general rules are followed, then the result will be an optimum handling of the equity constraints. The total budget to be spent or the total tax to be assessed will not be either undershot or overshot. The minimum and maximum constraints will be satisfied, and the bottom-line adjusted allocations or assessments will come as close as possible to the optimum allocations or assessments while still satisfying the constraints.

The problem shown in Table 8.1 can be handled by the Policy/Goal Percentaging software by using its optimizing methodology and then making the adjustments described above. The P/G% program is now being improved to include those adjustments, although they can be made with a hand calculator.

One might note that there seems to be no mathematical programming routine that can handle the problem of Table 8.1. The problem can be expressed in mathematical programming language as follows:

$$(X_1)^2 + (X_2)^1 = Y_1$$
$$(X_1)^1 + (X_2)^3 = Y_2$$
$$X_1 + X_2 = \$500$$
$$X_1 \geq \$240$$
$$X_2 \geq \$80$$

The first two equations express the two non-linear objective functions that are involved. The next three statements express the constraints. There are mathematical programming routines that can do non-linear programming. There are also mathematical programming routines that can do multi-objective programming. No routines, however, seem to exist that can do both non-linear and multi-objective programming.[3]

CONFLICTING CONSTRAINTS

Conflicting constraints can generally be resolved in various ways:

(1) **Prioritizing the constraints and then satisfying them in the order of their priorities.** That approach tends to result in only the first constraint being satisfied if the constraints are mutually exclusive. An example might be choosing among two different school busing programs. One may satisfy the constraint of achieving a minimum 60% integration score, and the other one may satisfy the constraint of not spending more than a maximum number of dollars. If there is a court order involved, the court is likely to say the integration constraint is the more important one to satisfy. The courts have rejected excuses that relate to the expensiveness of providing court-appointed counsel to indigent defendants in criminal cases. The courts are, however, more willing to compromise in light of the costs when statutory rather than constitutional interpretation is involved, as with satisfying requirements that relate to environmental protection or occupational safety.

(2) **Developing a compromise whereby each constraint is partly satisfied.** One kind of compromise involves splitting the difference where each constraint is considered equally important. This involves determining the result if only the first constraint were

satisfied, and then determining the result if only the second constraint were satisfied. An example is the situation dealing with satisfying the conflicting effectiveness constraints. The allocation that meets the maximum delay constraint does not meet the minimum respect constraint. On the other hand, the allocation that meets the minimum respect constraint does not meet the maximum delay constraint. That example involved splitting the difference because the delay constraint and the respect constraint were considered equally important. The compromise is the midpoint or the average between those separate results.

(3) Another kind of compromise involves **determining a weighted average between these separate results**. Each constraint is given a weight indicating its relative importance. The compromise result thus tends to be closer to the result which would occur if only the more heavily weighted constraints were considered. An example is the one dealing with satisfying minimum equity constraints where the sum of the minimums adds to more than the total budget. It seems fairer to allocate in proportion to the minimums than to treat each minimum constraint as being equally important. That kind of proportionate allocation in effect weights each constraint by the size of its minimum.

(4) Another method of resolving conflicting constraints which seems especially worth seeking is to **increase the total benefits or reduce the total costs so all the constraints can be satisfied**. That approach is worth multiple examples. One involves satisfying all the equity minimums by increasing the total budget through greater productivity, creativity, or whatever it takes to generate more resources. Another example involves switching to an additional alternative (such as criminal case diversion) when the existing alternatives (such as trials and pleas) cannot satisfy all the effectiveness constraints. Still another example is working additional trial hours in order to make going to trial as attractive to a client as accepting a settlement, or working to get a bigger settlement in order to make accepting a settlement as attractive to the lawyer as going to trial.

(5) Special solutions may exist for conflicting constraints in light of the **specific subject matters**. An example is the predictive situation involving religious activities in the public schools where the Supreme Court indicates that a purely educational purpose will make the activities constitutional, but a participation requirement will make the activities unconstitutional. The best way of

dealing with those possibly conflicting constraints might be to recognize they conflict only in a kind of truth table that shows all the possible combinations, but they are not likely to occur in reality given the interests of the groups that favor required religious activities. Many other conflict situations may also be unrealistic problems, or problems that have other situation-specific solutions.

In deciding among alternative ways of satisfying individual constraints or conflicting constraints, a decision matrix can be quite helpful, whereby the alternatives are put on the rows, the criteria for judging them are put on the columns, and relation scores are put in the cells, possibly on a 1–5 scale. The basic idea of thinking in terms of alternatives, criteria, and relations was done at least implicitly in discussing the following controversies:

(1) Deciding whether one should satisfy constraints first and then optimize, or optimize first and then satisfy the unsatisfied constraints.

(2) Meeting the equity minimums (where some budget categories are below their minimums and some are above) by giving the minimums to those who are below and then allocating the residue proportionately to those who are above, as contrasted to an approach that involves taking from those who are above in reverse proportionality and giving to those who are below.

(3) Deciding between splitting the difference evenly and working with weighted or proportionate constraints in resolving the conflicting effectiveness constraints of delay and respect, and in resolving the conflicting constraints of equity minimums and a budget maximum.

(4) Deciding between a non-linear and a linear approach to developing the production functions, in the example of the safety-net constraints.

(5) Deciding between a pollution tax and a marketable pollution right in view of their respective political feasibility and other characteristics.

(6) Deciding between public and private sector delivery systems for home ownership for the poor and other projects, in view of their respective administrative feasibility and other characteristics.

(7) Deciding between settling and going to trial, in light of the client's profit, the lawyer's profit, and other criteria.

(8) Deciding between predicting the Supreme Court decisions (in the cases involving religious activities in the public schools) on the basis of three versus four predictive criteria.

In deciding among alternative ways of satisfying individual constraints or conflicting constraints, various kinds of sensitivity analysis can be helpful for determining the effects of input changes on the conclusion as to which substantive or methodological alternative is best. Forms of sensitivity analysis in this context include:

(1) **What–if analysis.** This kind of analysis is especially associated with microcomputer spreadsheets. It can be applied to decision matrices like those just mentioned. It involves determining what would happen to the bottom-line conclusion if there were changes in the alternatives, criteria, constraints, weights, relations, or other inputs. An example is adding the diversion alternative to trials and pleas, or adding expense to the goals of delay-reduction and respect in the effectiveness example. Experimenting with different weights for the criteria would also be an example, as was mentioned in developing the predictive analysis. Experimenting with different relation scores is another example, such as different settlement offers, expected values, or trial hours in the ethical constraints situation. One can also experiment to see what would happen with different constraints, such as changing the maximum budget constraint or the equity minimum constraints in the budgeting situation.

(2) **Threshold analysis.** This kind of analysis is especially associated with the P/G% program. It generally involves determining what it would take to bring a second-place alternative up to first place. It can be illustrated by showing what it would take to bring a lawyer's second-place alternative of settling up to his or her first-place alternative of going to trial, or what it would take to bring a client's second-place alternative of going to trial up to his or her first-place alternative of settling. A quantitative constraint can also have a threshold value, above which the first-place alternative remains in first place, and below which the second-place alternative moves into first place.

(3) **Convergence analysis.** This kind of analysis is also associated with the P/G% program. It is normally used to determine at what point a criterion weight becomes large enough so that the criterion dominates all the other criteria. For example, if respect

were the only criterion in the analysis of criminal case disposi-
tions, then the allocation would be 75% to trials and 25% to
pleas, because trials receives a score of 6 on respect and pleas
receives a score of 2. The convergence weight of respect to delay
is a weight of 2.00 because at that weight, the allocation is 70%
and 30%. The 70%–30% allocation is within only five percentage
points of the 75%–25% allocation which would occur if respect
had a weight of infinity. Thus, a weight of 2 is roughly the
equivalent of infinity because it produces results that are within
five percentage points of the results produced by a weight of
infinity. A quantitative constraint can also have a convergence
value of, say, 3. At that value, the results are within five percentage points of what would occur if the constraint requires a
minimum or maximum of approximately 1 to 10 units for a goal
or an alternative.

(4) **Updating analysis.** This kind of sensitivity analysis shows how the
policy recommendation or decision rule changes as a result of
new events or new cases. For example, if various anti-pollution
bills are passed in Congress, then this may cause us to revise our
notions of the political feasibility of various kinds of anti-
pollution legislation, and to revise our policy recommendations.
Likewise, if various housing statutes are implemented successfully in the administrative agencies, this may cause us to revise
our notions of the administrative feasibility of various kinds of
housing legislature, and to revise our recommendations. Updating analysis is particularly important for developing and main-
taining decision rules where the updating involves inputting the
latest court decisions.

From this overall analysis, one can conclude that satisfying constraints in public policy analysis (even conflicting constraints) is not
so difficult from a methodological perspective, provided that one
proceeds in a systematic logical manner that is sensitive to the specific
subject matters involved. It is hoped that this chapter will shed light
on the distinctions between (1) constraints and goals, (2) different
types of constraints, (3) constraint-satisfying and optimizing, and (4)
prioritizing, compromising, and resource expanding in resolving conflicting constraints. It is also hoped that this chapter will shed light on
such important tools as the decision matrix and various forms of
sensitivity analysis for dealing with constraints and other aspects
of decision-making. In policy analysis, constraints do need to be

considered, but they do not need to be constraining with regard to rationality and creativity. They can be treated as another worthwhile challenge in the variety of problems encountered in doing systematic public policy evaluation.

SOME CONCLUSIONS

The title of this chapter is "Multiple and Possibly Conflicting Constraints". Looking back over the nine types of constraints that have been discussed, we can see a number of cross-cutting principles. Especially important are the principles or variations that deal with conflicting constraints. Those situations have generally been unnecessarily difficult to resolve in decision science.

A constraint is a condition that must be met in order for a policy recommendation to be adopted, regardless of the degree of other goal achievement. In a predictive context, a constraint is a condition that must be met in order for a prediction of victory, defeat, or other outcome to be meaningful, regardless of the scores on the other predictive criteria. All constraints have an element of minimum or maximum that cannot be violated. The minimums tend to refer to minimum benefits and the maximums tend to refer to maximum costs.

Constraints in public policy analysis can be classified as fitting into any one or more of nine categories. They refer to constraints that relate to (1) equity, (2) effectiveness, (3) overall budgets, (4) safety nets, (5) ratios, (6) political feasibility, (7) administrative feasibility, (8) ethical responsibility, and (9) predictive constraints. Those constraints were illustrated in this chapter mainly by examples that relate to allocating a criminal justice budget between the police and the courts.

Optimizing without constraints differs from optimizing with constraints. In pure optimizing, the allocating or choosing is done in proportion to or in light of how well the alternatives score on the criteria. The methodology tends to involve calculating percentages for allocation purposes or aggregate scores for choosing among discrete alternatives. When constraints are present, the methodology tends to involve algebraic solutions. If a minimum constraint is present, one usually sets an alternative or criterion equal to that minimum. One does not want to go below the minimum, or the constraint will be violated. One also generally does not want to go above the minimum, or unnecessary costs may be incurred. Likewise, if a maximum constraint is present, one usually sets an alternative or criterion equal to that maximum. One does not want to go above the maximum, or the constraint will be violated. One also generally does not want to go below the maximum, or benefits may be unnecessarily missed.

Notes and References

1. On dealing with constraints in public policy analysis in general, see S. Nagel, *Public Policy: Goals, Means, and Methods* (New York: St Martin's Press, 1984), especially the chapters on equity, effectiveness, human rights, discretion, economic structure, government structure, political feasibility, and ethical constraints. On quantitative constraints in allocation problems, see "Allocation Logic", in S. Nagel, *Policy Evaluation: Making Optimum Decisions* (New York: Praeger, 1982).
2. On the idea of optimizing first and then satisfying the constraints especially in the context of allocating to the police and courts, see S. Nagel "Optimally Allocating Money to Places and Activities", in Patrick Humphreys and Janos Vecsenyi (eds), *High Level Decision Support: Lessons from Case Studies* (Amsterdam: North-Holland, 1986). On the example of allocating to the police and the courts, see James Levine, Michael Musheno, and Dennis Palumbo, *Criminal Justice in America: Law in Action* (Wiley, 1985).
3. On equity constraints, see Douglas Rae *et al.*, *Equalities* (Cambridge, Mass. Harvard University Press, 1981); and S. Nagel, "Equity as a Policy Goal", in Nagel, *Public Policy: Goals. Means and Methods*.

9 The Need for Simplicity in Spite of All That Multiplicity

The purpose of this chapter is to explain how traditional optimizing can be improved by multiple criteria decision-making (MCDM) in general and the Policy/Goal Percentaging (P/G%) variation of MCDM in particular.

The essence of Policy/Goal Percentaging is the analyzing of public policy problems by:

1. Listing available alternatives on the rows of a two-dimensional matrix.
2. Listing criteria for judging the alternatives on the columns of the matrix.
3. Inserting scores in the cells showing how each alternative relates to each criterion.
4. Transforming the scores if necessary to consider that the goals may be measured on difference dimensions.
5. Aggregating the transformed scores across each alternative in order to arrive at a summation score for each alternative.
6. Drawing a conclusion as to which alternative or combination should be adopted.[1]

The forms of traditional optimizing that the above analysis can supplement or improve upon include:

1. **Payoff matrices**, which show alternatives on the rows, contingent events on the columns, and payoffs in the cells from each alternative given the occurrence or non-occurrence of the contingent event.
2. **Decision-trees**, which represent a combination of arrow diagrams and payoff matrices by showing a set of decision forks, probability forks, and other paths leading to a set of payoffs.
3. **Optimum level curves**, which show that too much or too little of a policy produces a hill-shaped or valley-shaped relation with benefits, costs, or benefits minus costs.

4. **Indifference curves and functional curves**, which are considered useful for allocating scarce resources.[2]

The P/G% approach is described above in terms of the decision matrix which is associated with it. It could have also been described in terms of the logical and mathematical algorithm that is associated with it. That algorithm emphasizes part/whole percentages for dealing with multi-dimensionality, and the use of criterion scores as proxies for non-linear elasticity coefficients. Likewise, the four forms of traditional optimizing could be described in terms of their mathematical characteristics. The first two relate to finite mathematics and probabilistic decision theory. The second two relate to classical calculus optimization and linear/non-linear programming.

COMPARISONS OF FOUR FORMS OF OPTIMIZING

Payoff Matrices

A problem involving decision-making under conditions of risk may be handled by both a payoff matrix and by an MCDM approach. The two approaches at first glance look somewhat similar. They both involve discrete alternatives on the rows and states of nature or criteria on the columns. Most MCDM approaches are capable of handling multiple alternatives as well as multiple criteria. A typical payoff matrix, however, can handle only one go/no–go alternative or two conflicting choices, and it can handle only one contingent event at a time.

Being able to consider multiple criteria and multiple alternatives makes the MCDM and P/G% approaches more validly in conformity with reality and not just a simplistic abstraction. The problem of whether to take an abused child away from its family is a good example. The payoff matrix approach tends to over-emphasize the probability of subsequent abuse as a criterion, and it may lead to undesirable decisions to take the child away. The MCDM approach involves a more balanced perspective by also explicitly considering (1) the need to preserve whatever love might exist within the family between the child, its parents, and its siblings, which is not so likely to be present in any other environment, and (2) the need to consider the extra costs to the taxpayer which may not be so warranted.

The MCDM and P/G% approaches are not only more valid but also simpler. They tend to make use of 1–5 scales, integer weighted criteria, computerized threshold analysis, and a logical way of analyzing a problem in terms of alternatives, criteria, and relations. These approaches thus combine increased validity with increased simplicity instead of presenting the more common tradeoff of having to sacrifice some precision for simplicity or some simplicity for precision.

Decision-Trees

To deal with multiple contingent events, decision-trees are often used. A good example is deciding whether to go to trial or accept a settlement in the field of litigation strategy. That type of problem could lead to many confusing branches when approached from a decision-tree perspective. Inputting all that information via a decision-tree program (like the Arborist published by The Scientific Press) is a complicated chore. It is even more complicated to try to manipulate such a decision-tree in order to determine the best choice and what it would take to bring the second-best choice up to first place.

The data from a complicated decision-tree can be easily handled by most MCDM software (including P/G%) by treating each scenario or path as a separate criterion in a matrix with two alternatives on the rows and the scenarios as criteria on the columns. There would also be a criterion covering the litigation costs and a criterion indicating the settlement offer. The probabilities would be treated as values for weighting the scores of each alternative on each scenario or criterion. Each probability or weight is the product of the component probabilities. The damages also need to be adjusted for collection fees and time discounting. The time discounting can also be done by MCDM software which allows for such transformations, as P/G% does.

With that matrix format, one can quickly determine the alternative that generates the most benefits minus costs. Such a format also facilitates determining the changes in the probabilities or present value scores that would bring the second-place alternative up to first place. That information can be helpful in deciding whether to have confidence in the first-place alternative and what critical inputs may require additional information. Knowing how close the breakeven values are to the actual values can also be helpful in litigation strategy by informing the lawyer advocate where to concentrate one's efforts in order to produce a more favorable decision.

The advantages of an MCDM matrix over a decision-tree include:

1. The MCDM matrix is **far easier to type** without the artwork of a decision-tree.
2. It is far simpler in terms of the number of rows since there are only **as many rows as there are options.**
3. It is **more consistent with the commonsense business practice** of picking the option that is most profitable, or that is positively profitable in a go/no–go situation.
4. It eliminates virtually all **rounding errors.**
5. It is far **easier to read.**
6. It allows for an **infinite number of degrees of damages.** In calculating an average, the damages can be any amount.
7. It allows for an **infinite number of degrees of delay**, not just two or four years on judgement, or one and three years on collection. In calculating average delay, the time periods can be any amount.
8. It easily allows for **more plaintiff choices** than just suing or not suing, such as sue with a jury trial, sue with a bench trial, settle with a structured settlement, settle with a flat payoff, or reject the case altogether.
9. It easily allows for a **defendant perspective** of defending with a jury trial request, defending with no jury trial request, offering various structured settlements, or offering various flat payoffs.
10. It easily allows for **sensitivity analysis** whereby any of the benefit or cost items can be expressed in terms of a **threshold value** that would make for a tie between suing and not suing at the bottom line.
11. It easily allows for **sensitivity analysis** whereby any of the benefit or cost items can be expressed as a **range between minimum and maximum values.**
12. It easily allows for **non-monetary benefits and non-monetary costs** which would be involved in criminal cases and possibly civil cases that do not involve damages.
13. The **arithmetic is much simpler.**
14. There is no **unnecessary disaggregation** into so many pieces. The MCDM table disaggregates the decision-making into benefit items, cost items and *B–C* net items. The MCDM table thus forces the decision-maker to think about each of those goal components in order to decide between the two options avail-

able. Delay and collection can be considered costs, negative benefits, or simply items that are relevant to determining the true benefits.

15. A MCDM table could show the degree of risk adverseness as a cost of suing, or show the degree of risk preference as a benefit of suing. Being risk adverse is, however, a non-monetary cost, and being a risk preferer is a non-monetary benefit. MCDM tables can deal with a **mix of monetary and non-monetary variables** by methods described in the references at the end of this chapter.

16. It easily allows for making **allocation decisions** as to how much time or money should be invested in alternative case activities or cases.

17. Decision-trees tend to encourage lots of branches concerning **relatively trivial matters** at the ending branches such as how long it takes to collect on a judgement that is already awarded, and a devaluing of **more important matters** like the diversity of factors that influence winning and losing at the initial branches.

18. The MCDM table can be easily handled with a microcomputer program which provides for **prompting and sensitivity analysis**.

19. The decision matrix or MCDM table can easily handle **multiple alternatives**, not just two alternatives.

20. The decision matrix can handle **non-monetary criteria**, not just monetary ones.

21. The decision matrix can add and subtract alternatives, criteria, and relations, and make other sensitivity changes with relative ease in order to see how they affect the **bottom-line conclusions**.

Optimum Level Curves

Many public policy problems involve finding an optimal level of activity where doing too much or too little is undesirable. This is true of all undesirable societal occurrences which are quite costly to eliminate or greatly reduce, such as highway deaths, violent crimes, terminal cancer, and harmful pollution. For each problem, too much is clearly undesirable, but achieving only a small occurrence may also be too costly.

The traditional optimizing perspective on these problems is some form of classical calculus optimization. That means trying to arrive at a level of occurrences where the marginal benefits equal the marginal costs, or where the marginal costs of allowing the undesirable activity to occur equals the marginal costs of seeking to eliminate the activity.

In order to find the equilibrium or optimum point, one generally needs to establish an equation for each of the two basic relations. The costs of allowing the occurrence might be expressed as $a(x)^b$, and the cost of fighting the occurrence might be expressed as $A(X)^B$. Thus we want to set the marginal costs equal to each other and solve for X to find the optimum level. That means solving for X in an equation like $ba(X)^{b-1} = BA(X)^{B-1}$.

That approach, however, is often meaningless to apply:

1. **No good data is available** for doing the statistical analysis on which the non-linear regression equations might be based.
2. The costs and benefits are often **non-monetary as well as monetary**.
3. There may be **spurious correlations** between the costs and the social indicator being examined by virtue of causal forces that are influencing both of them.
4. There may be problems of **reciprocal causation** whereby the level of expenditures influences the social indicator, but the social indicator also influences the level of expenditures.
5. There may be many costs and benefits requiring a **multi-criteria perspective**.

Virtually all optimum level problems can be converted into more meaningful MCDM problems. Doing so involves changing the nature of the question from "What is the optimum level of crime, pollution, cancer, or defendants released prior to trial?" The new question becomes, "What is the best combination of ways to reduce crime, pollution, cancer, or defendants being expensively held in jail prior to trial when other defendants are expensively committing crimes and not showing up while released?" Phrasing the question in those multi-criteria terms generates many alternatives and many criteria for judging them. More important, it frequently generates ideas for arriving at a solution that can be a super-optimum with regard to exceeding the best expectations of each of the contending interests in public policy problems.

For example, take the subject of what is the best pre-trial release system to have. Conservative solutions tend to emphasize holding people in jail in order to reduce crime committing and no-shows by released defendants. Liberal solutions tend to emphasize releasing people in order to reduce embittering experiences, arbitrary subjectivity in determining who will be held, jail riots due to overcrowding, and defendants pleading guilty in order to be released from pre-trial detention on probation or for a term equal to the time they have already spent in jail waiting for trial. If one just talks in terms of the optimum level to hold, then conservatives are going to be antagonized if the figure is too low, and liberals are going to be antagonized if the figure is too high, although either side might be mildly pleased that the figure is not worse. It was partly an MCDM perspective that led to bail reforms which emphasized releasing more defendants but simultaneously reducing crime committing and no-shows by (1) screening defendants to determine their degree of risk for being released, (2) having defendants show up once a week or so at the courthouse before trial, (3) notifying defendants shortly before trial, (4) selectively prosecuting no-shows, and (5) especially providing for speedy trials to reduce the time available for crime committing, disappearing, or running up an expensive pretrial detention bill.

Allocation Analysis

Traditional allocation analysis involves obtaining information on alternative allocations to see their statistical effects or marginal rates of return. For example, one might obtain data at many points in time showing (1) how much money City 1 allocated to fighting crime, and (2) how much crime occurred at each of those time points. With that data, one can derive the numerical parameters for City 1 in an equation of the form $Y_1 = a_1 + b_1 \log X_1$. Y is crime occurrence, and X is anti-crime dollars. Working with the logarithm of X_1 takes into consideration that anti-crime dollars reduce crime, but at a diminishing rate of return. One can modify the basic equation by using anti-crime dollars at a prior point in time (X_{t-1}) in order partially to control for reciprocal causation. One can also modify the basic equation by adding Y_{t-1} as an independent variable on the right side of the equation partially to control for other variables that influence crime occurrence besides anti-crime dollars. A similar analysis can be done for City 2, yielding an equation of the form $Y_2 = a_2 + b_2 \log X_2$.

Suppose we only have two cities, to which we want to allocate \$50. The logical way to do so with this information would be to allocate the \$50 in such a way as to have $X_1 + X_2 = \$50$, and to have the marginal rates of return of the two cities equal each other. Doing so will put the cities into an equilibrium, where there is nothing to be gained by shifting dollars from one city to another. We would not want to give all of the $50 to City 1, even if it has the highest semi-log regression coefficient. Diminishing returns mean that we would be receiving a lower marginal rate of return (MRR) on the last portion of the $50 allocation by giving it to City 1 than by giving the last portion as a starter to City 2. Equalizing the two MRRs means having a second equation of the form, $b_1/\text{Log } X_1 = b_2/\text{Log } X_2$ as one learns in elementary calculus. If one solves that pair of equations simultaneously, one finds that $X_1 = (\$50)(b_1)/(b_1 + b_2)$, and $X_2 = (\$50)(b_2)/(b_1 + b_2)$. That tells us to allocate to each city a portion of the $50 in proportion to the city's semi-log regression coefficient or in accordance with the ratio between its coefficient and the sum of the coefficients. As with optimum level analysis this kind of allocation analysis may produce meaningless coefficients due to reciprocal causation, spurious causation, and other factors that confound statistical analysis.

Traditional optimizing can be contrasted with multi-criteria decision analysis. For example, suppose we want to allocate $50 to two cities, and we do not trust the magnitude of the statistical coefficients in view of those confounding factors. We could ask knowledgeable people to score each city on a 1 to 10 scale as to how efficiently the police in each city use extra dollars to reduce crime. If City 1 scores an 8 and City 2 scores a 4, then logically we would give the first city 8/12 or 67% of the $50, and the second city 4/12 or 33%, assuming police efficiency is the only criterion. If we do the same thing with judicial efficiency, City 1 might receive a score of 3, and City 2 a score of five. Those numbers translate into part/whole percentages of 3/8 or 38% and 5/8 or 62%. We then could average the percentages and allocate (67% + 38%)/2 or 52% to City 1, and (33% + 62%)/2 or 48% to City 2. If our knowledgeable insiders consider police efficiency to be twice as important as judicial efficiency in reducing crime, then City 1 would receive an even bigger allocation when the percentages are weighted by 2 and 1, respectively, since City 1 scores higher on police efficiency.

COMPARISONS ON SIX METHODOLOGICAL PROBLEMS

An appropriate way to integrate the material comparing Policy/Goal Percentaging with traditional optimizing is first to indicate the key methodological problems involved in optimizing. We can then clarify how those problems are handled by P/G% and by the more traditional approaches.

In determining the key methodological problems, it is helpful to clarify the basic elements of optimizing, regardless whether we are referring to traditional optimizing or to newer varieties of optimizing that have been stimulated by MCDM and microcomputer software. One can define optimizing as the systematic processing of a set of (1) goals to be achieved, (2) alternatives for achieving them, and (3) relations between goals and alternatives in order to choose the best alternative or combination in light of the goals, alternatives, and relations.

Those basic elements relate to the following methodological problems regarding how to deal with (1) multiple dimensions on multiple goals, (2) multiple and possibly conflicting constraints, (3) multiple alternatives that are too many to determine the effects of each one, (4) complicated relations between goals and alternatives, (5) missing or imprecise information concerning such inputs as the weights of the goals or the relations between goals and alternatives, and (6) simplicity of analysis and presentation in spite of the above multiplicity and complexity.

Multiple Dimensions on Multiple Goals

The P/G% approach has a relatively distinct way of handling each of those problems which can be contrasted with traditional optimizing. Multi-dimensional criteria are handled by P/G% mainly by weighting the raw scores on different criteria in terms of the relative importance of the criteria and in light of the measurement units used. P/G% also handles multi-dimensional criteria by converting the raw scores into weighted part/whole percentages, which makes them into dimensionless numbers. That is especially useful when the criteria are abstract and measured on scales like 1–5 scales, rather than measured in concrete units like dollars, miles, years, pounds, etc.

Traditional optimizing, on the other hand, tends to deal with multi-dimensionality problem by working with single objective function or a composite goal. Multi-objective programming and arrow diagrams are exceptions since they do preserve the separate goals. Working with a composite goal moves the multi-dimensionality problem back to a process that is separate from the optimizing process. That compositing process often emphasizes measuring all the sub-goals in terms of dollars or some other common measurement unit, rather than preserving the distinctive measurement of each separate goal.

Multiple Constraints

Multiple constraints are handled by P/G% by optimizing without taking constraints into consideration, and then making adjustments if the optimizing solution does not satisfy all the constraints. (Traditional optimizing tries to satisfy the constraints first and then to optimize within those constraints or to do both simultaneously. Under such a system one may satisfy equity constraints by giving to each person, group, or place whatever minimums they are entitled to. The sum of those minimums is then subtracted from the grand total available to be allocated. By satisfying constraints before optimizing, the solution reached is likely to deviate more from the unconstrained optimum than by satisfying the constraints after optimizing. This is so because any person, group, or place that scores low on the criteria will receive minimum allocation plus a proportionate share of the residue of the grand total available to be allocated. Thus, any persons who would otherwise be entitled to only the bare equity minimums would unnecessarily receive more than the minimum, contrary to the optimizing criteria.

On the matter of conflicting constraints, the P/G% approach emphasizes handling such conflicts through a combination of prioritizing, compromising, and expanding the resources, alternatives, or criteria. Suppose there are minimum equity constraints which say Place 1 should receive $400 as a minimum, and Place 2 should receive $200. Suppose further that the total budget provides for only $500. Most traditional optimizing would deal with the above problem of conflicting constraints by reporting that the problem is unsolvable given those constraints. There is, for example, nothing inherent in decision theory, calculus optimizing, or mathematical programming as to how conflicting constraints are to be handled.

Multiple Alternatives

Multiple alternatives may be so many that one cannot determine the effects of all of them. This is especially in an allocation problem where the number of ways of allocating scarce monetary resources to three or more persons may be virtually astronomical. The P/G% approach handles such situations by converting the raw scores into part/whole percentages. Those part/whole percentages are used as allocation percentages to multiply against the grand total in order to determine the allocation for each person, group, or place.

Traditional optimizing is often not concerned with allocation matters because the alternatives are discrete rather than continuum alternatives. By definition, a discrete or lump-sum alternative is either chosen or not chosen, whereas a continuum alternative allows for degrees. Where allocation or degrees are involved, traditional optimizing tends to use a classical calculus optimization approach if one can obtain true derivatives or elasticity coefficients. In most policy evaluation problems, however, valid elasticity coefficients are virtually impossible to obtain due to reciprocal causation, spurious causation, interaction, and unsatisfactory data. As a result, P/G% uses part/whole percentages as proxies for elasticity coefficients. Traditional optimizing may also allocate via the reiterative guessing of mathematical programming. That approach may be unrealistic if it makes linear assumptions. Where non-linear programming is involved, the computer may get stuck in non-optimum solutions.

Relations Between Goals and Alternatives

The P/G% approach tends to determine relations between alternatives and goals by relying on the perceptions of knowledgeable insiders. Traditional optimizing prefers statistical or behavioral data analysis on the theory that such analysis is less biased than asking interested persons. Statistical analysis, however, often has the serious defects of not being able to deal with reciprocal causation, spurious causation, and interactions, as mentioned above. A typical time-series, for example, may show a positive relation between anti-crime expenditures and crime occurrence, not because the expenditures cause crime, but because crime occurrence causes expenditures. Even if the statistical analysis can get the direction of the relations correct, one cannot trust the magnitude of the relations regardless how accurate the original raw data is.

The P/G% approach also tends to rely more on deduced relations than statistical relations. This enables one to evaluate alternatives before they are adopted. That is also generally true of payoff matrices, decision-trees, and multi-objective programming, but not statistical curves for optimum level, indifference, or functional analysis. By deducing relations from known facts or reasonable premises, one thereby avoids such problems in empirical analysis as a lack of a sufficient experimental or control group, and lack of sufficient before or after data. Pre-adoption deductive modeling also avoids the problem of policies being adopted to the unnecessary detriment of people and the problem of bureaucratic inertia and newly vested interests interfering with changes if one has to rely on post-adoption evaluation.

Missing Information

Missing information is often handled under the P/G% approach by changing the questions. Asking for the exact value of an input item can be changed to asking whether the input item is above or below a threshold value. Threshold values are at a point where a higher or lower score will affect the alternative that is considered best. Most people find it easier to deal with questions that ask, for example, whether a probability is more or less than 0.70, rather than asking what is the probability.

Traditional optimizing tends to deal with missing information by finding the information that is missing. That can be needlessly expensive, and it can paralyze decision-making. Sometimes missing or imprecise information is dealt with by eliminating cases or variables. That can result in research over-emphasizing variables that are easily measured, even though they may be relatively unimportant.

Simplicity of Analysis and Presentation

Simplicity of drawing conclusions is promoted by having a user-friendly microcomputer program that requires virtually no technical knowledge in order to use the program, even though the program is based on principles of classical optimization. The P/G% program is like that, but that is not so with programs available for drawing conclusions in decision theory, calculus optimization, or mathematical programming.

On simplicity of presentation, the P/G% approach or the PG table presents results in terms of alternatives on the rows, criteria on the columns, and relations in the cells, with an aggregate total across each row. That approach is in conformity with Lotus 1–2–3 analysis which is the best selling software in the world. It is also in conformity with common sense, as contrasted to the more difficult presentation formats in traditional optimizing.[3]

CONCLUDING THOUGHTS

In the light of the above considerations, one can conclude that the P/G% and related MCDM analysis may have much to offer as supplements to traditional optimizing. MCDM approaches are relatively new compared to the more traditional methods. They are, however, catching on fast largely as a result of new microcomputer software. Programs with names like LightYear, Expert Choice, and PrefCalc are selling well and being widely used. P/G% is relatively new among the MCDM approaches.

In comparison to the other MCDM approaches, P/G% emphasizes:

1. **Part/whole percentaging for dealing with multi-dimensionality**, rather than forcing common measurement units on the goals.
2. **Post-optimizing constraint adjustments**, rather than trying to build into the program all possible constraint situations.
3. **Part/whole percentaging allocations**, rather than have a program that deals only with discrete or lump-sum alternatives.
4. **Relations determined by the user's knowledge** often on 1–5 attitude scales, rather than emphasizing relations that provide for more complicated measurement which tend to leave out important relations.
5. **Sensitivity analysis for dealing with missing information**, rather than requiring that missing information be filled in.
6. **Simplicity in drawing conclusions** by way of the user-friendly P/G% program and simplicity in presenting results by way of the PG table.

It is important to emphasize that P/G% seeks to be simple in order to encourage use of the program and the results, but being simple does not mean being simplistic. Being simplistic refers to being simple by leaving out important considerations. That is contrary to the way in which P/G% and most other MCDM programs work. Along with their simplicity, they actually provide greater detail by (1) separating out the sub-goals of the overall objective function,

(2) allowing for more goals and alternatives, and (3) being explicit in stating constraints, relative weights of the goals, and the nature of the relations.

One might also emphasize that the P/G% and MCDM software are in a state of rapid development, with new improvements being adopted as a result of new experiences. Microcomputer software does lend itself to experimentation and creative change. It is hoped that this chapter will thereby stimulate further insights as to how the new software can be made even more valid, versatile, and user-friendly. Such software can thus become even more of a contribution to the development of better decision-making in government, law, business, and elsewhere.

Notes and References

1. On Policy/Goal Percentaging, see S. Nagel, "P/G% Analysis: An Evaluation Aiding Program", *Evaluation Review*, 9: 209–14 (1985); S. Nagel, *Evaluation Analysis with Microcomputers* (Beverly Hills, Calif.: Sage, 1987); and Benjamin Radcliff, "Multi-Criteria Decision-Making: A Survey of Software", *Social Science Microcomputer Review*, 4: 38–55 (1986).
2. Traditional optimizing methodologies are described in such books as Samuel Richmond, *Operations Research for Management Decisions* (New York: Ronald, 1968); Warren Erickson and Owen Hall, *Computer Models for Management Science* (Reading, Mass.: Addison-Wesley, 1986); Elwood Buffa and James Dyer, *Management Science/Operations Research: Model Formulation and Solution Methods* (New York: Wiley, 1981) and Sang Lee and Laurence Moore, *Introduction to Decision Science* (Princeton, N. J.: Petrocelli/Charter, 1975).
3. The P/G% approach is consistent with incrementalism in policy analysis in view of the emphasis in P/G% on trial-and-error and sensitivity analysis. See Aaron Wildavsky, *Speaking Truth to Power: The Art and Craft of Policy Analysis* (Boston, Mass.: Little, Brown, 1979) and Charles Lindblom, *The Policy-Making Process* (Englewood Cliffs, N.J.: Prentice-Hall, 1980). This approach is also consistent with rationalism in policy analysis in view of its emphasis on systematically determining goals to be achieved, alternatives for achieving them, and relations between goals and alternatives in order to choose the best alternative, combination, or allocation. See Edward Quade, *Analysis for Public Decisions* (Amsterdam: North-Holland, 1983) and Duncan MacRae and James Wilde, *Policy Analysis for Public Decisions* (N. Scituate, Mass.: Duxbury, 1979).
4. For further details on MCDM and P/G% applied to prediction rather than prescription, see S. Nagel "Microcomputers and Improving Social Science

Prediction", *Evaluation Review*, 10: 635–60 (Symposium on "Microcomputers and Evaluation Research", 1986); S. Nagel "Using Microcomputers and P/G% to Predict Court Cases", *Akron Law Review*, 19: 541–74 (1985); and Samuel Bodily, " Spreadsheet Modeling as a Stepping Stone", *Interfaces*, 16: 34–42 (1986).

Part IV
Applications to Diverse
Fields

10 Public Policy Problems

The essence of decision-aiding software is that it is designed to process a set of:

1. goals to be achieved,
2. alternatives for achieving them, and
3. relations between goals and alternatives

in order to choose the best alternative, combination, or resource allocation in light of the goals, alternatives, and relations.

The main benefits of decision-aiding software are in accurately and quickly handling five key methodological problems in decision-making:

1. multiple dimensions on multiple goals; this is the "apples and oranges" program
2. multiple missing information
3. multiple alternatives that are too many to be able to determine the effects of each one
4. multiple and possibly conflicting constraints
5. the need for simplicity in drawing and presenting conclusions in spite of all that multiplicity.[1]

ADDING APPLES AND ORANGES

Decision-making problems often involve multiple goals measured on a variety of different dimensions, such as miles, hours, dollars, 1–5 attitude scales, yes–no dichotomies, etc.

Some of the ways in which multiple dimensions are handled are:

1. Multiply the apples by two if you like each apple twice as much as each orange. Then everything will be expressed in orange units.
2. Ask whether the gain in apples from choosing one alternative is worth more or less than the gain in oranges from choosing a second alternative.
3. Convert the apple units into percentages by dividing the raw

145

scores on the apple goal by the sum of the apples, and convert the orange units into percentages by dividing the raw scores on the oranges goal by the sum of the oranges.

These methods become clearer with the concrete illustrative example of choosing between two affirmative action programs for a medical school. One program produces a lot of minority students, but treats few patients. The other program produces few minority students, but treats a lot of patients. The example is shown in Table 10.1.[2]

MISSING INFORMATION

We often do not know relation scores of each alternative on each goal, and we often do not know the relative weights of the goals.

The key way in which missing information is handled is to allow the user quickly and accurately to determine the effects of inserting various values for the missing information. More specific techniques include:

1. **What–if analysis**, whereby the computer shows what would happen if we made changes in the goals, alternatives, and/or relations.
2. **Threshold analysis**, whereby the computer shows for each relation-score and goal-weight the value which would cause a tie between the second-place alternative and the first place alternative.
3. **Convergence analysis**, whereby the computer shows for each goal weight at what magnitude the goal tends to dominate the other goals such that nothing is to be gained by increasing the weight further.
4. **Best–worst analysis**, whereby the computer shows what the conclusion would be using values that most favor a given alternative, and then values that least favor a given alternative. The two conclusions are then averaged.

These methods become clearer with the concrete illustrative example of deciding between nuclear energy and solar energy in light of their long-term value and cost, as is shown in Table 10.2.[3]

Table 10.1   Four methods for dealing with multi-dimensional trade-offs

POLICY	RAW SCORE INCREMENTS		PART/WHOLE PERCENTAGING			
	Students Trained (S)	Patients Treated (P)	Students Trained $w=1$	Patients Treated $w=2$	Unweighted Sum	Weighted Sum
Policy A (X_1)	30	10	60%	36%	96%	132%
Policy B (X_2)	20	18	40%	64%	104%	168%
Total (Whole)	50	28	100%	100%	200%	300%
Difference (Increment)	$+ 10S \gg - 8P$?					
Threshold			$W60 + 36 = W40 + 64$ $W^* = 1.40$			

POLICY	PAIRED-COMPARISON MONETIZING			WEIGHTED RAW SCORES		
	Students Trained $\$Y = (S)^{0.92}$	Patients Treated $\$Y = (P)^{0.90}$	SUM	Students (Expressed in Terms of Patients) $W=2$	Patients	Sum
Policy A (X_1)	$22.85	$ 7.94	$30.79	60	10	70
Policy B (X_2)	$15.74	$13.48	$29.22	40	18	58
Total	$38.59	$21.42	$60.01	100	28	128
Threshold				$W30 + 10 = W20 + 18$ $W^* = 0.80$		

Notes:

1. Incremental analysis has the advantage of simplicity, especially where there are only a few policies and goals. It is also applicable to variables that are non-quantitative. It involves a minimum of transforming of the raw data. It reduces the value judgement to determining whether the incremental gain of one policy is preferred over the incremental gain of a second policy.
2. Percentaging analysis has the advantage of being applicable where there are many policies and goals. It reduces the value judgement to determining the relative weight of the goals.
3. Paired-comparison monetizing tends to consider all the values of the relevant decision-makers, although their values are not disaggregated into separate components. Working with monetized variables may also be more comfortable for many people. Paired-comparison monetizing reduces the value judgements to determining at what point a set of non-monetary benefits is equal to a quantity of dollars.
4. Weighted raw scores have the advantage of being relatively easy to apply where all the goals have tangible units like students or patients, rather than intangible units like scores on a 1–9 attitude scale, where part/whole percentaging tends to be easier to handle.

Table 10.2 Threshold values, insensitivity ranges, and change slopes

GOALS POLICIES	Long-term Value (Y_1)	Low Cost (Y_2)	WEIGHTED SUM
Nuclear (X_a)	a_1 +1 4 (3 to ∞)	a_2 +1 3 (2 to ∞)	7
Solar (X_b)	b_1 −1 5 (−∞ to 6)	b_2 −1 1 (−∞ to 2)	6
Weights	W_1 −1 1 (−∞ to 2)	W_2 +2 1 (0.5 to ∞)	

Notes:

1. The symbol in the upper left-hand corner of each cell shows (1) the identifying symbol of each relation, with the letter indicating the goal; (2) the identifying symbol of each weight, with the subscript indicating the goal to which the weight refers.
2. The number in the middle of each cell shows (1) the value of the relation on a 1–5 scale; (2) the value of the weight, with the least important goal having a weight of 1.
3. The number in the upper right-hand corner of each cell shows by how much the gap changes between the two alternatives being compared if the input increases by one unit.
4. The number other than infinity in parentheses in each cell is the threshold value for each point. At that value, there will be a tie in the weighted sum of the two alternatives being compared.
5. The range in parentheses in each cell is the insensitivity range. That range shows how far down and up each input can go without affecting which alternative is the winner.

ALLOCATING RESOURCES

Decision-aiding software can help in allocating resources, as contrasted to the generally easier problem of just finding a best alternative or combination.

A good way of allocating resources is to convert into percentages the raw merit scores of the objects to which the resources are to be allocated. One can then apply the percentages to the grand total available to be allocated. A good way to convert the raw scores into percentages is by dividing them by their total within the same goal in order to get part/whole percentages. Those percentages can then be summed across the goals, using a weighted sum where the goals have different weights.

Table 10.3A shows how the P/G% software can be used in an allocation problem where the bottom line consists of allocation percentages. The alternative methods shown are trials and plea bargains. Additional alternatives could be added such as diversions or dismissals. The goals shown are to reduce delay and to increase respect for the legal system. Additional goals could be added such as reducing expense and increasing the probability of innocent defendants being acquitted.

The raw data shows in our hypothetical court system, the average trial takes 120 days, and the average plea bargain takes 30 days from arrest to disposition. The data also shows that the trials alternative receives a respect score of 6 on a 0–10 scale in a rough survey of attorneys, and pleas receives a score of only a 2. It would not be meaningful to add 120 days to a respect score of 6 to get an overall score for trials because (1) delay is measured in days, and respect is measured on a 0–10 scale, necessitating a common measure in order to be able to add these scores, (2) delay is a negative goal where high scores are undesirable, and (3) a score of 2 on respect may be a negative score such that each additional plea bargain decreases respect for the system.

To deal with those problems, we do the following:

1. The delay scores are converted into part/whole percentages by dividing each score by the sum of the delay column, but after inverting for the negative goal.
2. The inversion is done by working with the reciprocals of the delay scores. That means working with 1/120 and 1/30 rather than 120 and 30. Doing so preserves the fact that trials are four times as bad as pleas on the goal of delay, while making the pleas score higher than the trials score. We are then working with speed rather than delay as a goal. Speed should be given a weight of +1 if delay has previously been given a weight of −1.
3. The respect scores are also converted into part/whole percentages by dividing each score by the sum of the respect column, but after adjusting for the fact that pleas may have a negative score.
4. That means determining the value of a true zero on the 0–10 scale and subtracting that value from the 0–10 scores. Thus, if a 5 is the

Table 10.3 Allocating cases to methods of resolving them

A. THE RAW DATA

	Delay (Days)	Respect (0–10 Scale)
Trials	120	6
Pleas	30	2
	150	8

B. THE TRANSFORMED RAW DATA

	Speed (1/Days)	Respect (−5 to +5)
Trials	1/120 or 0.00833	+1
Pleas	1/30 or 0.03333	−3
	5/120 or 0.04166	−2

separation point between positive scores and negative scores, then a 6 is the equivalent of a +1, and a 2 is the equivalent of a −3. Those transformed numbers are shown in Table 10.3B.

Table 10.3C converts the transformed data into part/whole percentages. Pleas is given 0% on respect because one would not want to allocate anything more than the minimum possible if pleas has a negative score and if more respect were the only criterion. We can now add across the percentages and obtain an aggregate percent of 120% for trials and 80% for pleas. We then divide by 2 to bring the sum of those percentages down to 100% because we cannot allocate more than 100%.

Table 10.3D takes into consideration that respect is considered to be twice as important as speed. That means multiplying the percentages in the respect column by 2. The new aggregate percentages are then 220% and 80%. We then divide by 3 or the sum of the weights to obtain the allocation percentages of 73% and 27%. Not all allocation

C. THE PART/WHOLE PERCENTAGES

	Speed P/W%	Respect P/W%	Aggregate P/W%	Allocation %
Trials	20%	100%	120%	60%
Pleas	80%	0%	80%	40%
	100%	100%	200%	100%

D. THE WEIGHTED P/W%s

	Speed $w = 1$	Respect $w = 2$	Aggregate P/W%	Allocation %
Trials	20%	200%	220%	73%
Pleas	80%	0%	80%	27%
	100%	200%	300%	100%

Notes:

1. The raw data is hypothetical, but realistic. The object is to decide on the optimum allocation of cases to trials versus pleas in light of the facts that (1) trials receive a score of 120 days on delay and pleas 30 days, and (2) trials receive a score of 6 on respect and pleas a score of 2.
2. Transforming the raw data involves (1) calculating the reciprocals for the raw score of the negative goals of delay; (2) recalculating the raw scores on respect using a scale that shows absolute zero. If N equals absolute zero, then subtract N from each of the original raw scores. For example, on a 0–10 scale the number 5 (or below) might be absolute zero.
3. Calculating the correct part/whole percentages involves (1) calculating the part/whole percentages on the inverted negative goal; (2) giving zero % to any alternative that has a negative raw score, then calculating the part/whole percentages for the other alternatives.
4. Calculating the allocation percentages involves (1) multiplying the part/whole percentages in each column by the relative weight of the goal to which the column pertains; (2) summing the weighted part/whole percentages across each alternative; (3) dividing those aggregate percentages by the sum of the weights. The results are the allocation percentages for each alternative or budget category.

problems involve multiple dimensions, negative goals, or negative scores. If, however, one can follow the allocation analysis of Table 10.3, then one can deal with simpler allocation problems.[4]

ADJUSTING FOR CONSTRAINTS

Decision-aiding software can help in dealing with constraints that require minimums or maximums on the alternatives or the goals or other conditions that must be met, regardless how high the scores are of an alternative on the goals.
The main ways in which constraints are handled are:

1. The constraints can be met **before** one allocates scarce resources or determines the relation scores. Doing so tends to result in giving an alternative more than it is entitled where it only deserves the minimum. That result cannot occur if adjustments are made **after** allocating so as to bring alternatives up to their minimums.
2. The best way of resolving conflicting constraints is to **expand the total benefits available** or **reduce the total costs to be imposed** so that all the constraints can be satisfied simultaneously. If that is not possible, then resolve conflicting constraints by developing compromises that satisfy each constraint in proportion to its importance. Other less desirable alternatives involve partially satisfying all constraints equally, or fully satisfying certain constraints in the order of their priority.

Adjusting for constraints is illustrated with the same problem as allocating a budget to police and courts in light of crime reduction and fair procedure. The constraints specify minimum amounts to the police and the courts, but those minimums may add to more than the total budget available.
A good way to adjust to satisfy the equity constraints with two, three, and four budget categories is as follows:

1. With two budget categories, suppose category A is below its minimum and category B is above its minimum. After allocating in proportion to their aggregate scores, then give category A its minimum. Give the rest of the total budget to category B.
2. With three budget categories, suppose A is below its minimum and B and C are above their minimums. Then give A its minimum. Divide the rest of the total budget between B and C in proportion to their aggregate scores, as in Table 10.4.
3. With four or more budget categories, one can reason by analogy to the three-category situation. No matter how many budget categories are below their minimums in the initial optimizing, give them their minimums and then remove them from further allocat-

ing. The remainder of the total budget then gets divided proportionately among the other budget categories.[5]

SIMPLICITY OF ANALYSIS

Decision-aiding software that is based on multi-criteria decision-making can greatly simplify the analysis of a variety of decision-aiding problems that have traditionally used more complicated and often less valid methods, such as arrow diagrams, payoff matrices, decision-trees, optimum level curves, indifference curves, functional curves, and multi-objective programming. The essence of MCDM software is that it works with a table, matrix, or spreadsheet with alternatives on the rows, evaluative criteria on the columns, relation scores in the cells, and a summation column at the right showing the overall score or allocation percent of each alternative.

A good illustration of the simplicity of MCDM and P/G% software is the decision whether to take away or leave an abused child with the child's family. Table 10.5A shows the problem analyzed with a traditional payoff matrix, and Table 10.5B shows the problem analyzed with a P/G% spreadsheet table. Both approaches show the alternatives on the rows. The payoff matrix shows contingent events and possibly their probabilities on the columns, whereas the P/G% approach shows goals and their relative weights on the columns. The payoff matrix shows relative payoffs in the cells, whereas the P/G% approach shows relation scores on a 1–5 scale in the cells between the alternatives and the goals. The payoff matrix shows benefits minus costs on the right side with each element discounted by the probability of its occurring, whereas the P/G% approach shows the weighted summation scores for each alternative at the right side.

Both approaches are applied to the same empirical situation in Table 10.5. The payoff matrix tends to lead to a decision to take the child away because the probability of severe abuse is likely to be greater than the threshold probability. The P/G% approach leads to a closer decision because it emphasizes multiple criteria of avoiding abuse, preserving family love, and saving the taxpayer cost. One could argue that those three criteria are taken into consideration in the relative payoffs in the cells of the payoff matrix. However, by lumping all three criteria together, their separate existences and sensitivity values get overwhelmed by the criterion of avoiding abuse. The payoff matrix may thus lead to results that are less valid in terms of the decision-maker's goals than the P/G% approach.

Table 10.4 Data for illustrating equity constraints and adjustments to satisfy them

ALLOCATION CRITERIA / BUDGET CATEGORIES	RAW SCORES		TRANSFORMED SCORES			ALLOCATION RESULTS				
	Crime Reduction	Fair Procedure	Aggregate Scores	Allocation Percentages		Optimum Allocations		Minimums	Adjusted Allocations	
				2-way	3-way	2-way	3-way		2-way	3-way
	(1)	(2)	(3)	(4a)	(4b)	(5a)	(5b)	(6)	(7a)	(7b)
Police	2.00	1.00	3.00	43%	39%	$214	$195	$240	$240 (Min.)	$240 (Min.)
Courts	1.00	3.00	4.00 / 7.00	57%	51%	$286	$255	$ 80	$260 (100% of $260)	$218 (84% of $260)
Corrections	0.50	0.25	0.75	N/A	10%	N/A	$ 50	$ 40	N/A	$ 42 (16% of $260)
TOTALS	—	—	7.75	100%	100%	$500	$500	$360	$500	$500

Notes:

1. Optimizing can be done first, and then adjustments are made to satisfy the constraints if they have not been satisfied already. In other words, if we optimally allocate without considering the minimums, we obtain what is shown in column *5a* (for two budget categories) and column *5b* (for three budget categories). If we then consider the minimums, we obtain what is shown in columns *7a* and *7b*.

2. There is $500 available to be allocated this year. There was $450 available to be allocated last year. *N/A* = Not Applicable.

3. The minimums in column *6* are equal to 80% of last year's budget. Last year, the police received $300, the courts received $100, and corrections received $50.

4. The numbers in columns *1* and *2* are based on a rough survey of a small sample of some people who are knowledgeable about the criminal justice system.

5. The formulas for the numbers in the other columns are:

   (3) = (1) + (2)
   (5b) = (4b) ($500)

   (4a) = (3)7.00
   (6) = 80% of last year's allocation

   (4b) = (3)7.75
   (5a) = (4a) ($500)

6. The best way to make the adjusted allocations of *7a* and *7b* is to give any budget category its minimum (from column 6). If its optimum (from column *5a* or *5b*) falls below its minimum, then divide the residue among the other budget categories in proportion to their aggregate scores (from column 3).

Table 10.5 Comparing a payoff matrix with P/G% on decision-making under conditions of risk (e.g., deciding whether to take away or leave an abused child)

A. The payoff matrix

	Severe subsequent abuse Would not Occur	Would occur	
			Benefits − Costs
Take away	(a) −50	(b) +100	$(P)(100) - (1-P)(50)$
Leave	(c) +50	(d) −100	

Notes:

1. The cell entries are arrived at by asking the decision-makers the following questions:

(1) Of the four possible occurrences, which ones are desirable (marked +), and which ones are undesirable (marked −)?
(2) Of the desirable occurrences, which one is the most undesirable (marked −100)?
(3) How much more undesirable is the most undesirable occurrence in comparison to the less undesirable occurrence (marked −50 to show cell (d) is twice as bad as cell (a))?

2. With that information, one can determine the threshold probability as follows:

(1) At the threshold, the discounted benefits equal the discounted costs (i.e., $100P = 50 - 50P$).
(2) The solution for P in that equation is $P^* = d/(a+d)$ or $P^* = 100/50 + 100) = 0.33$.
(3) That means if the probability is greater than 0.33 that there will be severe subsequent abuse, then the child should be taken away.

B. The P/G% approach

	Avoid Abuse ($w = 2$)	Preserve Family Love ($w = 1$)	Save Taxpayer Cost ($w = 1$)	Weighted Sum
Take away	4	2	2	12
Leave	2	4	4	12

Notes:

1. The scoring of each alternative on each criterion is on a 1–5 scale where 5 = highly conducive to the goal, 4 = mildly conducive, 3 = neither conducive nor adverse, 2 = mildly adverse to the goal, and 1 = highly adverse. Decimal scores can be given between these numbers where appropriate.
2. Avoiding abuse is considered to be twice as important as preserving whatever family love might exist or saving taxpayer cost.
3. By considering multiple criteria rather than emphasizing the probability of severe subsequent abuse, the decision is a much closer decision, and more dependent on the specific facts or scores on the first two criteria than on a general threshold probability.
4. If the criteria are given equal weight and a threshold analysis is performed, then leaving the child wins 10 points to 8 points. The threshold or tie-causing values of the weights are 2, 0 and 0. The threshold values of the relation scores are then 6, 4, 4, 0, 2 and 2, reading across the matrix.

The advantages of the P/G% approach over a payoff matrix include:

1. P/G% can explicitly consider any number of criteria such as the three shown above.
2. P/G% can explicitly consider any number of alternatives such as, take away to an institution, take away to a foster home, take away to a relative's home, leave with counselling, or leave without counselling.
3. Being able to consider multiple criteria and multiple alternatives makes the P/G% approach more validly in conformity with reality, and not just a simplistic abstraction.
4. P/G% is also simpler with its 1–5 scales, weighted criteria, computerized threshold analysis, and logical way of analyzing a problem in terms of alternatives, criteria, and relations.[6]

SOME CONCLUSIONS

As mentioned at the beginning of this chapter, the main benefits of the decision-aiding software are its accuracy and speed in handling the five key methodological problems in evaluation analysis. Fully to appreciate the relevance of the software, it is necessary actually to use it; we can, however, briefly describe how the software applies to each problem.

On the matter of **multiple dimensions on multiple goals**:

1. In comparing any two alternatives, one can show for each goal the **incremental gain of the better alternative over the other alternative**. This can be more easily done by putting the goals on the rows and the two alternatives on the columns since the software subtracts across the rows. One can then pick the alternative that has the more desired set of increments.
2. One can specify the **importance of each goal relative to the least important goal**. Those weights can consider both importance and the nature of the measurement units where raw scores are used.
3. The software is capable of working with the relations either as **raw scores or part/whole percentages** by exercising an option on the data management menu.

On the matter of **missing information**:

1. The software can do **what–if analysis** by allowing the user to change any of the inputs and quickly see how those changes affect the bottom-line conclusion.
2. The main menu gives the user an option to do a **threshold analysis** or a **convergence analysis** to determine the critical values for relation scores or goal weights, above which one alternative would be better and below which another alternative would be better.
3. In specifying the criteria, one can divide each criterion into a **best version** and a **worst version**, such as the best possible cost on each alternative and the worst possible cost. The computer can then show the overall best score, the overall worst score, and the midpoint for each alternative.
4. The software can also draw **indifference curves** or **threshold curves** showing the combination of scores on two or more variables which would lead to a tie between any two alternatives.

On the matter of **allocating resources**:

1. The user can specify the **grand total available** to be allocated. The program will multiply that grand total by the allocation percentages for each alternative or budget category.
2. The allocation percentages are calculated by obtaining an overall score for each alternative and then dividing each overall score by the sum of the scores in order to obtain **part/whole allocation percentages**.

3. The program can **transform the raw scores** by determining their reciprocals where negative goals are involved, or by subtracting the value of absolute zero from each raw score where negative scores are involved. Those transformations may, however, be easier to do with a calculator, and then just enter the results into the data matrix.

On the matter of **adjusting for constraints**:

1. The user can enter **minimum constraints for each alternative**, and the program can guarantee they will be met in whatever allocation is done. A better approach, though, would be to optimize ignoring the constraints, and then make adjustments for any alternative or criterion that violates its minimum or maximum.
2. The ease of doing what–if analysis facilitates resolving conflicting constraints and conflicting decision-makers by enabling both sides or a mediator to try different alternatives, criteria, weights, constraints, relations, and other inputs until a **mutually satisfying solution** is found.

On the matter of **simplicity**:

1. The essence of the software is the idea of putting alternatives on the rows of a spreadsheet matrix, criteria and weights on the columns, relations in the cells, and overall scores for the alternatives in the right-hand column.
2. That system is in conformity with a great deal of systematic decision-making, as indicated by the popularity of spreadsheet software, payoff matrices, decision trees, and other formats that can be reduced to a decision matrix.

This kind of evaluation analysis could be done with pencil and paper or even implicitly in one's mind. The analysis is, however, substantially facilitated by the availability of the software and microcomputers. The software encourages thinking more explicitly about evaluation problems without confining the user to quantitatively measured variables. It facilitates creativity by allowing changes to be so easily made. We may be at the advent of new ways of thinking about program evaluation, policy analysis, and decision-making to the benefit of the decision-makers and those who are affected by their decisions.[7]

Appendix: Examples of Specific Public Policy Applications

HUMAN RESOURCES

Table A10.1 Alternative policies for providing public aid, especially for dependent children

GOALS / POLICIES	Low Taxpayer Burden		Encourage Recipients to Advance Themselves	Politically Feasible	No Artificial Migration	No Unconstitutional Unfairness	Sums
	Direct	Indirect					
No Public Aid (1)	5	1	2	1	3	3	15
The Poor House (2)	1	2	2	1	3	2	11
Unreformed ADC (3)	2	2	2	4	2	2	14
ADC Plus Work Incentives (4)	2	3	4	4	2	2	17
The Above Plus the Working Poor (5)	2	2	4	4	2	2	16
The Above Plus National Minimums (6)	2	2	4	4	4	2	18
The Above Plus Due Process & NIT (7)	2	2	4	4	4	4	20
Broaden Survivorship under OASDHI (8)	2	4	4	1	4	4	19
Demogrant or Children's Allowance (9)	1	3	2	1	4	4	15

Notes:

1. If political feasibility requires at least a 2 rather than a 1, then alternatives *1*, *2*, *8*, and *9* are politically *un*feasible.
2. The best alternative seems to be number 7 which is in effect the Nixon Family Assistance Plan. It involves adding work incentives, the working poor, and national minimums to basic ADC system, along with the minimum due process required by the Supreme Court.
3. Reformed Aid to Dependent Children (ADC) includes (1) allowing recipients to keep the first $60 per month which they earn plus $1 out of every $2 thereafter up to a certain amount, as a work incentive; (2) allowing ADC to be received by families in which there is a working father and mother present although their combined income is below the poverty level; (3) providing for a minimum benefits level across all 50 states, and (4) providing minimum due process.
4. Minimum due process includes (1) being informed as to what wrong one allegedly committed; (2) being able to present witnesses on one's behalf; (3) being able to cross-examine one's accusers; (4) having a judge who is not one of the accusers; and (5) having assistance from appointed counsel.
5. The abbreviation NIT stands for negative income tax, which is a system whereby people whose incomes fall below a certain level receive a monthly check in the mail from the Internal Revenue Service. The abbreviation OASDHI stands for Old Age, Survivors, Disability, and Health Insurance. That is the US social security system, which could be broadened to define survivorship as including children who have been abandoned by their fathers even though their fathers are still alive.

CIVIL RIGHTS

Table A10.2 Alternative public policies toward race relations

GOALS / POLICES	Stimulating Minority Advancement	Always Favouring the One with the Higher Score	Never Favouring One Who is Unqualified	SUM
1. Requiring Segregation or Discrimination	1	1	1	3
2. Allowing Discrimination (same as doing nothing)	2	2	2	6
3. Outlawing Discrimination	4	4	4	12
4. Requiring Affirmative Action	5	4	4	13*
5. Requiring Preferential Hiring	4	2	4	10
6. Allowing Reverse Racism	2	2	2	6

Notes:

1. Discrimination in this context means requiring or allowing a white with a score of 40 to be preferred over a black with a score of 60, where 50 is the minimum score for one who is qualified, or where both are qualified but the white is preferred even though the black applicant is substantially more qualified.
2. Affirmative action in this context means only hiring blacks who are qualified but actively seeking out qualified blacks through (1) advertising, (2) locating one's physical plant, (3) removing requirements that are racially correlated, but not correlated with job performance, and (4) providing on-the-job-training for all but especially to overcome lack of training by blacks
3. Preferential hiring means only hiring blacks who are qualified, but preferring qualified blacks over moderately less qualified whites, generally as a temporary measure to offset prior discrimination.
4. Reverse racism is the same as discrimination, except blacks are favored.
5. The summation column tends to indicate that the optimum policy level for achieving the desired goals is to move away from discrimination to requiring affirmative action, but not to requiring preferential hiring except as a short-term remedy for prior discrimination.

CRIMINAL JUSTICE

Table A10.3 Crime reduction

ALTERNATIVE POLICIES (X's)	GOALS TO BE ACHIEVED (Y's)					OVERALL SCORES			
	Protect the Innocent (L)	Increase Probability of Arrest, Conviction or Punishment (N)	Decrease Crime Benefits (N)	Increase Crime Costs (N)	Save Money (C)	Liberal Score	Neutral Score	Conservative Score	Total Score
Decrease Legal Technicalities	1	1	0	0	3	8	10	12	30
Increase the professionalism of CJ Decision-makers	3	2	0	0	2	15	14	13	42
Harden Crime Targets	2	0	2	0	2	12	12	12	36
Change Peer Group Values	2	0	2	0	2	12	12	12	36
Increase Sentence Length and Prison Hardship	1	0	0	2	2	3	10	11	30
Increase the Opportunity Costs i.e. the Lost Opportunities from Committing Crimes	2	0	0	3	1	13	12	11	36
TOTAL	11	3	4	5	12	63	70	71	210

Notes:

CJ stands for criminal justice; *L* for liberal; *N* for neutral; and *C* for conservative.

NATURAL RESOURCES AND ENVIRONMENTAL PROTECTION

Table A10.4 Alternative ways of dealing with the problem of pollution

POLICIES \ GOALS	Pollution Reduction	Political Feasibility	SUM
Marketplace	1	5	6
Regulation	3	3	6
Pollution Taxes	5	1	6

Notes:

1. At first glance, the analysis appears to lead to a three-way tie.
2. At second glance, the analysis indicates that relying on the marketplace does not satisfy a minimum level of pollution-reduction, because neither private firms nor municipalities have an incentive to reduce pollution since doing so will mean an increase in expenses with no increase in income.
3. At second glance, the analysis also indicates that relying on pollution taxes (that are proportionate to the amount of pollution generated) does not satisfy a minimum level of political feasibility, because pollution taxes generate too much opposition from private firms and municipalities.
4. The analysis thus leads to the conclusion that regulation is the best alternative for dealing with pollution, including a system of permits, inspection, and prosecution for violating the permits granted.
5. This analysis is an example of minimum constraints on the goals, as contrasted to minimum constraints on the alternatives.
6. One might also note that in this substantive context, the bottom line as to who wins is insensitive to the weights of the goals or the measurement categories, since only one alternative meets the minimum constraints. For example, suppose pollution reduction is scored 2, 4, and 5 on market place, regulation and pollution taxes. Suppose further that political feasibility is scored 4, 4, and 3. One would still arrive at the same conclusion that regulation is the best alternative if one requires better than a 2 on pollution reduction and better than a 3 on political feasibility.
7. The political feasibility scores shown in the above table are as of about 1970 when water and air pollution legislation was first being proposed at the federal level. As of 1987 the political feasibility of going to a total marketplace solution should be substantially lower since it would mean repealing existing federal regulation. As of 1987, pollution taxes are even more politically unfeasible as a result of observing how they have been defeated at the federal, state, and local levels.
8. There are many more alternatives for dealing with the problem of pollution than just the marketplace, regulation, and pollution taxes. See the more detailed Table 12.2 entitled "Comparing Alternative Incentives for Reducing Pollution" which contains 19 alternatives that lend themselves to various combinations including the alternative of selling and buying marketable pollution rights which in effect combines policies of relying on the marketplace, regulation, and pollution taxes.

GOVERNMENT AND BUSINESS

Table A10.5 P/G% applied to economic problems: unemployment/inflation
(economics)

POLICIES \ GOALS	Reduce Unemployment to 3 per cent	Reduce Inflation to 3 per cent	Equitable Distribution of Unemployment and inflation	Free Enterprise	SUM
1. Doing Nothing	3	3	2	4	12
2. Increase Money Supply Decrease Interest Rates	4	2	3	3	12
3. Decrease Money Supply Increase Interest Rates	2	4	3	3	12
4. Increase Government Spending Decrease Taxes	4	2	3	3	12
5. Decrease Government Spending Increase Taxes	2	4	3	3	12
6. Job Creation Price Control	4	4	4	1	13
7. Decrease Taxes Decrease Domestic Spending	4	4	3	3	14
8. Tax Breaks and Subsidies Decrease Defense Spending	5	5	3	3	16

Notes:

1. Policy *1* of doing nothing causes too much harm at least in the short run.
2. Policies *2–3* and *4–5* assume that periods of high unemployment and inflation do not occur simultaneously, which is no longer so.
3. Policy *6* is too expensive and too restrictive on marketplace incentives compared to the alternatives.
4. Policy *7* has the defect that merely decreasing taxes will not necessarily stimulate productivity without strings attached. Decreasing domestic spending may not be enough to avoid large government deficits which can stifle low interest rates needed for technological and business innovation.
5. Policy *8* presumes that tax breaks and subsidies will increase productivity which will reduce the work week and thereby make more jobs available while not reducing take-home pay. Increased productivity also means reduced inflation since workers and producers will be giving more for the increased wages and prices charged.
6. A score of 5 in a cell means the policy is highly conducive to the goal; a score of 4 means the policy is mildly conducive to the goal; a 3 means the policy is neither conducive nor adverse to the goal; a 2 means the policy is mildly adverse to the goal; and a 1 means the policy is highly adverse to the goal.

GOVERNMENT AND SCIENCE

Table A10.6 Deciding an optimum level of cancer in the light of the prevention and damage costs

GOALS ALTERNATIVES (X)	Lost Productivity $Y_1 = 0.1(X)$	Patient Medical Care $Y_2 = (X)^{0.5}$	Prevention Cost $Y = 1M(X)^{-2}$	SUM
$0	$0	$0	$ ∞	$ ∞
100	10	10	100	120
200	20	14	25	59
300	30	17	11	58
400	40	20	6	66
500	50	22	4	76

Notes:

1. As cancer cases increase, lost productivity goes up at a constant rate and patient medical care goes up at a diminishing rate. In order to get cancer down, prevention cost has to go up at an increasing rate.
2. Considering these three relevant costs and the above data, the optimum cancer level is 300 cases per whatever population is under consideration. At that level, the total costs are minimized at 58 monetary units.
3. An important point is that the optimum level of cancer is zero cases only if the costs of achieving zero cases is low, which it is not. The zero category would be the optimum category if the prevention costs at that point were 57, which would be contrary to having a higher prevention cost with 100 cancer cases.
4. The symbol $ ∞ stands for infinite dollars or the equivalent of a tentatively impossible relation.

NATIONAL SECURITY

Table A10.7   International law: arms control

GOALS POLICIES	Low Burden on the Economy	Avoidance of Nuclear War	Avoidance of Being Conquered	Political and Technological Feasibility	SUM
1. Encourage War to Bring an Armageddon	2	1	2	1	6
2. First Strike With no Retaliation	1	2	4	1	8
3. Arms Buildup	1	1	4	3	9
4. Wait for Bilateral Reduction Without Stimuli	2	2	4	4	12
5. Wait for Bilateral Reduction With Stimuli	2 (4)	3 (4)	4	4	13 (16)
6. Supervisable Freeze	3	4	3	4	14
7. Temporary Unilateral Freeze	3	4	3	3	13
8. Permanent Unilateral Freeze	4	4	2	1	11
9. Unilateral Disarmament	4	3	2	1	10

Notes:

1. This table originated in 1986. The numbers in parentheses show changes in the scores as of 1988.
2. The policy alternatives are arranged from the most war-oriented at the top to the most pacifist at the bottom. The criteria are arranged in random order.
3. The criteria are tentatively given equal weight. If they were given liberal weights, then the second criterion would be given more weight than the third criterion. If they were given conservative weights, then the third criterion would be given more weight than the second criterion. Either way, Alternative 5 would still receive the highest summation score.

LABOR RELATIONS

Table A10.8 Relating labor policies to societal goals

GOALS / POLICIES	Reduce Abuse of Workers	Stimulate Business		Taxpayers		Consumers on Price and Quality	SUM
		Short Run	Long Run	Direct	Indirect		
Maximum Hours	4	2	4	3	2	3	18
Minimum Wages, Including Supplements	4	3	$3\frac{1}{2}$	3	2	3	$18\frac{1}{2}$
No Child Labor	4	2	4	3	2	3	18
No Discrimination	4	2	4	3	2	3	18
No Unsafety	4	2	4	3	2	3	18
No Management Abuses in re Unions	4	2	4	3	3	3	19
No Union Abuses in re Management	3	4	4	3	3	3	20
No Union Abuses in re Members	4	4	$2\frac{1}{2}$	3	3	4	$20\frac{1}{2}$
Delayed Emergency Strikes	3	4	4	3	3	4	21

Notes:

1. Reduced profits is a short-run effect of policies to reduce abuse of workers. Increased profits is a long-run effect since such policies stimulate the adoption of labor-saving equipment which tends to increase productivity and profitability.

2. Increased taxes is frequently a short-run effect of new government policies, but not so much policies that regulate, as contrasted to those that subsidize. Decreased taxes may be the indirect or long-run effect if the regulation results in enabling workers to be healthier and more productive and less likely to become welfare dependents, especially due to premature aging or disability.

3. All of the goals are stated in a positive way so that a plus on the taxpayer's goal means a favorable effect from the taxpayer's perspective, rather than an increase in the taxpayer's burden.

4. All the policies in table A10.8 seem to cross a minimum threshold of desirability, especially if one notes that the summation score for each policy when divided by six goals comes out to be 3 or higher, indicating that each policy represents a net benefit, or neither a benefit nor a cost overall.

Notes and References

1. For further details on optimizing in terms of goals, policies, relations and conclusions, see S. Nagel, *Public Policy: Goals, Means, and Methods* (New York: St Martin's Press, 1984) and Edward Quade, *Analysis for Public Decisions* (Amsterdam: North-Holland, 1983). These two books could be referred to for any of the eight principles. The first book uses numerous legal examples. Other books that take an optimizing perspective toward law include Richard Posner, *Economic Analysis of Law* (Boston, Mass.: Little, Brown, 1977), and Gordon Tullock, *The Logic of the Law* (New York: Basic Books, 1971).

2. On dealing with non-monetary benefits and costs, see Mark Thompson, *Benefit–Cost Analysis for Program Evaluation* (Beverly Hills, Calif.: Sage, 1980); and Edward Gramlich, *Benefit–Cost Analysis of Government Programs* (Englewood Cliffs, N.J.: Prentice-Hall, 1981), although they may overemphasize monetizing non-monetary variables, rather than working with them in their original form or close to it. Also see S. Nagel, "Nonmonetary Variables in Benefit-Cost Evaluation", *Evaluation Review*, 7: 37–64 (1983) and S. Nagel, "Economic Transformations of Nonmonetary Benefits in Program Evaluation", in James Catterall (ed.), *Economic Evaluation of Public Programs* (San Francisco: Jossey-Bass, 1985).

3. On dealing with missing information without having to gather additional information, see Mark Thompson, *Decision Analysis for Program Evaluation* (Cambridge, Mass.: Ballinger, 1982); and Clifford Harris, *The Break-Even Handbook* (Englewood Cliffs, N.J.: Prentice-Hall, 1978). Also see S. Nagel "Dealing with Unknown Variables in Policy/Program Evaluation", *Evaluation and Program Planning*, 6: 7–18 (1983), and S. Nagel, "New Varieties of Sensitivity Analysis", *Evaluation Review*, 9: 772–9 (1986).

4. On diverse methods for dealing with the multiplicity of alternatives in allocation problems, see Philip Kotler, *Marketing Decision Making: A Model Building Approach* (New York: Holt, 1971) (calculus and statistical analysis); Claude McMillan, *Mathematical Programming: An Introduction to the Design and Application of Optimal Decision Machines* (New York: Wiley, 1970) (reiterative guessing and operations research); and S. Nagel, *Policy Evaluation: Making Optimum Decisions* (New York: Praeger, 1982) (variations on part/whole percentaging in Chapters 10–13). Also see S. Nagel, "Optimally Allocating Federal Money to Cities", *Public Budgeting and Finance*, 5: 39–50 (1985).

5. On dealing with constraints in public policy analysis in general, see Nagel, *Public Policy: Goals, Means, and Methods* especially the chapters on equity, effectiveness, human rights, discretion, economic structure, government structure, political feasibility, and ethical constraints. On quantitative constraints in allocation problems, see "Allocation Logic", in S. Nagel, *Policy Evaluation: Making Optimum Decisions* (New York: Praeger, 1982), where the problem of allocating to police, courts, and corrections is also discussed.

6. On the matter of simplicity in drawing and presenting conclusions in

evaluation analysis see S. Nagel, "Comparing Multi-Criteria Decision Making and P/G% with Traditional Optimizing", in Yoshikazu Sawaragi (ed.), *Multiple-Criteria Decision Making* (Berlin: Springer-Verlag, 1987) and "Simplifying Basic Methods", in Nagel, *Public Policy: Goals, Means, and Methods*. On the subject of taking away abused children, see 160 "Neglect", in George Cooper, *et al.*, *Law and Poverty: Cases and Materials* (St Paul: West, 1977).

7. On Policy/Goal Percentaging and the P/G% software, see Benjamin Radcliff, "Multi-Criteria Decision Making: A Survey of Software", *Social Science Microcomputer Review*, 4: 38–55 (1986); S. Nagel, "P/G% Analysis: An Evaluating-Aiding Program", *Evaluation Review*, 9: 209–14 (1985); and S. Nagel, "A Microcomputer Program for Dealing with Evaluation Problems", *Evaluation and Program Planning*, 9: 159–68 (1987). On the applicability of P/G% to all five analytic problems, see S. Nagel, *Evaluation Analysis with Microcomputers* (Greenwich, Conn.: JAI Press, 1988).

11 Law Problems

The purpose of this chapter is to describe how microcomputers can aid in making law decisions, including decisions that relate to the judicial process, law practice, and law management.

Those three kinds of law decisions are subdivided into eight examples. The material on the judicial process deals with computer-aided (1) case synthesizing, (2) fact synthesizing, and (3) law evaluation. The law practice material deals with computer-aided (4) counseling, (5) negotiation, and (6) advocacy. The law management material deals with (7) judicial administration, and (8) legal administration. Each of those eight types of computer-aided law decisions is described along with a concrete example and an illustrative visual aid.

The idea of computer-aided law decisions is a law variation on computer-aided manufacturing (CAM) and computer-aided design (CAD), which are becoming increasingly important in the American economy. Computer-aided law decisions have in common a systematic procedure for processing a set of (1) goals to be achieved or predictive criteria, (2) alternatives for achieving the goals or alternative situations, and (3) relations between criteria and alternatives in order to choose a best alternative, combination, allocation, or predictive decision-rule.[1]

Computer-aided decisions thus differ substantially from computer-aided clerical work like word processing, file management, litigation support, document drafting, citation access, or law office bookkeeping.[2] At the other extreme, computer-aided decisions differ from the idea of computers making decisions in place of appellate judges, trial judges, legislators, legal counselors, law negotiators, lawyer advocates, judicial administrators, or law firm administrators.[3] Computerized clerical work is highly possible and useful, but it is not lawyer work. Computers as decision-makers without judges, lawyers, and other legal personnel is probably not possible and of questionable value if it were possible.

Microcomputers can be helpful in processing goals, alternatives, and relations, especially for indicating what it would take to bring a second-place alternative up to first place, or what it would take to improve a predictive decision-rule. The microcomputer software described in this chapter belongs in the general categories of multi-criteria decision-making, expert systems, and artificial intelligence.

The specific software is called Policy/Goal Percentaging (P/G%) because it relates policies or decisions to goals or criteria, and it uses part/whole percentaging to deal with the goals being measured in different ways.

COMPUTER-AIDED JUDICIAL PROCESS (CAJP)

Computer-aided Case Synthesis (CACS)

Table 11.1 provides an example of synthesizing a set of appellate cases using the P/G% software. The appellate cases consist of nine cases dealing with legislative redistricting from *Colegrove* v. *Green* = (1948) to *Baker* v. *Carr* = (1962). Each case is scored yes with a 2 and no with a 1 on each of the four predictive criteria. The criteria include (1) whether equality is explicitly required by the relevant federal or state constitution, (2) whether a state or federal legislature is involved, (3) whether the degree of equality violation is big or little, and (4) whether a federal or state court is involved. The yes answer is the one that favors a decision for the side that is attacking the existing redistricting system.

The last column shows how each case was decided in terms of whether the winner was the defender or the attacker of the existing redistricting system. The second-to-last column shows the sum of the raw scores. It leads to a decision–rule that says, "if there is a total raw score of 7 or above, then the attacker wins; and if there is a total raw score of 6 or below, then the defender wins". That decision rule, however, has one inconsistency. It is the Grills case (1960), in which there were only 6 points, but the attacker still won.

To eliminate such inconsistencies, one can do a variety of legitimate things, as indicated in the notes below Table 11.1. The most meaningful approach is generally to give the predictive criteria different weights to indicate their relative importance. In this context, the most important criteria are the first criterion (which deals with the nature of the law) and the third criterion (which deals with the key facts). Of the two, the equality requirement is the most important since the degree of equality violation would mean little if there is no equality requirement. Giving the equality requirement a weight of 2 doubles all the numbers in the first column. Doing so changes the summation scores. The new weighted summation scores now lead to a decision–rule that says, "if there is a total raw score of 8 or above,

Table 11.1 Synthesizing appellate cases: legislative redistricting

CRITERIA CASES	Equality Requirement W = 1 (or 2)	State Legislature W = 1	Equality Violation W = 1	Federal Court W = 1	SUM (Weighted)	OUTCOME	
						Winner	Award
Colegrove	1 (2)	1	1	2	5 (6)	D	$0
Grills	2 (4)	2	1	1	6 (8)	A	2
Maryland	1 (2)	2	2	1	6 (7)	D	0
Scholle	1 (2)	2	2	1	6 (7)	D	0
WMCA	1 (2)	2	1	2	6 (7)	D	0
Asbury	2 (4)	2	2	1	7 (9)	A	6
Dyer	2 (4)	1	2	2	7 (9)	A	8
Baker	2 (4)	2	2	2	8 (10)	A	9
Magraw	2 (4)	2	2	2	8 (10)	A	10

Notes:

1. A *1* in columns 1 to 4 means No. A 2 means Yes. An "*A*" in the outcome column means that the attacker wins. A "*D*" means that the defender wins.

2. The decision-rule that the above data initially generates is the following:

   (1) If a redistricting case during the time period covered has a summation score of 7 or above, the attacker wins.

   (2) With a summation score of 6 or below, the defender wins.

3. That decision-rule generates one inconsistent case. The inconsistency can be eliminated by (1) changing the decision-rule to say that a summation score of 6 leads to an unclear outcome; (2) giving the first variable a weight of 2, which would be consistent with the importance of requiring equality; (3) adding a fifth variable called "Deciding after the Maryland case" (4) eliminating the Grills case, but that does not seem justifiable; (5) changing the measurement on the first variable from no–yes to a 1–3 scale and giving Grills a score of 3; (6) finding that Grills really deserves a relation score of 2 on the third of the four variables.

4. Each predicted criterion is initially given an equal weight of 1. If the equality requirement is given a weight of 2 in view of its substantive importance, then the Grills case would no longer be an inconsistently low-scoring case in which the attacker won. The new predictive decision rule would be the following:

   (1) If a redistricting case has a weighted summation score of 8 or above, the attacker wins.
   (2) If the weighted summation score is 7 or below, the attacker loses.

5. The dollar amounts in the last column represent hypothetical data showing how many thousands of dollars the successful attacker received in the form of damages. That information is useful for illustrating how the methodology can predict a continuum outcome as contrasted to a dichotomous outcome of winning versus losing.

then the attacker wins; and if there is a total raw score of 7 or below, then the defender wins". That new decision-rule results in no inconsistencies. The set of cases have thus been synthesized into a meaningful decision-rule.[4]

Computer-aided Fact Synthesis (CAFS)

Table 11.2 provides an example of synthesizing a set of facts in a trial decision using the P/G% software. This is a criminal case in which the key question is whether the defendant is guilty or not. For the sake of simplicity, there are two pieces of evidence. One is a defense witness who offers an alibi for the defendant. That witness has an 80% probability of telling the truth, which would favor the defendant being found not guilty. The second piece of evidence is a prosecution witness who claims to have seen the defendant at the scene of the crime. There is a 70% probability that the witness is telling the truth when one just analyzes that witness alone without considering the testimony of related witnesses.

Not all witnesses or pieces of evidence are of equal importance. An alibi witness is more important than a witness who saw the defendant at the scene of the crime. If the alibi witness is telling the truth, then the defendant cannot be guilty. If the crime-scene witness is telling the truth, then the defendant could still be innocent, since being at the scene of the crime does not mean that the defendant committed the crime. Therefore, give the alibi statement a weight of 2 or a multiple of 2.

The synthesizing then involves adding 0.40 to 0.70 in order to obtain a weighted sum for the alternative that the defendant is not guilty. Those two weighted sums should then be divided by the weights (which are 2 and 1) in order to obtain probabilities that add to 1.00. The bottom line thus shows there is a 0.37 probability that the defendant is guilty in light of the analysis and a 0.63 probability that the defendant is not guilty. It would therefore be appropriate to acquit the defendant since the probability of guilt should be higher than about 0.90 in order to justify a conviction.[5]

Computer-aided Law Evaluation (CALE)

Table 11.3 provides an example of using the P/G% software to arrive at a conclusion as to what policy ought to be adopted in light of a set of goals to be achieved. The subject matter is how should illegally obtained evidence be treated by the courts in criminal cases. The four alternatives listed consist of (1) the good-faith exception to excluding the evidence, (2) the suspension – dismissal exception to excluding the evidence, (3) the prevailing rule of excluding illegally seized evidence from criminal proceedings, and (4) the previous emphasis on the possibility of damage suits and prosecution to deter illegal searches. The goals to be achieved include (1) decreasing illegal police searches, (2) not encouraging lying by the police, (3) decreasing crime occurrence, and (4) feasibility in being capable of being adopted.

Table 11.3 also shows how each alternative is scored on each criterion using a 1–3 scale, where 3 = relatively high on the goal, 2 = middling on the goal, and 1 = relatively low on the goal. On the goal of decreasing illegal police searches, the alternatives of suspensions–dismissals and damages–prosecution are the strongest deterrents if applied. On not encouraging lying, the good-faith exception does not do so well compared to the other alternatives. On decreasing crime occurrence, the good-faith exception scores highest because it allows the police the freest hand. On the matter of feasibility, the good-faith exception may be questionable as to its constitutionality. Suspensions–dismissals lacks legislative feasibility, and damages–prosecution lacks judicial feasibility.

If one adds across each alternative without giving different weights to the goals, then the scores of the alternatives are 5 for the good-faith exceptions and a three-way tie for the other three alternatives. Even with different weights for the goals to consider the liberal, neutral, and conservative positions, there is still a three-way tie between suspension–dismissal, the exclusionary rule, and damages–prosecution. The bottom-line conclusion is that the exclusionary rule is the best of the tied alternatives because it is the only one that passes the feasibility constraint. It is feasible in the sense that it has been widely adopted across the 50 states. The other three alternatives have not been widely adopted, and there is considerable doubt as to whether they ever could be.[6]

Table 11.2 Synthesizing trial facts: a criminal case

Criteria / ALTERNATIVES	(1) Defense Statement (Alibi) $W_1 = 2$	(2) Prosecution Statement (Scene of Crime) $W_2 = 1$	(3) SUM $(1)+(2)$	(4) $\dfrac{\text{SUM}}{N}$ $(3)/2$	(5) Weighted Sum $(1.5)+(2)$	(6) Weighted Sum / Sum of Weights $(5)/3$
Defendant is Guilty	0.20 (0.40)	0.70	0.90	0.45	1.10	0.37*
Defendant is Not Guilty	0.80 (1.60)	0.30	1.10	0.55	1.90	0.63
	1.00 (2.00)	1.00	2.00	1.00	3.00	1.00

Notes:

1. The numbers in columns 1 and 2 are probabilities. They indicate the degree of accuracy or truth associated with the statements in the direction of establishing the defendant's guilt. Thus, the 0.20 probability means that there is a 0.80 probability that the defense statement is true, and the 0.20 complement is in the direction of establishing the defendant's guilt. These are probabilities of truth, not probabilities of guilt.

2. The weights indicate the degree of importance of the evidence items. Thus an alibi statement is quite important (if true) in establishing innocence. A statement saying the defendant was at the scene of the crime is less important because even if it is true, it does not establish the defendant's guilt. The numbers in parentheses in column 1 are weighted probabilities.

3. The numbers in column 3 are the sum of the two weighted probabilities. The numbers in column 5 are the sums of the two weighted probabilities.

4. The numbers in column 4 are unweighted average probabilities. The numbers in column 5 are weighted average probabilities. the numbers in column 6 are an approximation of Bayesian conditional probabilities especially when one only has probabilities of truthfulness and degrees of importance to work with.

5. If the probability in the upper right-hand corner is greater than 0.90, then the judge, juror, or other perceiver of these two items of evidence should vote to convict assuming (1) 0.90 is accepted as the threshold probability interpretation of beyond a reasonable doubt, and (2) these are the only items of evidence. If the starred probability is 0.90 or less, then one should vote to acquit.

6. With two alibi witnesses, each might receive a weight of 1.5 if one witness receives a 2. They do not both receive a 2 because they partly reinforce each other.

7. No set of weights will cause the weighted average to exceed 0.90 with probabilities of 0.20 and 0.70. Thus, there is no threshold value for either W_1 or W_2.

8. The difficulty of obtaining a set of evidence items across the prosecution and the defense that average better than a 0.90 probability may indicate that jurors and judges generally operate below the 0.90 threshold, even though judges and commentators say that 0.90 is roughly the probability translation of "beyond a reasonable doubt".

Table 11.3 Law evaluation: evidence illegally obtained

ALTERNATIVE POLICIES	GOALS TO BE ACHIEVED			Feasibility	OVERALL SCORES							
	Decrease Illegal Police Searches (L)	Not Encourage Lying by Police (N)	Decrease Crime Occurrence (C)		Liberal Score		Neutral Score		Conservative Score		Total	
					B	A	B	A	B	A	B	A
1. Good Faith Exception	1	1	3	1	8	11	10	13	12	15	30	39
2. Suspension–Dismissal	3	2	2	1	15	18	14	17	13	16	42	51
3. Exclude Evidence	2	2	1	3	11	20	10	19	9	18	30	57
4. Damages–Prosecution	3	2	2	1	15	18	14	17	13	16	42	51
TOTALS												

Notes:

1. The four alternatives are (1) allow the evidence in if the police testify they did not intend to engage in illegal behavior, (2) allow the evidence in if the state adopts a system of suspensions on the first offense and dismissal on the second offense, (3) exclude illegally seized evidence from criminal proceedings, and (4) emphasize damage suits and prosecution to deter illegal searches.

2. Conservatives are considered as giving the relatively conservative goals a weight of 3, neutral goals a weight of 2, and liberal goals a weight of 1. Liberals are considered as giving the conservative goals a weight of 1, neutral goals a weight of 2, and liberal goals a weight of 3. Neutrals are considered as giving all the goals a weight of 2. Feasibility is assumed to be worth a weight of 3 in view of its importance.

3. The scoring of the alternatives on the goals is done on a 1–3 scale. A 3 means conducive to the goal. A 2 means neither conducive nor adverse. A 1 means adverse to the goal.

4. An overall score is calculated by summing the products of the relation scores multiplied by the weights across each row or policy. For example, the liberal score of 8 is arrived at by summing (1×3) plus (1×2) plus (3×1), or $3 + 2 + 3 = 8$.

5. The liberal, neutral, conservative, and total scores are shown before (B) and after (A) adding the feasibility criterion. Without that criterion, the exclusionary rule comes out third or fourth out of the four alternatives. With that criterion, the exclusionary rules comes out first on all four value systems.

6. The other three alternatives are relatively lacking in feasibility because (1) the good-faith exception has questionable constitutionality, since it may provide too little deterrence against illegal search and seizure; (2) a system of suspensions and dismissals would require approval by state legislators or police administrative boards, which is unlikely; (3) prosecution of police officers for illegal searches without physical violence is unlikely, and the probabilities are quite low of an innocent or guilty person suing for damages, winning, and collecting anything substantial.

COMPUTER-AIDED LAW PRACTICE (CALP)

A. Computer-aided Counseling (CAC)

We can best illustrate CALP by considering Table A11.2 (p. 199). Table A11.2 in the appendix to Chapter 11 provides an example of computer-aided counseling in the field of will drafting. There are computer programs available that will convert decisions concerning estate allocation into the proper legal form to serve as a valid will, such as the WillWriter program. Those programs, however, are not for helping the testator decide how to divide his or her estate. They assume that such decisions have already been made. They are useful in providing checklists as to what decisions should have been made, or need to be made.

In this example, the testator is trying to decide among three possible beneficiaries, namely his son, daughter, and wife. In using the P/G% program to aid in making such decisions, the lawyer and the testator together can list the possible beneficiaries. The testator with the aid of the lawyer can tentatively decide on a set of criteria for evaluating the potential beneficiaries. In this case, there are two criteria. One is need, and the other is deservingness.

Need is scored on a 1–5 scale. A 5 in this context means highly needy, and a 4 means mildly needy. At the other extreme, a 1 means highly well-off or the opposite of highly needy, and a 2 means mildly well-off or the opposite of mildly needy. A 3 thus means neither needy nor well-off, but somewhere in the middle. On such a scale, the wife scores a 5. The daughter scores a 4, and the son scores a 2. Deservingness is also scored on a 1–5 scale. A 5 in this context means highly deserving; a 4 means mildly deserving; a 3 means neither deserving nor undeserving; a 2 means mildly undeserving; and a 1 means highly undeserving. Deservingness can especially refer to how nice the potential beneficiary has been to the testator, or refer to the good the beneficiary might do with the bequest, although those could be two separate criteria. On the deservingness scale, the son scores a 4. The wife scores a 3, and the daughter scores a 2.

The object now is to use that jointly-determined information to derive meaningful allocation percentages for each of the three beneficiaries. A simple way to do that is to add each person's two scores in order to arrive at an overall score for each person. Doing so gives the wife an overall score of 8. Both the son and the daughter receive overall scores of 6 apiece. The sum of those three scores is 6 + 6 + 8, or 20. With a total evaluative pie of 20, the son and daughter should logically receive 6/20 or 30% apiece. The wife should receive 8/20, or 40%.

Those allocations, however, are only tentative. They represent a first cut or initial analysis, subject to change depending on what is revealed as a result of making changes in the inputs. An appropriate change to experiment with might involve additional beneficiaries, such as other relatives, friend, or charities. Doing so might suggest additional criteria, such as the extent to which the bequest might be appreciated, or might result in the testator receiving favorable publicity. One might also experiment with other ways of measuring need or deservingness besides a 1–5 scale, although the methodology changes if the two criteria are measured on two different scales.

An especially useful tool for analyzing the effects of changes in the scores is the threshold analysis shown in Table A11.2C. This shows the changes in the scores that would have to occur to bring the son or daughter up to the allocation level of the wife, or to bring the wife down to the level of the son or daughter. This is useful where the testator is having doubts as to whether the beneficiaries should receive equal or different amounts. Table A11.2C shows that for the son to share equally with the wife, one of four scores or a combination would have to change, namely (1) the son's 2 on need would have to be a 4, (2) the son's 4 on deservingness would have to be 6 which is impossible on a 1–5 scale, (3) the wife's 5 on need would have to drop to a 3 or be misestimated by that much, or (4) the wife's deservingness would have to be a 1 instead of a 3. If all those possibilities seem unrealistic, then one can feel more confident in giving the extra allocation to one's wife. The analysis also shows that the son should be given the same allocation as the wife if the testator values deservingness as being 3 times as important as need, or if need is considered 1/3 as important as deservingness. The same kind of a determining what it would take to bring the daughter up to the same allocation as the wife.

The P/G% program has other useful features for estate allocation or for any kind of allocation. It can deal with negative criteria such as keeping administrative costs down. It can work with 1–5 scales, dollars, percentages, years of service, or other measurement dimensions. It can show at what weight a criterion becomes strong enough that the bottom-line allocations are within five percentage points of what the allocations would be if that were the only criterion. The program can be used to help allocate partnership profits among the members of a law firm, to allocate time or money to various activities or places, and to allocate taxes to various governmental programs.[7]

Computer-aided Negotiation (CAN)

Table 11.4 provides the data for an example of computer-aided negotiation in a damages case. The alternatives basically are either to go to trial or to settle out of court. This example is presented from a plaintiff's perspective although it could have also been presented from a defense perspective. The example involves a contingency fee arrangement, although it could have been shown with an hourly rate or a flat fee. Table 11.4B shows the criteria for deciding between trial and settlement from both the lawyer's perspective (L) and the client's perspective (C). The lawyer here happens to be a female, and the client is a male. The criteria can also be classified as those which involve benefits (positive weights) and those which involve costs (negative weights). They can also be classified in terms of whether the criteria relate to the trial alternative (1–4) or the settlement alternative (5–8).

The weights in Table 11.4B indicate the following:

1. The 0.22 shows that there is an estimated 0.65 probability of winning and that the lawyer gets 0.33 of what is won. That probability could also be discounted for time, using the time-discounting provisions of the P/G% program.
2. The 0.43 shows that there is an estimated 0.65 probability of winning, and the client gets 0.67 of what is won.
3. The $30 indicates that the lawyer feels her litigation hours are worth $30 an hour to her.
4. The −1 shows that the client has litigation costs that are figured as a lump amount, not by the hour.
5. The 0.20 indicates that the lawyer retains 20% of the settlement.
6. The 0.80 indicates that the client retains 80% of the settlement.
7. The $20 indicates that the lawyer feels her settlement hours are worth $20 an hour to her,
8. The −1 shows that the client has settlement costs (if any) that are figured as a lump amount, not by the hour.

Table 11.4   Computer-aided negotiation: a damages case

A. The Alternatives of Trial Versus Settlement
Alternative
1. Go to Trial
2. Settle

B. The Criteria and Weights of the Benefits and Costs

Criterion	Meas. Unit	Weight
1 (L) Dams. if Won	$	0.22
2 (C) Dams. if Won		0.43
3 (L) Lit. Hours		−30.00
4 (C) Lit. Costs		−1.00
5 (L) Set. Offer		0.20
6 (C) Set. Offer		0.80
7 (L) Set. Hours		−20.00
8 (C) Set. Costs		−1.00

C. Scoring the Alternatives on the Criteria for Trial

	(L) Dams.	(C) Dams.	(L) Lit. H.	(C) Lit. C.
Go To Trial	3000.00	3000.00	20.00	400.00
Settle	0.00	0.00	0.00	0.00

D. Scoring the Alternatives on the Criteria for Settlement

	(L) Set. O	(C) Set. O	(L) Set. H	(C) Set. C.
Go To Trial	0.00	0.00	0.00	0.00
Settle	1000.00	1000.00	5.00	0.00

E. The Overall Results from the Lawyer's Perspective

	(L) Dams.	(L) Lit. H	(L) Set. O.	(L) Set. H.	Combined Rawscores
Go To Trial	650.00	−600.00	0.00	−0.00	50.00
Settle	0.00	−0.00	200.00	−100.00	100.00

F. The Overall Results from the Client's Perspective

	(C) Dams.	(C) Lit. C	(C) Set. O.	(C) Set. C.	Combined Rawscores
Go To Trial	1300.00	−400.00	0.00	−0.00	900.00
Settle	0.00	−0.00	800.00	−0.00	800.00

G. What It Would Take to Get the Client to Settle

	Go to Trial	Settle	Weight
(C) Dams. if Won	2769.23		0.400
(C) Lit. Costs	500.00		
(C) Set. Offer		1125.00	0.900
(C) Set. Costs		−100.00	

H. What It Would Take to Get the Lawyer to Trial			
	Go to Trial	Settle	Weight
(L) Dams. if Won	3230.77		· 0.233
(L) Lit. Hours	18.33		−27.500
(L) Set. Offer		750.00	0.150
(L) Set. Hours		7.50	−30.000

Table 11.4C and 11.4D show how each alternative scores on each criterion as follows:

1. The damages if won are estimated at $3,000.
2. The lawyer's litigation hours are estimated at 20 hours.
3. The client's litigation costs are estimated at $400.
4. The settlement offer thus far is $1,000.
5. The lawyer's settlement hours are estimated at 5.
6. The client's settlement costs are nothing.

In light of the above data, Table 11.4E shows the lawyer would do better to settle, rather than go to trial. For the lawyer, the $3,000 damages income (discounted by the 0.65 probability of victory and the 0.33 contingency fee rate) becomes $650. If she subtracts $600 in litigation costs ($30 times 20 hours), there is a net profit of $50. On the other hand, a $1,000 settlement means $200 income at 20%. If she subtracts $100 in settlement costs ($20 times 5 hours), there is a net profit of $100 for settling. Table 11.4F, however, shows the client would be better off going to trial, rather than settling. For the client, the $3,000 damages income (discounted by the 0.65 probability and the 0.67 complement of the contingency fee rate) is $1,300. If he subtracts $400 in litigation costs, there is a net profit of $900. On the other hand, a $1,000 settlement means $800 income at 80%. If he subtracts nothing in settlement costs, there is a net profit for settling that is $100 less than the estimated trial net profit.

The P/G% program is especially useful for computer-aided negotiation because it can so conveniently indicate what it would take to bring a second-place alternative up to first place. Table 11.4G, for example, shows that settlement would become more profitable to both the client and the lawyer than going to trial if the lawyer can get the insurance company to raise its offer from $1,000 to anything higher than $1,125. If the insurance company is unwilling to go higher than $1,125, then the lawyer has an ethical obligation to go to trial, assuming the estimated inputs are reasonably accurate. If, however, the estimated damages amount is as low as $2,769, then the lawyer should settle in the client's best interests, or if the client's litigation costs are more than $500. The lawyer should also accept the $1,000 settlement if the combination of victory probability and contingency complement are as low as 0.40 rather than 0.43, or if the client is allowed to keep 90% of the settlement rather than 80%, although then the lawyer may not be so enthusiastic about settling.

Table 11.4H shows from the lawyer's perspective what it would take to make going to trial more profitable than settling. There are eight answers plus combinations of them, as indicated by the eight breakeven values shown in Table 11.4H. If any of the original scores change to the scores shown in Table 11.4H, then going to trial becomes more profitable. Those changes include increased damages, decreased litigation hours, decreased settlement, increased settlement hours, increased probability of victory, increased contingency fee, decreased litigation hourly rate, decreased settlement percentage, or increased settlement hourly rate. Table 11.4H shows exactly what increase or decrease will generate a tie between the profitability of going to trial and the profitability of settling.

With that kind of information, the lawyer can negotiate better with the insurance company over the settlement offer and possibly with the client over the contingency fee. The lawyer can also see from these figures what margin of error there is on the estimates. Thus, if it is better for the client's interests to go to trial with an estimated damages higher than $2,769, then the lawyer need not anguish over whether the damages are likely to be $3,000 or $5,000 since either figure is over $2,769, and likewise with the other estimates.[8]

Computer-aided Advocacy (CAA)

Table 11.5 provides an example of a case brief using the P/G% software. The case is *San Antonio* v. *Rodriguez*, 411 US Supreme Court 1 (1973). The case dealt with the extent to which a state is required to help equalize expenditures per student across school districts within the state. The first part of the brief (Table 11.5A) shows that the Supreme Court was faced with the four basic alternatives of (1) no equality required, (2) equal expenditures per student, (3) a minimum amount of expenditures per student, but otherwise allowing for inequality, or (4) a requirement of equality but at a high

Table 11.5 Computer-aided advocacy: *San Antonio* v. *Rodriguez*

A. THE ALTERNATIVES AND THE CRITERIA

Alternative	Previous Outcome	Criterion	Meas. Unit	Weight
NO EQUALITY REQD.	YES	1 EDUCATED POP.	1-3	1.00
= $ PER STUDENT	NO	2 –DISCONTENT		1.00
MIN. $ PER STUDENT	NO	3 –DOWNGRADING		1.00
HIGH $ PER STUDENT	NO	4 ADMIN. EASE		1.00
OTHER	?	5 CONSIST. W/CASES		1.00
		6 –EXPENSE		1.00

B. THE SCORES OF THE ALTERNATIVES ON THE CRITERIA

	EDUCATED	–DISCON	–DOWNGR	ADMIN. EA	CONSIST.	EXPENSE
NO EQUALITY REQD.	1.00	1.00	3.00	3.00	2.00	3.00
= $ PER STUDENT	2.00	2.00	1.00	1.00	2.00	2.00
MIN. $ PER STUDE	2.00	2.00	2.00	1.00	2.00	1.50
HIGH $ PER STUD	3.00	3.00	2.00	1.00	1.00	1.00

C. THE TOTAL SCORES OF THE ALTERNATIVES

Alternative	Combined Rawscores	Previous Outcome
NO EQUALITY REQD.	13.00	YES
= $ PER STUDENT	10.00	NO
MIN. $ PER STUDENT	10.50	NO
HIGH $ PER STUDENT	11.00	NO

D. WHAT IT WOULD TAKE TO BRING THE SECOND PLACE ALTERNATIVE UP TO FIRST PLACE

	NO EQUALIT	MIN. $ PER	Weight
EDUCATED POP.	–1.50	4.50	3.500
– DISCONTENT	–1.50	4.50	3.500
– DOWNGRADING	0.50	4.50	–1.500
ADMIN. EASE	0.50	3.50	–0.250
CONSIST. W/CASES	–0.50	4.50	??
– EXPENSE	0.50	4.00	–0.667

level. The first part of the brief also shows that the court answered yes to the first alternative, but no to the others.

The second part of the brief (Table 11.5B) shows that there are about six relevant criteria including, (1) having an educated population, (2) decreasing discontent due to educational disparities, (3) avoiding the downgrading of affluent schools, (4) administrative ease, (5) consistency with prior cases, and (6) avoiding heavy taxpayer expense. The third part of the brief (Table 11.5B) shows how each alternative scores on each criterion using a simple 1–3 scale, where 3 = highly conducive to the goal, 2 = neither conducive nor adverse, and 1 = adverse to the goal. The fourth part of the brief (Table 11.5C) shows the combined raw scores for each alternative using the apparent scoring of the Supreme Court. The alternative with the highest combined raw score is "no equality required", which is the alternative that the Supreme Court adopted.

The fifth part of the brief (Table 11.5D) is the threshold analysis. It shows what it would take to bring the second-place alternative up to first place. There was a gap of 2.50 points between first and second place on the combined raw scores. That gap would be eliminated if the "no equality" alternative were to drop by 2.50 points on any of the six criteria. That would be too big a drop on any one criterion since the criteria cannot go below 1.00. The gap would also be eliminated if the second-place alternative of having a "minimum number of dollars per student" were to increase by 2.50 points on any of the six criteria. That would be too big an increase on any one criterion since the criteria cannot go above 3.00. The gap would also be eliminated if the Supreme Court were to place substantially more weight on having an educated population or on decreasing discontent due to educational inequalities. Those are two areas which the advocates of a "minimum-dollars" position should emphasize. The gap would be eliminated if the other criteria were given negative weights which is unlikely. Changing the weight would not help with regard to consistency with prior cases, since both alternatives scored the same on that criterion.[9]

COMPUTER-AIDED LAW MANAGEMENT (CALM)

Computer-aided Judicial Administration (CAJA)

Table 11.6 shows how one can systematically view the problem of assigning judges to case types. This hypothetical problem involves two judges named Fox and Wolf. It involves the case types of criminal and civil cases. Each judge is expected to spend 10 hours in trial in an average week. In such a week, there are about 8 criminal hours and 12 civil hours of trial work.

Judge Fox received a score of 4 for criminal cases on a 1–5 scale, and Judge Wolf a 2. On civil cases, they both received a score of 3. The scoring was done by having each judge or all the judges in the system anonymously score each other. Each judge also scored himself or herself on degree of interest in the case types on a 1–5 scale. The ability scores and interest scores were averaged to give the scores of 4, 2, 3, and 3. What is the best allocation of these two judges to these two case types?

"Best" in this context means an allocation or assignment that will result in as large an overall quality score as possible within the row and column constraints. The overall quality score is the sum of each

Table 11.6   Judicial administration: assigning judges to types of cases

CASES JUDGE	CRIMINAL		CIVIL		Hours per Judge
	Quality Score	Hours Assigned	Quality Score	Hours Assigned	
FOX	4	a	3	b	10
WOLF	2	c	3	d	10
Hours per Casetype		8		12	20

Notes:

1. The allocation system is shown in its simplest form with two judges and two casetypes. Each judge is expected to put in ten hours a week to satisfy the average weekly total of 20 hours of trial time. Criminal cases constitute 40% of the total or 8 hours, and civil cases constitute 60% or 12 hours. Judge 1 receives scores of 4 and 3 on the two casetypes, and Judge 2 receives scores of 2 and 3.

2. A logical way to resolve the optimum allocation with this relatively simple example is to reason as follows:

   (1) Judge Wolf does a bad job on criminal cases. Therefore, give Judge Wolf 0 criminal hours. That means Judge Wolf gets 10 civil hours to add across to 10. Judge Fox must then get 8 criminal hours to add down to 8. Judge Fox must also get 2 civil hours to add across to 10 and down to 12.

   (2) Judge Fox does a good job on criminal cases. Therefore, give Judge Fox as many hours as possible on criminal cases which is 8. That means Judge Wolf gets 0 criminal hours to add down to 8. Judge Wolf must then get 10 civil hours to add across to 10. Judge Fox must also get 2 civil hours to add across to 10 and down to 12.

3. On a more general level, resolve the optimum allocation by reasoning as follows:

   (1) Pick out all the quality scores that are 1s or 2s. Give those cells as few hours as possible.

   (2) Pick out all the quality scores that are 5s or 4s. Give those cells as many hours as possible.

   (3) Make logical adjustments so that all the columns add down to what they should, and all the rows add across to what they should.

   (4) Also try to minimize the number of casetypes per judge rather than have every judge do at least a little bit of everything.

4. The optimum allocation is defined as allocating the total number of hours to each cell so as to satisfy the row constraints, the column constraints, and any cell constraints, while at the same time maximizing the sum of the products of the quality score times the hours assigned for each cell. A cell includes a quality score of a judge on a casetype and a quantity of hours assigned to a judge on a casetype.

product of a judge's quality score times the hours assigned for a given case type. In this context the overall quality score is equal to $4a + 2c + 3b + 3d$. The object is to solve for a, b, c, and d so as to maximize that overall score while satisfying the constraints.

The best way to proceed if one does not have a computer is to give as few hours as possible to those cells which have quality scores of 1 or 2, and as many hours as possible to those cells which have quality scores of 5 or 4, while satisfying the constraints. Doing so results in an allocation of 0 hours to c, 8 hours to a, 2 hours to b, and 10 hours to d.

That method can be meaningful for a substantial number of judges and case types. One can, however, solve big judicial assignments faster and with more accuracy by using a linear programming routine. Such routines are easy to use on microcomputers. One simply informs the computer of the row totals, the column totals, and the quality scores. The computer then generates the optimum allocations. The program will also indicate (1) how much each quality score can vary without affecting the optimum result, (2) how much each row total and column total can vary, and (3) how much of a change in the overall quality score would occur as a result of a one-unit change in the hours assigned or in any of the inputs.[10]

Computer-aided Legal Administration (CALA)

Table 11.7 shows an example of computer-aided legal administration in the field of optimum sequencing of law cases. The illustrative problem is, "What is the best order in which to handle three cases that involve an estimated 10, 20, and 30 hours and that are predicted to generate $21, $61, $80 in billing?" For the sake of simplicity, assume we have a one-lawyer firm who works a 40-hour week. With three cases labeled A, B, and C, there are six ways in which they can be ordered consisting of ABC, ACB, BAC, BCA, CAB, and CBA. Which is the best order?

A more general way to view the problem is in terms of five different methods that are frequently proposed for ordering cases in a law firm, a government agency, or elsewhere. Those alternative methods arranged randomly are:

1. Take the cases in the order of the **highest benefits first**. That means CBA.
2. Look to the cases with the **lowest costs first**. That means ABC.
3. Take them **first come, first served**. That also means ABC.

Table 11.7   Law firm administration: sequencing cases
(*Problem*: What is the best order to handle three cases that involve 10, 20, and 30 hours and that generate $21, $61, and $80 in billing?)

A. *The Alternatives: Five Sequencing Methods*
   Alternative
   1 Highest Bs First
   2 Lowest Cs First
   3 1st Come, 1st Served
   4 Highest B–C First
   5 Highest B/C First

B. *The Criteria: Two Weeks of Profit*

Criterion	Meas. Unit	Weight
1 1st Week Profit	$	2.00
2 2nd Week Profit	$	1.00

C. *The Profit Obtained by Each Alternative for Each Week*

Alternative/Criteria Scoring	1st Week	2nd Week
Highest Bs First	70.50	31.50
Lowest Cs First	68.67	33.33
1st Come, 1st Served	68.67	33.33
Highest B–C First	70.50	31.50
Highest B/C First	74.33	27.67

D. *The Overall Score for Each Sequencing Method*

Alternative	Combined Rawscores
1 Highest Bs First	172.50
2 Lowest Cs First	170.67
3 1st Come, 1st Served	170.67
4 Highest B–C First	172.50
5 Highest B/C First	176.33

Notes:

1. The above computer printout shows that by taking the first three cases in the order of the highest benefit/cost ratio first, one thereby maximizes overall benefits minus costs.
2. This is so because the B/C order results in more profit being earned earlier, and that profit is thus available to draw interest or to be reinvested, more so than if it is earned later.

4. Prefer the **most profitable first**, meaning the ones with the highest benefits minus costs. That means *C* ($80–30), *B* ($61–20), and then *A* ($21–10).

5. Take them in the order of their **benefit/cost (B/C) ratios**. That means *B* ($61/20, or 3.05), *C* ($80/30, or 2.67), and then *A* ($21/10, or 2.10).

We want to pick the best ordering criterion in terms of maximizing the profits of the law firm, while operating within ethical constraints. At first glance, one might think the order of the cases will make no difference in the profit that can be made from these three cases. The cases are going to consume a total of 60 hours regardless of the order in which they are handled. Likewise, the order will not affect the fact that they will collectively bring in $162 in billings. If we assume that one hour is worth $1 or one monetary unit, then their net profit will be $162 minus $60, or $102 regardless of the order in which they are processed.

At second glance, however, we realize that one method may bring in more money earlier than another method. The method that brings in the most money as early as possible is the most profitable because that early money can be invested in the firm or elsewhere, thereby drawing interest which might otherwise be a missed opportunity. Table 11.7B shows that the criterion for judging these methods should be how much profit they generate in the first week, the second week, and so on, with more weight given to the profit of the first week than the second week.

Table 11.7C shows for each method how profitable it is in terms of the separate weekly profits, rather than the overall profit which is the same $102 for all the methods. The winning method is taking the cases in the order of their benefit/cost ratios. That method generates $74.33 in the first week, which is about $4 higher than its nearest competitor. If we assume that these numbers are $1,000 units, then by not taking the cases in their B/C order, the firm may be losing the interest that could have been made on $4,000 invested for one week. If that kind of loss is multiplied by 52 weeks and 30 cases rather than three cases, then a lot of money may be needlessly lost.

The $74.33 is calculated by noting that case *B* has the highest B/C ratio, and thus comes first. Case *B* takes 20 hours and generates a net profit of $41. We then go to case *C*, which has the second best B/C ratio. It takes 30 hours, but we only have 20 hours left in the week. We therefore do 2/3 of the case, and thus earn 2/3 of the $50 profit which is $33.33. If we add that to $41, the first week generates $74.33 profit. The second week brings $27.67 in profit, or the remainder of the $102. This assumes that the measurement units or the monetary units are really $1,000 units rather than $1 units.

One can contrast that optimally profitable sequencing with any of the other less profitable methods. For example, if the cases are processed in terms of their individual profitability, we would take case *C* first, rather than case *B*. Doing so would consume 30 hours for a profit of $50. We would then have time for only 10 of 20 hours of case B, which is the next most profitable case. That would earn half of the $41 profit, or $20.50. If we add $50 to $20.50, then we get only $70.50, or $70,500, rather than $74.33, or $74,333. The $70,500 and the $74,333 assume that the measurement units or the monetary units are really $1,000 units rather than $1 units.

To be more exact we could time discount the profits of the second week using the time-discounting provisions of the P/G% program. That would give a more accurate overall score than giving the first week's profits a weight of 2. The time discounting, however, would not change the rank order as to which is the best sequencing method.

A computer can aid in implementing the B/C sequencing method by questioning the relevant lawyers as the cases come in as to their estimates of the expenses and income for each case. The computer can then arrange the cases each week in the order of the B/C ratios, and then display that order to aid in deciding which case to take next. To prevent cases with a low B/C ratio from being unreasonably delayed, the computer can flag cases for immediate processing in time to meet the statute of limitations, other deadlines, or an ethical constraint that says no case should have to wait more than a given time to reach a certain stage.

By following such procedures, the law firm administration will not only be maximizing the law firm's profits, but it will also be maximizing the happiness of the clients collectively. This is so if we assume that $1 in billing activity generates the equivalent of one happiness unit. That way the B/C method thus generates more client happiness earlier than the alternative methods do. The estimated total happiness units per week can be calculated by adding 40 to the numbers given in the first column of Table 11-7C, and adding 20 to the numbers in the second column. The B/C method thus generates 114.33 happiness units, which is higher than any of the other methods. It is pleasing when law-firm administrative methods can be found that maximize both the interests of the law firm and the interests of the clients.[11]

SOME CONCLUSIONS

The essence of computer-aided decision making is the processing of goals, alternatives, and relations between goals and alternatives in order to choose a best alternative. This is the basic model or methodology. The essence of law decisions is judging, lawyering, and the administration of judging and lawyering. This is the basic substance.

What are the benefits of using computer-aided decision-making which justifies their general use in law decisions? The benefits include the following:

1. Working with the basic model encourages being more explicit about goals to be achieved, alternatives for achieving them, and relations between goals and alternatives.
2. The model leads to choosing the alternative, combination, or allocation that is best in light of the goals, alternatives, and relations.
3. The model leads to choosing predictive decision-rules that are capable of separating the past cases into winners and losers in light of their characteristics. That separation is relevant to predicting or explaining future cases accurately.
4. The model facilitates making changes in order to determine the effects on the bottom line of different goals, alternatives, relations, and other inputs.
5. The model informs the users what it would take in order to bring second-place alternatives or other alternatives up to first place.
6. The model allows and encourages the users to inject their knowledge of the subject matter, rather than impose substance on the users.
7. The model lends itself to being used with microcomputers in order to simplify arithmetic, record keeping, and manipulation of the data.
8. The model stimulates new insights into causal and normative relations that might otherwise be overlooked.

Costs involved in obtaining these benefits are mainly a willingness to think differently and more explicitly about the judicial process and lawyering than one may be accustomed to. The benefits do seem to substantially outweigh these costs, especially if these models are considered supplements to traditional perspectives, rather than substitutes. What is especially needed is to spread an awareness of these decision-aiding methods and applications, because to know them is to find them useful. It is hoped that this chapter will facilitate that purpose of making these models better known, so they can be made even more useful.

Appendix : Examples of Specific Law Applications

COMPUTER-AIDED LAW DECISIONS: ADDENDUM

The purpose of this brief addendum is to provide three specific examples of lawyers who have made use of the P/G% software to aid in arriving at lawyer-like decisions. The first example is E. Fremont Magee, a partner in the firm of Piper and Marbury of Baltimore, Maryland. He says:

"I regularly make use of P/G% for the selection of candidates for arbitration panels in medical malpractice claims here in Maryland. Before a medical malpractice matter can be tried in court in Maryland, it must first be submitted to a statutory three member arbitration panel. Each side is given sketchy resumes of five potential candidates to serve as panel chairmen. Each of these is an attorney. In addition, there are five candidates to serve as the lay member and five health care providers to serve as the health care provider member. Each side has the opportunity to strike two candidates from each list. Generally, the biographical information of the lawyers includes date of birth, year of admission to the bar, undergraduate school, graduate school, trial frequency, number of years of litigation experience, medical malpractice experience, arbitration experience, association with health providers, nature of practice and related matters. I use the program to rank the five potential candidates based on the various values I assign to these various criteria" (letter to the author, February 19, 1985).

The second example is C. Howard Thomas, Jr, a partner in the firm of Saul, Ewing, Remick, and Saul of Philadelphia. He presented two interesting uses of P/G% made by his law firm at the Legal Tech '86 Conference in Philadelphia. One use involved deciding where to move the offices of the firm. The firm had to move because it needed larger quarters. There were about five key places to choose among. There was considerable emotion in arguing over the five places. The partners decided to be explicit on the criteria the firm was seeking to achieve and how each place scored on each of those criteria. By doing that, the emotional subject could be handled more rationally. The analysis showed a certain place to be the tentative winner. A sensitivity analysis was then performed to see what changes in the relative weights of the criteria and in the scores of the alternatives on the criteria would be necessary to bring each other place up to the same desirability level as the first-place alternative. It was decided that all of the needed changes were unreasonable. The partners then felt pleased they had made the right choice as to where to move the law firm. The firm has also made use of P/G% in deciding whether to litigate or settle out of court. The analysis in at least one big case was shared with the client to convince the client that accepting the settlement was a wise decision.

The third example is Karen S. Dickson and John Finan of the Akron

University Law School. They analyzed a dozen key cases which involved the issue of whether a worker is an employee or an independent contractor. The analysis involved scoring each case on seven criteria as to whether the criterion was present or absent. Each case was given a summation score by adding its points on the criteria. The cases in which the total points were nine or more consistently found the worker to be an employee. The cases in which the total points were eight or less consistently found the worker to be an independent contractor. That consistent pattern was established after noting the need to give extra weight to whether the principal has control of the details of the agent's work, as compared to the other criteria. Dickson and Finan thus used the P/G% prediction methodology inductively to operationalize the concepts of employee and independent contractor more clearly than the courts had previously verbalized those concepts.

PRIVATE LAW

Contracts

Table A11.1   Allocating profits under a partnership contract for a law firm

---

A. LISTING OUT THE PARTNERS

	Alternative
1	PARTNER #1
2	PARTNER #2
3	
4	
5	
6	
7	
8	
9	
10	
11	
12	
13	
14	
15	PARTNER #15

B. LISTING OUT THE ABBREVIATED CRITERIA

Criterion	Criterion
1 YEARS AS PARTNER	1 ATTRACT CLIENTS
2 AGE	2 RETAIN CLIENTS
3 YEARS AS LAWYER	3 MANAGEMENT
4 YEARS WITH FIRM	4 COMMITTEES
5 BILLABLE HOURS	5 TEACHING
6 BILLINGS THIS YEAR	6 PUBLISHING
7 BILLINGS LAST YEAR	7 BAR ACTIVITIES
8 COLLECTIONS THIS YEAR	8 COMMUNITY ACTIV.
9 COLLECTIONS LAST YEAR	9 REL. W/ASSOCIATES
10 $ MANAGED THIS YEAR	10 REL. W/STAFF
11 $ MANAGED LAST YEAR	11 RESPECT/COMMUNITY
12 TURNOVER TO CASH	
13 REALIZATION ON UNB	
14 REALIZE ON BILLED	
15 TECHNICAL ABILITY	

Notes:

1. The partners should be listed by name. Minimums per partner, if any, can be specified. The actual column is for showing last year's share of the profits for comparison with this year.
2. For further details on each criterion, see John Iezzi, "Partner Compensation", *Legal Economics*: 29–32 (March/April 1985).
3. The measurement units may be in years, dollars, a 1–5 scale, or whatever seems meaningful.
4. All the criteria can be weighted equally, or some criteria can be given a weight of 2 or 3 depending on how important some criteria are considered to be relative to other criteria by the partners deciding collectively.

Property Law

Table A11.2   Estate Allocation

A. *Scoring the Beneficiaries on Need and Deservingness*

	Need	Deservingness
Son	2.00	4.00
Daughter	4.00	2.00
Spouse	5.00	3.00

Note:
Table A11.2A shows that the alternative beneficiaries are a son, a daughter, and a spouse. The criteria for allocating are need and deservingness. Each beneficiary is scored on each criterion on a 1–5 scale. A 5 means highly conducive to the criterion. A 4 means mildly conducive. A 3 means neither conducive nor adverse. A 2 means mildly adverse, and a 1 means highly adverse.

B. *Allocating in Proportion to How Well the Beneficiaries Score on Each Criterion*

	Need	Deservingness
Son	18.18	44.44
Daughter	36.36	22.22
Spouse	45.45	33.33

Note:
Table A11.2B shows in the first column how the estate would be allocated if only need were considered. The son then receives 2/11 or 18%, the daughter 4/11 or 36%, and the spouse 5/11 or 45%. Likewise with the second column on deservingness.

C. *Averaging the Separate Allocations to Determine the Overall Allocations*

	Allocation	P/W%
Son	$313.13	31.31
Daughter	$292.93	29.29
Spouse	$393.94	39.39

Note:
Table 11.2C averages the allocations based on need and deservingness to determine an overall allocation. Thus, the son gets 31% overall which is the average between 18% on need and 44% on deservingness. Likewise with the daughter and the spouse. The averages in Table A11.2C are based on treating need and deservingness as having equal weight or importance. One could arrive at a weighted average for each beneficiary if the criteria had different weights or degrees of relative importance. One can also specify minimum allocations for each beneficiary. If a beneficiary fails to receive the minimum percentage in step A11.2C, then give the beneficiary that minimum and reallocate the remainder to the other beneficiaries.

continued on page 200

Table A11.2 *continued*

D. **What it Would Take To Bring a Second Place Alternative Up to First Place**

	Son	Spouse	Weight
Need	3.60	3.00	0.407
Deservingness	6.00	1.86	2.455

Note:
Table A11.2D shows the scores the son or spouse would have to receive on each criterion to justify the son receiving the same allocation as the spouse. It also shows that there would be a tie in the allocation if the weight of need were cut more than half from 1.00 to 0.41, of if deservingness were more than doubled from 1.00 to 2.46. A similar table could be generated for the daughter and spouse or for the son and spouse. Table A11.2D can be helpful to someone who is advocating an increased percentage to one of the beneficiaries. It can also be helpful to the will-maker in deciding whether he or she really wants a certain beneficiary to have more or less than another beneficiary.

E. **The Weights at Which Each Criterion Dominates the Other Criteria**

Weight

Need	5.00	Stopping difference set at:
Deservingness	5.00	5.1 percentage points

Note:
Table A11.2E shows that if the weight of need is raised from 1 to 5, then the allocation percentages in Table A11.2C will be within 5 percentage points of the percentages on the left side of Table A11.2B. Likewise if the weight of deservingness is raised from 1 to 5, then the allocation percentages in Table A11.2C will be within 5 percentage points of the percentages on the right side of Table A11.2B.

Family Law

Table A11.3   Divorce issues

A. DECIDING WHETHER TO GET A DIVORCE			
Alternatives	Criteria	Meas. Unit	Weight
1 Stay Married As Is	1 – Alcohol/Addict	1–5 Scale	1.00
2 Develop Agreement	2 – Violence		1.00
3 Living Apart	3 Remarriage		1.00
4 Full Divorce	4 Privacy/Ind.		1.00
	5 Economic Status		1.00
	6 Colleagues/		1.00
	Relationships		
	7 Children		1.00
	8 Companionship		1.00

B. DECIDING ON A PROPERTY SETTLEMENT			
Alternatives	Criteria	Meas. Unit	Weight
1 Sell All/Div. 1/2	1 Equal Division	1–5 Scale	1.00
2 House Kept/$ Rest	2 Child Interests		1.00
3 Keep All/Div. 1/2	3 H or W Needs		1.00
4 Keep Some/Pay $			

C. DECIDING ON CHILD CUSTODY			
Alternatives	Criteria	Meas. Unit	Weight
1 Mother Gets All	1 Child Interests	1–5 Scale	2.00
2 Some Kids to Each	2 Mother Interests		1.00
3 Some Time to Each	3 Father Interests		1.00
4 Father Gets All			

D. DECIDING ON CHILD SUPPORT			
Alternatives	Criteria	Meas. Unit	Weight
1 $50/2 Weeks	1 – Child Needs	1–5 Scale	1.00
2 $100	2 – Spouse Ability		1.00
3 $150			1.00
4 $200			1.00
5 $250			
6 $300			
7 $350			
8 $400			
9 $450			
10 $500			

Tort Law

Table A11.4   Predicting who will win in civil cases

A. THE PREVIOUS CASES, THEIR OUTCOMES, AND THE PREDICTIVE CRITERIA

Alternatives	Previous Outcome	Criteria	Meas. Unit	Weight
1 Johnson (D)	D – $0	1 Elected Judge	1/No – 2/Yes	1.00
2 Park (P)	P – $70	2 No Fault Law		1.00
3 Dixon (D)	D – $0	3 Urban Place		1.00
4 Crawford (P)	P – $65	4 Male Plaintiff		1.00
5 Hudson (P)	P – $78			

B. HOW THE CASES SCORE ON EACH OF THE PREDICTIVE CRITERIA

Alternatives	Elected Judge	No Fault Law	Urban Place	Male Plaintiff
Johnson (D)	1.00	1.00	1.00	1.00
Park (P)	2.00	1.00	2.00	2.00
Dixon (D)	2.00	1.00	1.00	1.00
Crawford (P)	2.00	2.00	2.00	1.00
Hudson (P)	2.00	2.00	2.00	2.00

C. THE OVERALL SCORES OF THE CASES

Alternatives	Combined Rawscores	Previous Outcome
1 Johnson (D)	4.00	D – $0
2 Park (P)	7.00	P – $70
3 Dixon (D)	5.00	D – $0
4 Crawford (P)	7.00	P – $65
5 Hudson (P)	8.00	P – $78

D. BRINGING THE HIGHEST LOSER UP TO THE LEVEL OF THE LOWEST WINNER

Criteria	Dixon (D)	Park (P)	Weight
Elected Judge	4.00	0.00	??
No Fault Law	3.00	–1.00	??
Urban Place	3.00	0.00	–1.000
Male Plaintiff	3.00	0.00	–1.000

PUBLIC LAW

Criminal Law

Table A11.5 Data for Predicting Conviction or Acquittal

A. THE CASES AND THE PREDICTIVE CRITERIA

Alternatives	Previous Outcome	Criterion	Meas. Unit	Weight
1 JONES (C)	CONVICT	1 MISD. v. FELONY	2/YES – 1/NO	1.00
2 SMITH (C)	CONVICT	2 LOW GNP v. HIGH		1.00
3 BROWN (A)	ACQUIT	3 REP. JUDGE v. DEM.		1.00
4 GREEN (A)	ACQUIT	4 BLACK DEF. v. WHITE		1.00
5 MILLER (A)	ACQUIT			

B. HOW THE CASES SCORE ON THE PREDICTIVE CRITERIA

	MISD. V.F	LOW GNP	REP. JUDG	BLACK DE
JONES (C)	2.00	2.00	2.00	1.00
SMITH (C)	2.00	2.00	1.00	1.00
BROWN (A)	1.00	1.00	1.00	1.00
GREEN (A)	2.00	1.00	1.00	2.00
MILLER (A)	1.00	1.00	1.00	2.00

C. THE OVERALL SCORES OF THE CASES BEFORE AND AFTER ADJUSTING THE WEIGHTS

Alternative	Combined Rawscores	Previous Outcome	Alternative	Combined Rawscores	Previous Outcome
1 JONES (C)	7.00	CONVICT	1 JONES (C)	9.00	CONVICT
2 SMITH (C)	6.00	CONVICT	2 SMITH (C)	8.00	CONVICT
3 BROWN (A)	4.00	ACQUIT	3 BROWN (A)	5.00	ACQUIT
4 GREEN (A)	6.00	ACQUIT	4 GREEN (A)	7.00	ACQUIT
5 MILLER (A)	5.00	ACQUIT	5 MILLER (A)	6.00	ACQUIT

D. REVERSING THE WEAKEST ACQUITAL OR CONVICTION

	GREEN (A)	SMITH (C)	Weight
MISD. v. FELONY	3.00	1.00	??
LOW GNP v. HIGH	1.50	1.50	1.000
REP. JUDGE v. DEM.	2.00	0.00	??
BLACK DEF. v. WHITE	3.00	0.00	2.000

Notes:

1. The case names, predictive criteria, and the scores of the cases on the criteria are hypothetical. That hypothetical data first appeared in S. Nagel, "Using Simple Calculations to Predict Judicial Decisions", *American Behavioral Scientist*, 4: 24–8 (1960) and *Practical Lawyer*, 7: 68–74 (1961).
2. If the predictive criteria are given equal weight, then inconsistent predictions occur. There are two cases with total scores of 6, but one resulted in a conviction and one an acquittal. If, however, area income is given extra weight as a predictive criterion, then the inconsistencies are eliminated.
3. The decision-rule generated by this data is that if there are 8 or more points, there will be a conviction, but if there are 7 or less points, there will be an acquittal.

Constitutional Law

Table A11.6 Developing predictive decision-rules in equal protection cases

CASE TYPES	Criteria Score on Rights	Score on Groups	Sum	Outcome
1. Consumers/Region	1	1	2	D
2. Consumers/Economic Class	1	2	3	D
3. Employment/Region	2	1	3	D
4. Consumers/Sex	1	3	4	D
5. Employment/Economic Class	2	2	4	D
6. Housing/Region	3	1	4	D
7. Employment/Sex	2	3	5	D
8. Housing/Economic Class	3	2	5	D
9. Schools/Region	4	1	5	D
10. Housing/Sex	3	3	6	D
11. Schools/Economic Class	4	2	6	D
12. Consumers/Race	1	6	7	P
13. Criminal Justice/Region	6	1	7	?
14. Schools/Sex	4	3	7	?
15. Criminal Justice/Economic Class	6	2	8	P
16. Employment/Race	2	6	8	P
17. Voting/Region	7	1	8	P
18. Criminal Justice/Sex	6	3	9	P
19. Housing/Race	2	6	9	P
20. Voting/Economic Class	7	2	9	P
21. Schools/Race	4	6	10	P
22. Voting/Sex	7	3	10	P
23. Criminal Justice/Race	6	6	12	P
24. Voting/Race	7	6	13	P

Notes:

1. The above data can generate two compatible **decision-rules**. One rule is:

   (1) If an equal protection case has a summation score of 7 or higher, then the plaintiff will win.
   (2) If the case has a score of 6 or lower, then the defendant will win.

2. The alternative decision-rule is:

   (1) If an equal protection case has a summation score greater than 7, then the plaintiff will win.
   (2) If the case has a score of exactly 7, then the outcome is questionable.
   (3) If the case has a score of 6 or lower, then the defendant will win.

3. Each **case type** is defined in terms of:

   (1) The rights that are allegedly being denied, which can relate to voting, criminal justice, schools, housing, employment, or consumer rights in that order of importance.

(2) The group that is allegedly being given unequal treatment, which can relate to race (which generally means being black), sex (which generally means being female), economic class (which generally means being poor), or region (which generally means being urban, inner city, or poor) in that order of importance.

4. To determine the score of each case type on the **rights**, the six rights are arranged in rank order with the most important right receiving a score of 6. Slight adjustments are then made to recognize there is more distance between the top two rights and the bottom four than there is between the other rights.

5. To determine the score of each casetype on the **groups**, the four groups are arranged in rank order with the most important group receiving a score of 4. Slight adjustments are then made to recognize there is more distance between the top group and the bottom three than there is between the other groups.

6. The first decision-rule **implies** that the court would decide in favor of the plaintiff if the state provided grossly unequal right to counsel from one county to another, or if women were denied admission to an all-male public school, although the court has not yet done so.

7. The second decision-rule **implies** that being black scores slightly higher than a 6. That caused 12 to score slightly higher than 7, and thus to be distinguishable from the questionable cases.

8. **Landmark cases** or constitutional amendments that correspond to the casetypes include *Gomillion* v. *Lightfoot* (1956) (Casetype 24), *Powell* v. *Alabama* (1934) (23), *Nineteenth Amendment* (1920) (22), *Brown* v. *Board of Education* (1954) (21), *Harper* v. *Virginia* (1964) (20), *Shelley* v. *Kramer* (1950) (19), *Taylor* v. *Louisiana* (1976) (18), *Reynolds* v. *Sims* (1964) (17), *Jones* v. *Mayer* (1968) (12 and 16), *Gideon* v. *Wainwright* (1960) (15), and *Rodriguez* v. *San Antonio* (1973) (9 and 11).

9. The data for this table comes from Nagel, "Case Prediction by Staircase Tables and Percentaging", *Jurimetrics*, 25 (1985).

Economic Regulation

Table A11.7   Changing the measurement of the relations predicting welfare cases

A. THE ORIGINAL 1–3 MEASUREMENT ON THE PROCEDURAL CRITERION

Alternative		SUBSTANC	PROCEDUR	Combined Rawscores	Previous Outcome
1–ELIGIBLE,	–LAWYER	1.00	1.00	2.00	L
2–BENEFITS,	–LAWYER	2.00	1.00	3.00	L
3–ELIGIBLE,	–HEARING	1.00	2.00	3.00	L
4–TERMINATE,	–LAWYER	3.00	1.00	4.00	L
5–BENEFITS,	–HEARING	2.00	2.00	4.00	?
6–ELIGIBLE,	–REASONS	1.00	3.00	4.00	W
7–CRIM. PROS,	–LAWYER	4.00	1.00	5.00	W
8–TERMINATE,	–HEARING	3.00	2.00	5.00	W
9–BENEFITS,	–REASONS	2.00	3.00	5.00	W
10–CRIM. PROS,	–HEARING	4.00	2.00	6.00	W
11–TERMINATE,	–REASONS	3.00	3.00	6.00	W
12–CRIM. PROS,	–REASONS	4.00	3.00	7.00	W

B. THE NEW .99–3.01 MEASUREMENT ON THE PROCEDURAL CRITERION

Alternative		SUBSTANC	PROCEDUR	Combined Rawscores	Previous Outcome
1–ELIGIBLE,	–LAWYER	1.00	0.99	1.99	L
2–BENEFITS,	–LAWYER	2.00	0.99	2.99	L
3–ELIGIBLE,	–HEARING	1.00	2.00	3.00	L
4–TERMINATE,	–LAWYER	3.00	0.99	3.99	L
5–BENEFITS,	–HEARING	2.00	2.00	4.00	?
6–ELIGIBLE,	–REASONS	1.00	3.01	4.01	W
7–CRIM. PROS,	–LAWYER	4.00	0.99	4.99	W
8–TERMINATE,	–HEARING	3.00	2.00	5.00	W
9–BENEFITS,	–REASONS	2.00	3.01	5.01	W
10–CRIM. PROS,	–HEARING	4.00	2.00	6.00	W
11–TERMINATE,	–REASONS	3.00	3.01	6.01	W
12–CRIM. PROS,	–REASONS	4.00	3.01	7.01	W

Notes:

1. A "*W*" in the outcome column means that the welfare recipient wins. An "*L*" means that the welfare recipient loses. The Goldberg case is case type 8, and the Argersinger case is case type 7.
2. The decision-rule that the above data generate is the following:

   (1)   If a welfare case involves a summation score of 4.01 or above, the welfare recipient wins.
   (2)   With a summation score of 3.99 or below, the welfare recipient loses.
   (3)   With a score of 4.00, the outcome is unclear.
3. The leading case is *Goldberg* v. *Kelly* (1967). It involved a summation score of 5.00, and the welfare recipient won. Therefore, one would expect the welfare recipient to win even more with scores higher than 5.00. That covers case types 9, 10, 11, and 12. The outcome of case 7 is known from the Argersinger case (1970). The outcomes of case types 1, 2, 3, 4, and 6 are known from things said in the Goldberg case, not from *a fortiori* deduction.
4. With the 1–3 measurement, there are three inconsistent cases, all of which received an overall score of 4.00. One case was a loser; one was a winner; and the outcome of the third is unknown. With the 0.99–3.01 measurement, there are no inconsistencies. The losing case gets a score of 3.99; the winning case gets a score of 4.01; and the questionable case gets a score of 4.00.
5. The justification for changing the scale from 1–3 to 0.99–3.01 is secondarily to remove the inconsistencies. The primary justification is because the changes make substantive sense. Giving no reasons is practically the ultimate in deprivation of procedural due process. It should therefore score higher than 3 on a 1–3 scale. Not having an attorney in a civil matter is relatively minor compared to not having reasons or a hearing. It should therefore score lower than a 1 on a 1–3 scale.

International Law

Table A11.8 The US as an international litigant

CASETYPES / CRITERIA	Source of Law	US Opponent	SUM	OUTCOME
1. Foreign Law and Less Industrial Opponent	1	1	2	40%
2. Foreign Law and Non-country Opponent	1	2	3	48
3. Treaty and Less Industrial Opponent	2	1	3	51
4. Foreign Law and Equal Opponent	1	3	4	62
5. International Law and Less Industrial Opponent	3	1	4	56
6. Treaty and Non-country Opponent	2	2	4	58
7. International Law and Non-country Opponent	3	2	5	63
8. Treaty and Equal Opponent	2	3	5	73
9. US Law and Less Industrial Opponent	4	1	5	70
10. International Law and Equal Opponent	3	3	6	78
11. US Law and Non-country Opponent	4	2	6	78
12. US Law and Equal Opponent	4	3	7	92

Notes:

1. The decision-rule that the above data generate is $Y = 0.20 + 0.10(X)$, where Y is the probability of the United States winning and X is the summation score.
2. The above decision rule could also be expressed as a series of if – then statements like (1) If X is 1, then Y is 0.30; (2) If X is 2, Y is 0.40; (3) If X is 3, Y is 0.50; (4) If X is 4, Y is 0.60; (5) If X is 5, Y is 0.70; (6) If X is 6, Y is 0.80; and (7) If X is 7, Y is 0.90.
3. Table A11.8 deals with only two of the seven variables in the international law cases. The two are the main source of law and the industrial power of the US opponent. The source of law includes US law, international law, a treaty, and foreign law. The US opponent can be equal to the United States, not a country, or less than the United States in industrial power.
4. Only two variables are used in Table A11.8 rather than seven, partly because of the temporary limitation to 15 alternatives. One can handle all seven variables through multiple runs with 15 case types per run. The number of case-types, however, is 163,800 since the number of categories per variable is 4, 13, 6, 5, 3, and 7, respectively. Under those circumstances, one would not want to list all the case-types. Instead, one would want to know what the probability of US victory is for

continued on page 208

Table A11.8 *Notes continued*

any combination of seven categories. To estimate that, simply average the seven probabilities of US victory.

5. The outcome figures shown above come from averaging the two probabilities from the two variables used for each case-type. Thus, the combination of US law and equal power has a 0.92 probability because US law has an 0.85 probability and equal power has a 1.00 probability. This gives an approximation to a Bayesian conditional, especially where we only have the main probabilities to work with.

6. The above prediction equation comes from observing the relation between the summation scores and the outcome probabilities in Table A11.8. One can determine the prediction equation more accurately by using a statistical calculator that can easily arrive at such an equation for 12 pairs of inputs. One can also think in terms of six pairs of inputs for the summation scores from 2 to 7. Thus a score of 4 has an average outcome of 0.57 since case type 6 has an outcome of 0.56 and case type 8 had an outcome of 0.58.

7. Table A11.8 provides a good illustration of an outcome that is not a dichotomy of win or lose, but rather a continuum outcome of 9 to 1.00.

Notes and References

1. For general materials on multi-criteria decision-making applied to the legal process, see S. Nagel, *Using Personal Computers for Decision-Making in Law Practice* (Westport, Conn.: Greenwood Press, 1986). An earlier version is available from the Committee on Continuing Professional Education of the American Law Institute and the American Bar Association. On the general methodology, see S. Nagel, *Microcomputers, Evaluation Problems and Policy Analysis* (Beverly Hills, Calif.: Sage Publication, 1986), and the "Policy/Goal Percentaging" program, Decision Aids, Inc., 361 Lincoln Hall, University of Illinois, Urbana, Illinois 61801.

2. For discussions of computer-aided clerical work, see Mary Ann Mason, *An Introduction to Using Computers in the Law* (St Paul: West, 1984); and Daniel Remer, *Computer Power for your Law Office* (Berkeley, Calif.: Sybex, 1983). Relevant software includes "WordStar" (word processing), "DBase II" (file management), "Evidence Master" (litigation support), Matthew Bender (document drafting), "WestLaw" and "Lexis" (access to citations and case excerpts), and "Data Law" (billing and bookkeeping).

3. For articles that optimistically, pessimistically, or jokingly view computers as partly replacing judges and lawyers, see Paul Bartholomew, "Supreme Court and Modern Objectivity", *New York State Bar Journal*, 33: 157–64 (1961); Hugh Gibbons, "Using Computers to Analyze Legal Questions", in Thomas Rasmusson (ed.), *System Science and Jurisprudence* (Lansing, Mich.: Spartan Press, 1986); and Reed Lawlor, "Stare Decisis and Electronic Computers", in Glendon Schubert (ed.), *Judicial Behavior: A Reader in Theory and Research* (Chicago: Rand McNally, 1964).

4. On applying multi-criteria decision-making to synthesizing sets of appellate cases, see S. Nagel, "Using Microcomputers and P/G% to Predict Court Cases", *Akron Law Review*, 18: 541–74 (1985); S. Nagel, "Case Prediction by Staircase Tables and Percentaging", *Jurimetrics Journal*, 25: 169–96 (1985); and S. Nagel, *Causation, Prediction, and Legal Analysis* (Westport, Conn.: Greenwood Press, 1986). Also see Karl Llewelleyn, *The Common Law Tradition: Deciding Appeals* (Boston: Little, Brown, 1960). Relevant software for inductively synthesizing appellate cases could include statistical analysis software, such as "SPSS-PC", from 444 N. Michigan Avenue, Chicago, Illinois 60611.

5. On systematic synthesizing of facts in trial decisions, see Jerome Frank, *Courts on Trial: Myth and Reality in American Justice* (Princeton, N.J.: Princeton University Press, 1950); Bruce Sales (ed.), *The Trial Process* (New York: Plenum Press, 1981); and Norbert Kerr and Robert Bray (eds), *The Psychology of the Courtroom* (New York: Academic Press, 1982). Relevant software for calculating probabilities includes the Bayesian probabilities program in the package called "Computer Models for Management Science", from Addison-Wesley, Reading, Massachusetts.

6. On legal policy evaluation, see Richard Posner, *Economic Analysis of Law* (Boston: Little, Brown, 1977); Lawrence Friedman and Stewart Macaulay (eds), *Law and the Behavioral Sciences* (Indianapolis, Ind.: Bobbs-Merrill, 1977); S. Nagel, *Policy Evaluation: Making Optimum Decisions* (New York: Praeger, 1982); and S. Nagel, *Law, Policy, and Optimizing Analysis* (Westport, Conn.: Greenwood Press, 1986). Relevant software for evaluating policies in light of given goals includes those packages discussed in Benjamin Radcliff, "Multi-Criteria Decision Making: A Survey of Software", *Social Science Microcomputer Review*, 4: 38–55 (1986), such as "Expert Choice", from Decision Support Software, 1300 Vincent Place, McLean, Virginia 22101.

7. On allocating money or other resources to activities, places, or people, see S. Nagel, "Optimally Allocating Money to Places and Activities", in P. Humphreys and J. Vecsenyi (eds), *High Level Decision Support: Lessons from Case Studies* (Amsterdam: North-Holland, 1986). Microcomputer programs relevant to estate allocation include "WillWriter" of Nolo Press, 950 Parker St, Berkeley, CA 94710; "Fiduciary Accountant" of the Institute of Paralegal Training, 1926 Arch St, Philadelphia, PA 19103; and "Estate Tax Planner", of Aardvark-McGraw-Hill, 1020 North Broadway, Milwaukee, WI 53202. None of the three specifically deal with how to divide an estate. The first one converts allocation decisions into a will. The second aids in probating and administering a will. The third makes tax calculations for various decisions.

8. The data for the above example comes mainly from S. Nagel, "Applying Decision Science to the Practice of Law", *Practical Lawyer*, 30: 13–22 (April 1984). On computer-aided negotiation, see S. Nagel and M. Mills, "Microcomputers, Policy/Goal Percentaging and Dispute Resolution" in Cheryl Cutrona (ed.), *Bringing the Dispute Resolution Profession Together* (Washington, D.C.. Society of Professionals in Dispute Resolution, 1986); S. Nagel, "Microcomputers, Risk Analysis, and Litigation Strategy", *Akron Law Review*, 19: 35–80 (1985); and S. Nagel, "Lawyer

Decision-Making and Threshold Analysis", *University of Miami Law Review*, 36: 615–42 (1983). Microcomputer programs relevant to litigation negotiation include "The Art of Negotiating", Experience In Software, Inc., 2039 Shattuck Avenue, Suite 401, Berkeley, CA 94704; and "SettleMate", Lawyers Technology Inc., 339 15th St, #200, Oakland, CA 94612. The first one is basically a checklist of suggestions for improving one's negotiating skills, although it leaves out systematically comparing the benefits minus costs of going to trial versus the benefits minus costs of settling. The second program is useful for determining the value of different types of injuries.

9. On systematic case briefing, see Harry Jones *et al.* (eds), *Legal Method: Cases and Text Materials* (Mineola, N.Y.: Foundation, 1980); William Statsky and John Wernet, *Case Analysis and Fundamentals of Legal Writing* (St Paul: West, 1977); and Wayne Thode *et al.* (eds), *Introduction to the Study of Law: Cases and Materials* (Mineola, N.Y.: Foundation, 1970). Relevant software includes programs designed to teach law students how to analyze cases, as described in Russell Burris, Robert Keeton, Carolyn Landis, and Roger Park, *Teaching Law with Computers: A Collection of Essays* (Denver, Colo.: Westview Press, 1979).

10. Assigning judges to casetypes is briefly discussed in Task Force on the Administration of Justice, *The Courts* (Washington, D.C.: President's Commission on Law Enforcement and Administration of Justice, 1967): 88–90 and 165–7; and the ABA Commission on Standards of Judicial Administration, *Standards Relating to Trial Courts* (Chicago: American Bar Association, 1976): 86–93. Also see the more general literature and software on assigning people to tasks, such as Warren Erickson and Owen Hall, *Computer Models for Management Science* (Reading, Mass.: Addison-Wesley, 1986). On assigning lawyers to casetypes, see S. Nagel and M. Mills, "Allocating Attorneys to Casetypes", *Capital University Law Review* (1986).

11. On computer-aided sequencing of law firm cases and other jobs, see S. Nagel "Sequencing and Allocating Attorney Time to Cases", *Pepperdine Law Review*, 13: 1021–39 (1986); and S. Nagel, Mark Beeman, and John Reed, "Optimum Sequencing of Court Cases to Reduce Delay", *Alabama Law Review* (1986). Also see the more general literature on efficient sequencing, such as Richard Conway *et al.*, *Theory of Scheduling* (Reading, Mass.: Addison-Wesley, 1967). On allocating time per case regardless of the order of the cases, see S. Nagel, "Attorney Time Per Case: Finding an Optimum Level", *University of Florida Law Review*, 32: 424–41 (1980). The software that is most relevant to optimum sequencing is probably docketing software such as "Docket" by Micro-Craft, 2007 Whitesburg Drive, Huntsville, Alabama 35801.

12 All Fields of Knowledge

The P/G% software was presented in a special workshop at the 1987 annual meeting of the American Association for the Advancement of Science. That workshop was partly designed to bring out how the decision-aiding software could be applied to natural science, social science, and the humanities.

Five examples were used from the natural sciences. For physics, the example was choosing among alternative energy policies, such as nuclear, oil, coal, synthetic fuels, and solar. For chemistry, the example was comparing alternative incentives for reducing pollution, such as increasing the benefits of rightdoing, reducing the costs of rightdoing, increasing the costs of wrongdoing, reducing the benefits of wrongdoing, and increasing the probability of the benefits and costs occurring. For geology, the example was prioritizing earthquake policies that relate to hazard mitigation, long-term earthquake preparation, prediction/warning, relief operations, and long-term recovery. For astronomy, the example was deciding on research and deployment for the star wars defense. For biology, the example was deciding an optimum level of cancer in light of the prevention and damage costs.

Four examples were used for the social sciences. For psychology, the example was deciding whether to take away or leave an abused child with its family. For sociology, the example was deciding among alternative public policies toward race relations, especially between requiring the welcoming of minorities and having preferential hiring. For economics, the example was deciding among alternative unemployment and inflation policies, such as monetary policy, fiscal policy, controls, supply-side Reaganomics, and industrial policy. For political science, the example was evaluating alternative democratic and undemocratic ways of relating the government to the electorate.

There were four examples from the humanities. For philosophy, the example was evaluating ways of relating the government to the economy, including capitalism, socialism, and various combinations of the two. For language and literature, the example was evaluating alternative ways of handling freedom of communication, including restricting freedom of speech only when another fundamental right is jeopardized. For art and music, the example was evaluating alternative public policies toward subsidizing and regulating the arts. For history, the example was explaining historical behavior in the context of the motives of John Marshall in establishing the principle of judicial review of the constitutionality of legislative and executive acts.

The 13 examples can be best illustrated by presenting the computer-generated Tables 12.1–12.9 which follow. Those tables cover 13 problems (5 of which are discussed in chapter 10, see p. 145) across all fields of knowledge. They clarify for each field and problem the goals to be achieved, the alternatives available for achieving them, and the relations between goals and alternatives in order to choose or explain the best alternative, combination, allocation, or predictive decision-rule. Some of the tables also clarify what it would take to bring a second-place or other-place alternative up to first place.[1]

Table 12.1 Raw data for choosing energy policies (physics)

GOALS / POLICIES	Long-term Value	Cost	How soon Available	Safety	Environmental Protection	International Security/ Cooperation	SUM FOR Six GOALS
Nuclear	3½	3	3	2	3	2	16½
Oil	2	4	4	4	2	2	18
Coal	3	4	4	4	1	3	19
Synthetic Fuels	4	2	3	4	2	3	18
Solar	5	1	2	3½	4	4	19½
Totals	17½	14	16	17½	12	14	91

Notes:

1. One should note that each policy has subpolicies which are not shown here:

    (1) Nuclear can be divided into uranium (the most common form), plutonium and hydrogen.
    (2) Oil can be divided into known deposits and unknown deposits.
    (3) Coal can be divided into high polluting (the most common form) and low polluting.
    (4) Synthetic fuels can be divided into natural (like oil shale) and artificial (like garbage).
    (5) Solar can be divided into small-scale and large-scale.

2. One should note the big drawback for each energy source:

    (1) Nuclear lacks sufficient safety, especially nuclear wastes.
    (2) Oil lacks long-term value.
    (3) Coal is bad on pollution.
    (4) Synthetic fuels have high ongoing costs.
    (5) Solar has high start up costs for large-scale operations.

3. The choices can be best viewed in terms of three tracks:

    (1) Oil is best on the short-term track.
    (2) Coal and synthetic fuels make the most sense on the intermediate track, with a need for developing more economic synthetic fuels.
    (3) Solar and nuclear make the most sense on the long-term track, but there is a need for developing safer nuclear energy and for research on implementing large-scale solar energy.

Table 12.2   Comparing alternative incentives for reducing pollution
(chemistry)

CRITERIA ALTERNATIVES	Political Feasibility	Effectiveness in Reducing Pollution	Clean up Funds
I. Increase benefits of rightdoing			
1. Reward subsidies to cities	2	5	3
2. Reward subsidies to businesses	1	5	3
3. Pollution tax reduction	1	4	4
4. New government contracts	3½	4	3
5. Selling marketable pollution rights	3½	4	3
II. Reduce costs of rightdoing			
6. Tax deductions	4	3½	3
7. Cost subsidies to cities	4	3½	3
8. Cost subsidies to businesses	2	3½	3
III. Increase costs of wrongdoing			
9. Damage suits	4	4	3
10. Publicize wrongdoers	3½	4	3
11. Pollution tax	1	5	4
12. Fines	4	3	3
13. Jail	2	3	3
14. Loss of government contracts	2½	4	3
15. Buying marketable pollution rights	3½	4	3
16. Padlock injunction	2	4	3
IV. Reduce benefits of wrongdoing			
17. Confiscate profits	2	5	3½
V. Increase probability of benefits and costs			
18. Improve monitoring	4	4	3
19. Bounties for reporting	4	4	3

Cost to General Taxpayers	Cost to Consumers or Workers	Public Participation	Predictability and Due Process	SUM
1	3	3	4	21
1	3	3	4	20
3	2	3	4	21
2½	3	3	4	23
3	2	3	4	22½
2	3	3	4	22½
2	3	3	4	22½
2	3	3	4	20½
3	2	4	2	22
2½	3	4	2	22
4	2	3	4	23
3	2	3	2	20
2	3	3	2	18
2½	3	3	2½	20½
3	3	3	4	23½
3	2	3	2	19
3	3	3	2	21½
2	3	3	2	21
3	3	4	2	23

continued on page 216

Table 12.2   *Notes continued*

Notes:

1. The alternatives that score relatively high (meaning 23 points or higher) include:

   (1) Giving government contracts to business firms that satisfy or excel on meeting pollution requirements.
   (2) The pollution tax system although it may not be able to meet a minimum political feasibility level.
   (3) The buying and selling of marketable pollution rights as a cost to polluters and an income reward to non-polluters.
   (4) Bounties for reporting wrong-doing whereby the general public shares in fines that are levied.

2. The alternatives that score relatively low (meaning 20 or below) include:

   (1) Reward subsidies to business are opposed as being too expensive to the taxpayer.
   (2) Fines tend to be treated as a petty business expense that are passed on to taxpayers.
   (3) Jail sentences are unlikely to be imposed and thus relatively ineffective.
   (4) Padlock injunctions that are opposed because they result in loss of employment and production.

3. If the criteria are going to be weighted differently, political feasibility can be considered a constraint such that any alternative with a double-minus is considered unfeasible. Of the other criteria, effectiveness in reducing pollution is probably the most important, followed by cost to the general taxpayers.
4. The alternatives relate to incentives for reducing pollution. One could do a similar analysis concerning government structures for reducing pollution. The structure alternatives might be divided into those that relate to federalism, separation of powers, and relations between government and people.
5. Predictability in this context tends to refer to the extent to which formulae are followed for determining who gets benefits or costs. Due process refers to the extent to which the alternatives allow for those who are denied benefits or made to bear costs to receive a formal hearing to show they are being wrongly treated.

Table 12.3   Public policy relevant to earthquakes and related natural disasters (geology)

A THE ALTERNATIVE PUBLIC POLICIES

Alternative	Alternative
1 *Hazard mitigation*:	1 *Relief operations*:
2 Protect critical facilities	2 Therapy community
3 Land-use planning	3 Emergency health care
4 Upgrade structures	4 Interorganizational coordination
5 Enforce new codes	5 Plan for unanticipated
6 *Long-term earthquake preparation*:	6 *Long-term recovery*:
7 Sensitize public opinion	7 Mental health problems
8 Organize neighbourhoods	8 Legal–political problems
9 Sensitize and organizational groups	9 Unemployment–business problems
10 Sensitize business	10 Loans and housing
11 Media cooperation	11 Interorganizational coordination
12 Earthquake insure	12 Regional–national impact
13 *Predict and warn*:	
14 Prediction methods	
15 Warning routines	

B THE CRITERIA FOR EVALUATING THEM

Criterion	Meas. Unit	Weight
1 – Tax cost	1–5 scale	1.00
2 Lives saved		1.00
3 Property saved		1.00
4 –Economic disruption		1.00

Notes:

1. The alternative public policies for dealing with natural disasters are divided into five groups covering (1) hazard mitigation, (2) long-term earthquake preparation, (3) prediction and warning, (4) relief operations and (5) long-term recovery.
2. The criteria for evaluating the relative importance of the alternative public policies include reducing taxpayer costs, saving lives, saving property and minimizing economic disruption.
3. This particular analysis still needs to show how each alternative and/or group of alternatives is related to each criteria. One can then better determine the priorities, allocations and other choices.

Table 12.4 Deciding on research and deployment for the star wars defense (astronomy)

A THE ALTERNATIVES AND THE CRITERIA FOR EVALUATING THEM

Alternative	Criterion	Meas. unit	Weight
1 Research and Deploy	1 – Economic burden	1–5 scale	1.00
2 + Research but – Deploy	2 – Nuclear war		1.00
3 – Research and – Deploy	3 – Being conquered		1.00
	4 Politically feasible		1.00
	5 Technically feasible		1.00
	6 + Reagan's ego		1.00
			1.00

B HOW THE ALTERNATIVES SCORE ON THE CRITERIA

	–Economic burden	– Nuclear	–Being Conquered	Politically Feasible	Technically Feasible
Research and Deploy	1.00	2.00	2.00	3.00	4.00
+ Research but – Deploy	3.00	3.00	3.00	4.00	5.00
– Research and – Deploy	5.00	3.00	3.00	3.00	5.00

C THE OVERALL SCORES OF THE ALTERNATIVES

Alternative	Combined Rawscores	%
1 Research and Deploy	12.00	24.49
2 + Research but – Deploy	18.00	36.73
3 – Research and – Deploy	19.00	38.78

D WHAT IT WOULD TAKE TO BRING THE SECOND PLACE ALTERNATIVE UP TO FIRST PLACE

	– Research and Deploy	+ Research but –	Weight
– Economic Burden	4.00	4.00	0.500
– Nuclear war	2.00	4.00	??
– Being Conquered	2.00	4.00	??
Politically Feasible	2.00	5.00	2.000
Technically Feasible	4.00	6.00	??

Notes:

1. The alternatives are (1) have both research and deployment, (2) have research but not deployment and (3) have neither research nor deployment.

2. Research plus deployment is considered as having an adverse relation to avoiding nuclear war because deployment may cause the Soviet Union to take preventive action before the deployment can occur. Such preventive action is likely to mean nuclear war in which the dispersed Soviet Union may be more likely to have some surviving citizens than the United States.

3. The political feasibility of star wars research and especially deployment may have gone down substantially, as a result of late 1986 deterioration in the prestige and possible power of the Reagan administration. The technological feasibility may have gone up, as a result of partially successful experiments.

4. If one adds the criterion of Reagan's ego and gives it enough weight, then star wars research and even deployment become the winning alternative. Research without deployment can become the winning alternative by giving a little more weight than equal weight to political feasibility and popularity.

Applications of decision-aiding software in the fields of biology, psychology, sociology, and economics are given elsewhere in the book. To be more specific:

1. **Biology**. This includes biomedical matters, such as deciding an optimum level of cancer in light of the prevention and damage costs (see Table A10.6).
2. **Psychology**. This includes child abuse matters, such as deciding whether to take away or leave an abused child (see Table 10.5).
3. **Sociology**. This includes race relations, such as alternative public policies toward race relations (see Table A10.2).
4. **Economics**. This includes alternative policies for dealing with unemployment and inflation (see Table A10.5).

Table 12.5 Evaluating alternative ways of relating the government to the electorate (political science)

GOALS / POLICIES	Multiple Sources of Ideas	Popular Responsiveness	Fast, Unquestioned Decisions	SUM
1. No universal Voting Rights, and no Minority Political Rights	− (1)	− (1)	+ (4)	6
2. Universal Voting Rights, but no Minority Political Rights	− (2)	+ (4)	0 (3)	9
3. Minority Political Rights, but no Universal Voting Rights	+ (4)	− (1)	0 (3)	8
4. Universal Voting Rights, and Minority Political Rights	++ (5)	++ (5)	− (2)	12

Notes:

1. Universal voting rights mean all adults have the right to vote, but only one vote per person, and candidates are chosen by majority vote. Minority political rights especially refer to the right of minority viewpoints to have access to the media in order to try to convert the majority.

2. Democracy is generally defined as universal voting rights accompanied by minority political rights. Pure dictatorship involves no majority rule and no rights of minorities to convert the majority. Between those two categories are Policies 2 and 3 which involve various combinations of majority rule and minority rights.

3. With the above three goals, the policy of universal voting rights and minority political rights scores the best, even if the goals are unweighted. If the goals are weighted with more weight to multiple source of ideas and popular responsiveness, then Policy 4 would win by an even wider margin.

Table 12.6 Alternative ways of relating the government to the economy (philosophy)

POLICIES \ GOALS	1. Equality of Opportunity	2. More Opportunity to go Further	3. More Gross National Product	4. More Security	5. More Initiative to Take Chances	6. More Political Freedom and Popular Control	7. More Enterprise Freedom and Consumer Sovereignty	SUM
Capitalism	2	4	4	2	4	2	4	22
Mixed Economy	3	3	4	3	3	3	3	22
Socialism	4	2	4	4	2	4	2	22

Notes:

1. Socialism refers to government ownership and public policy designed to facilitate equality of income and wealth. Capitalism refers to private ownership with no public policy designed to facilitate equality of income and wealth.

2. Table 12.6 indicates that the policy which is best depends greatly on the relative weight assigned the goals. If one weights the goals 1, 4 and 6 more heavily than 2, 5 and 7 then socialism scores higher. Otherwise, capitalism scores higher.

3. One could conceivably talk in terms of four policies of (1) private ownership and no equality, (2) private ownership and equality, (3) government ownership and no equality, and (4) government ownership and equality. The two elements of capitalism do tend to go together, and likewise with the two elements of socialism.

4. One can have democratic or dictatorial capitalism and democratic or dictatorial socialism, depending on whether there are universal voting rights, and minority political rights. The democracy versus dictatorship issue is analysed in Table 12.7.

5. One can have responsive or non-responsive capitalism and responsive or non-responsive socialism. Responsiveness in this context refers to being responsive to consumers and workers. Socialism is traditionally thought of as being more responsive to consumers and workers. If one weights responsiveness heavily, then responsive capitalism and responsive socialism would be undesirable. Table 12.6 may, however, be helpful in deciding between responsive capitalism and responsive socialism.

Table 12.7 Alternative ways of handling freedom of speech (language/literature)

POLICIES	GOALS					SUMS
	Allow Creative Ideas	Encourage Constructive Criticism of Government	Protect due Process, Privacy and Equity Rights of Others	No undue Burden on the Taxpayer	Political or Constitutional Feasibility	
1. Provide funding and facilities for minority viewpoints	5	5	4	2	1	17
2. Allow unlimited free speech	4	4	2	3	2	15
3. Limit free speech only when another fundamental right is jeopardized	4	4	5	3	3	19*
4. Limit free speech when no fundamental right of others is jeopardized, but when the speech does not do anything constructive concerning societal improvement	2	2	3	3	4	14
5. Limit free speech when it is critical of prevailing government religion or other establishment ideas	1	1	2	2	1	7

continued on page 224

Table 12.7 Notes continued

Notes:

1. A policy that involves government funding and facilities for minority viewpoints would facilitate creative ideas and constructive criticism of government, but it seems politically unfeasible since the Supreme Court does not require it and a majoritarian Congress is not so likely to appropriate funds. The closest provision is probably requiring radio and TV stations to give minority parties free time when the major parties receive free time, and likewise with federal presidential funding provided that the minority parties are substantial.

2. Unlimited free speech would allow invasions of privacy, prejudicial pretrial publicity, and unlimited campaign expenditures, which neither the courts nor Congress endorse. Those rights of privacy, due process, and minimum equality in political campaigning are the fundamental rights which allow free speech limitations under Policy 3.

3. Examples of limitations under Policy 4 include pornography, libel, false pretenses, and advocacy that leads to physical harm. All those free speech exceptions have been substantially limited over the last 20 or so years.

4. Policies 2 through 5 are mutually exclusive. Policy 3 outscores the others on the above goals.

Table 12.8 Public policy toward the arts (art/music)

A THE ALTERNATIVE POLICIES

Alternative   Alternative

1 Art museums   7 Tax deductions
2 Public art display   8 – Censorship
3 Public music performances   9 – Discrimination
4 Public radio-TV   10 Public school education
5 Public libraries   11 Cultural exchange
6 Art/music/literature grants

B THE CRITERIA FOR JUDGING THE POLICIES

Criterion	Meas. Unit	Weight
	1–5 scale	
1 Arts availability		1.00
2 – Tax cost		1.00
3 Inspiration		1.00
4 Job opportunities		1.00
5 Geographic prestige		1.00
6 Appreciation of arts		1.00

continued on page 226

Table 12.8 continued

C RELATIONS BETWEEN THE ALTERNATIVES AND THE CRITERIA

	Arts Availability	– Tax Cost	Inspiration	Job Opportunities	Geographic Prestige	Appreciation of Arts
Art museums	0.00	0.00	0.00	0.00	0.00	0.00
Public art display	0.00	0.00	0.00	0.00	0.00	0.00
Public music performances	0.00	0.00	0.00	0.00	0.00	0.00
Public radio-TV	0.00	0.00	0.00	0.00	0.00	0.00
Public libraries	0.00	0.00	0.00	0.00	0.00	0.00
Arts/music/literature grants	0.00	0.00	0.00	0.00	0.00	0.00
Tax deductions	0.00	0.00	0.00	0.00	0.00	0.00
– Censorship	0.00	0.00	0.00	0.00	0.00	0.00
– Discrimination	0.00	0.00	0.00	0.00	0.00	0.00
Public school education	0.00	0.00	0.00	0.00	0.00	0.00
Cultural exchange	0.00	0.00	0.00	0.00	0.00	0.00

Notes:

1. This particular analysis still needs to show how each alternative is related to each criterion.
2. One can then better determine priorities, allocations and other choices.

Table 12.9 The motives of John Marshall in *Marbury v. Madison* (history)

A THE ISSUES AND OUTCOMES

Alternative	Previous Outcome
1 Disqualify oneself	No
2 No juris/with merits	Yes
3 Uphold/statute not apply	No
4 Uphold/const. allow	No
5 Appt. continuity	Yes
6 Judicial supremacy	Yes
7 Judicial review judicial only	No
8 Justice of the peace is pub. minister	No
9 Cong. change juris	No
10 Grant appointment	No

B THE GOALS, SCALES, AND WEIGHTS

Criterion	Meas. Unit	Weight
1 Attack Jefferson	1–3 scale	3.00
2 Avoid non-comply		2.00
3 Judicial review establish		4.00
4 Legal consistent		1.00

C HOW SAYING YES ON EACH ISSUE SCORES ON THE GOALS

	Attack Jefferson	Avoid Non-comply	Judicial Review Estab.	Legal Consistent
Disqualify oneself	1.00	3.00	1.00	3.00
No juris/with merits	3.00	2.00	2.00	1.00
Uphold/statute not apply	1.00	3.00	2.00	3.00
Uphold/const. allow	2.00	2.00	2.00	2.00
Appt. continuity	2.00	2.00	2.00	3.00
Judicial supremacy	2.00	2.00	3.00	2.00
Jr judicial only	2.00	2.00	2.00	2.00
Jp is pub. minister	2.00	2.00	2.00	1.00

continued on page 228

Table 12.9 continued

Cong. change juris	2.00	2.00	1.00
Grant appointment	3.00	1.00	2.00

D TOTAL SCORES OF SAYING YES ON EACH GOAL

Alternative	Combined Raw-Scores	Previous Outcome
1 Disqualify oneself	16.00	No
2 No juris/with merits	22.00	Yes
3 Uphold/statute not apply	20.00	No
4 Uphold/const. allow	20.00	No
5 Appt. continuity	21.00	Yes
6 Judicial supremacy	24.00	Yes
7 Jr judicial only	20.00	No
8 Jp is pub. minister	19.00	No
9 Cong. change juris	15.00	No
10 Grant appointment	17.00	No

Notes:

1. This is an analysis of the motives of John Marshall in the case of *Marbury v. Madison* which held that the courts could declare unconstitutional acts of Congress and the President.
2. Each alternative is a separate issue in the case on which there could be a yes or no answer. Each criterion is a hypothesized goal of John Marshall along with a set of tentative priorities or relative weights.
3. The analysis leads to a decision-rule which says that if a yes answer on an issue generates 21 points or more, then the issue should be decided affirmatively in order to be consistent with the hypothesized goals and their relative weights. If a yes answer on an issue generates 20 points or less, then the issue should be decided negatively.
4. Table 12.9D shows that the way in which John Marshall actually answered each issue is perfectly consistent with the decision-rule. That lends substantial confirmation to the idea that the hypothesized goals and their weights were Marshall's actual goals.

SOME CONCLUSIONS

Microcomputers can be used to aid people in all fields of science in reaching decisions. Decision-aiding software is especially relevant to processing a set of goals to be achieved, alternatives for achieving them, and relations between goals and alternatives in order to choose the best alternative, combination, or allocation of scarce resources.

Decision-aiding software can be useful in dealing with such analytic problems as (1) multiple dimensions on multiple goals, (2) multiple missing information, (3) multiple alternatives that are too many to determine the effects of each one, (4) multiple and possibly conflicting constraints, and (5) the need for simplicity in view of all that multiplicity.

Using decision-aiding software can enable us to (1) avoid the drudgery of arithmetic, (2) be prompted into clarifying goals, alternatives, and relations, (3) try numerous changes to see their effects, and (4) have our creativity stimulated in developing better explanations of why things happen the way they do, and better decisions as to what should be done.[2]

Notes and References

1. This program is related to the field of multi-criteria decision-making. That field includes such literature as W. Edwards and R. Newman, *Multi-Attribute Evaluation* (Beverly Hills, Calif.: Sage Publications, 1982), T. Saaty, *The Analytic Hierarchy Process: Planning, Priority Setting, Resource Allocation* (New York: McGraw-Hill, 1980), and M. Zeleny, *Multiple Criteria Decision-Making* (New York: McGraw-Hill, 1982). In comparison to those methods, the P/G% program is both simpler to use and more realistic in its procedures. The program is also related to spreadsheet analysis, but it is more focused on evaluating alternatives and informing the user as to what changes will make a difference as well as what difference they will make. See T. Henderson, *Spreadsheet Software: From VisiCalc to 1–2–3* (Indianapolis, Ind.: Que, 1982).
2. For further information concerning this multi-criteria decision-aiding tool, write or phone Stuart Nagel, 361 Lincoln Hall, University of Illinois, Urbana, Illinois, 61801, 217-359-8541. The microcomputer program is based on S. Nagel, "Multiple Goals and Multiple Policies". Nagel, *Public Policy: Goals, Means, and Methods* (New York: St Martin's Press, 1984). A copy of the program, the present manual, and the periodic updates can be obtained without charge by buyers of this present book on *Decision-Aiding Software*. A copy of the current manuscript for the relevant 500-page book entitled *Evaluation Analysis with Microcomputers* can also be obtained for the cost of photocopying and mailing.

Part V
Supplementary Materials

13 The Menu-tree for the Decision-aiding Software

This menu-tree shows how each option in the Best Choice program is related to each other option. The program consists of five main parts covering data, choosing, allocating, predicting, and special decision-making. Each of those parts contains major options. Each major option contains suboptions. Options exist on four different levels in the overall hierarchy and five different parallel parts. There is also a help part, which provides help for all the options. As of 1 July 1988, there are 37 options in the data part, 36 options in the choosing part, 45 in the allocating part, 57 in the predicting part, 29 under special decision-making, and 9 in the help part for a total of over 200 options.

DATA

Main Menu	2nd Menu Level	3rd Menu Level	4th Menu Level
		: Create	
		: Save	
	: File	: List	
	: Management	: Retrieve	
	:	: Delete	
	:	: Help	
	:		: Add
	:		: Delete
	:	: Alternatives ------	: Names
Data ---------------- :	:		: Help
	:	:	
	:		: Add
	:		: Delete
	:		: Names
	:	: Criteria ------------	: Measurement
	:	:	: Weights
	:	:	: Help
	: Changes --------- : Relations	:	
	:	:	
	:		: Constant
	:		: PV
	:		: FV
	:	: Transform --------	: Reciprocal
	:	:	: Log
	:	:	: Anti-Log
	:	:	: Help
	:	:	
	:		: All
	:		: Prior
	:	: Select -------------	: New
	:	:	: Help
	:	: Help	
	: Help		

CHOOSE

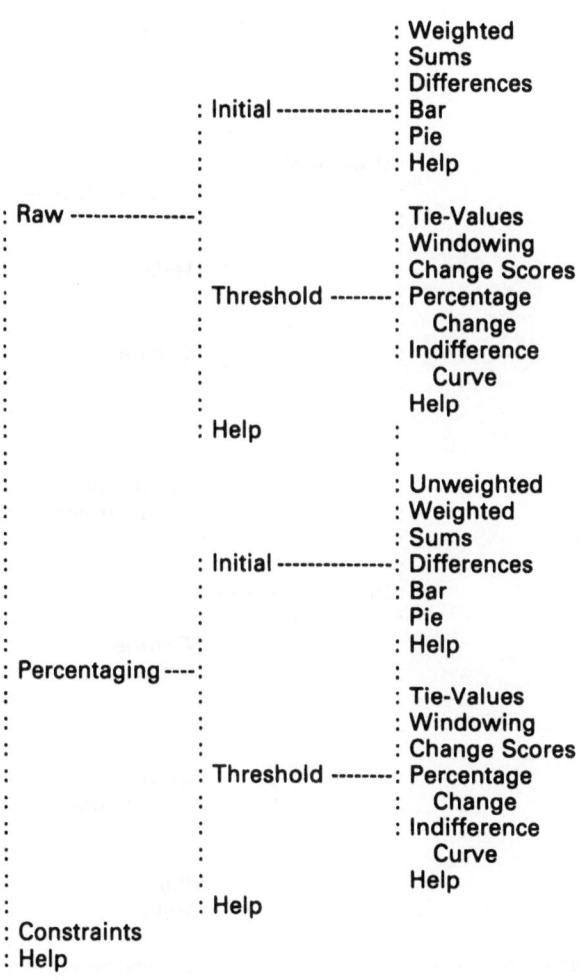

```
                                                    : Weighted
                                                    : Sums
                                                    : Differences
                                : Initial ---------: Bar
                                :                   : Pie
                                :                   : Help
                                :
              : Raw ----------:                     : Tie-Values
              :                :                    : Windowing
              :                :                    : Change Scores
              :                : Threshold -------: Percentage
              :                :                   :   Change
              :                :                   : Indifference
              :                :                       Curve
              :                :                       Help
              :                : Help             :
              :                                   :
              :                                   : Unweighted
              :                                   : Weighted
              :                                   : Sums
              :                : Initial ---------: Differences
              :                :                     Bar
              :                :                     Pie
              :                :                   : Help
Choose        :                :
              : Percentaging --:                   :
              :                :                   : Tie-Values
              :                :                   : Windowing
              :                :                   : Change Scores
              :                : Threshold -------: Percentage
              :                :                   :   Change
              :                :                   : Indifference
              :                :                       Curve
              :                :                       Help
              :                : Help
              : Constraints
              : Help
```

ALLOCATE

```
                                    : Budget
                                    :                   : Weights
                                    :                   :    Negative
                                    :                   : Relations
                                    :                   :    Negative
                  : Pre-Initial --------: Data          : Both
                  :                 :  Transform -----:    Negative
                  :                 :                  : All Positive
                  :                 :                  : Help
                  :                 : Help
                  :
                  :                                     : Unweighted
                  :                 : Ordinary ----------: Weighted
                  :                 :                   : Sums
                  :                 :
                  :                 :                   : Discrete
                  :                 :                   : Equity
                  :                 : Alternative-      : Ratio-
                  :                 :  Constraint -----:    Alternatives
                  :                 :                   : Help
                  :                 :
                  : Initial --------------:              : Effectiveness
                  :                 :                   : Ratio-Criteria
                  :                 : Criteria-         : Safety-Net
                  :                 :  Constraint -----: Help
                  :                 :
                  :                 :                   : Task Allocation
                  :                 : Both-            : Other Combos
                  :                 :  Constraint -----: Help
                  :                 :
                  :                 :
                  :                 : Pie
                  :                 : Help
                  :                 :                   : Weights
 Allocate -----------:              : Convergence ----: Relations
                  :                 :                   : Help
                  :                 : Differences
                  :                 : Mult Unknown
                  :                 :
                  : Post-Initial -------:              : Ranking
                  :                 :                   : Proportional
                  :                 : Inconsistencies : Expansion
                  :                 :                   : Help
                  :                 : Help
                  : Help
```

PREDICT

```
                                                      Linear
                                                    : Diminishing
                                                    :   Returns
                                  : If–Then Rule-------: U-shaped
                                  :                   : S-shaped
                                  :                   : Help
                                  :
                                  :                   : Linear
                                  :                   : Diminishing
                                  :                   :   Returns
                                  : Equation ------------: U-shaped
                                  :                   : S-shaped
                                  :                   : Help
                 : Raw-------------------:
                 :                :                   : Linear
                 :                :                   : Diminishing
                 :                :                   :   Returns
                 :                : Residuals ------------: U-shaped
                 :                :                   : S-shaped
                 :                :                   : Help
                 :                :
                 :                :                   : Linear
                 :                :                   : Diminishing
                 :                :                   :   Returns
                 :                : Graph----------------: U-shaped
                 :                :                   : S-shaped
                 :                : Help              : Help
                 :                                    : Linear
                 :                                    : Diminishing
                 :                                    :   Returns
                 :                : If–Then Rule-------: U-shaped
                 :                :                   : S-shaped
                 :                :                   : Help
Predict----------------:          :
                 :                :                   : Linear
                 :                :                   : Diminishing
                 :                :                   :   Returns
                 :                : Equation ------------: U-shaped
                 :                :                   : S-shaped
                 :                :                   : Help
                 :                :
                 : Percentaging -------:               : Linear
                 :                :                   : Diminishing
                 :                :                   :   Returns
                 :                : Residuals ------------: U-shaped
                 :                :                   : S-shaped
                 :                :                   : Help
                 :                :
                 :                :                   : Linear
                 :                :                   : Diminishing
                 :                :                   :   Returns
                 :                : Graph----------------: U-shaped
                 :                :                   : S-shaped
                 :                :                   : Help
                 :                :
                 :                :                   : Initial
                 :                : Percent Table ------: Threshold
                 :                :                   : Help
                 :                :
                 :                : Help
                 : Help
```

SPECIAL DECISION-MAKING

```
                              : Data
                              : Initial
            : Risk Analysis----: Threshold
            :                 : Help
            :
            :                              : Constraint
            :                 : Time-Save--------: Analysis
            :                 :                 : Help
            :                 :
Special ------------:         :                 : Constraint
            :                 : Profit Max-     : Analysis
            :                 :   monetary      : Help
            :                 :
            :                 :
            : Sequencing------:                 : Constraint
            :                 : Profit Max-     : Analysis
            :                 :   non-monetary  : Help
            :                 :
            :                 :
            :                 :                 : Retreive
            :                 : File            : Save
            :                 :   Management    : Help
            :                 :
            :                 : Help
            :
            :                 : Weighted
            :                 :   Averages
            : Group DM--------: Bar Graph
            :                 : Help
            : Help
```

HELP

```
                                        : File
                                          Management
                    : Data ------------------:              : Alternative
                    :                   : Changes ------------: Criteria
                    :                                         : Transform
                    :                                         : Select
                    :
                    :                   : Raw-------------------: Initial
                    :                   :                       : Threshold
                    : Choose --------------:
                    :                   :                       : Initial
                    :                   : Percentaging -------: Threshold
                    :
                    :                                         : Budget
                    :                   : Pre-Initial -----------: Data-Transform
                    :                   :
                    :                   :                     : Ordinary
                    :                   :                     : Alternatives-
                    :                   :                       Constraint
                    :                   : Initial -----------------: Criteria-Constraint
                    :                   :                     : Both-Constraint
  : Partial-------: Allocate ---------------:                : Convergence
  :                 :                   : Post-Initial-----------: Inconsistencies
  :                 :
Help :             :                                         : If–Then Rule
  :                 :                                         : Equation
  :                 :                   : Raw-------------------: Residuals
  :                 :                   :                       : Graph
  :                 : Predict----------------:
  :                 :                   :                       : If–Then Rule
  :                 :                   :                       : Equation
  :                 :                   : Percentaging         : Residuals
  :                 :                   :                       : Graph
  :                 :                   :                       : Percent Table
  :                 :
  :                 :                   : Risk Analysis
  :                 :
  :                 :                   :                       : Time Save
  :                 : Special --------------: Sequencing ---------: Prof Max-
  :                 :                   :                           monetary
  :                 :                   :                       : Prof Max-
  :                 :                   :                           non-monetary
  :                 :                   :                       : File
  :                 :                                             Management
  :                                     : Group DM
  :
  : All
  : Menu Tree
```

14 Testimonials for the Software

GOVERNMENTAL DECISION-MAKING

Public Administration

1. The 1985 ASPA Workshop on
   Using P/G% in Public Administration

   12 of 14 respondents said the workshop was excellent or good as a useful learning format.
   15 of 15 respondents said they thought the information presented was excellent or good.
   12 of 14 thought the workshop exceeded or met their expectations.
   14 of 15 said the overall effectiveness of the workshop instructor was excellent or good.
   10 of 13 said they would participate in a follow-up workshop.

2. President of the International Association of Schools
   and Institutes of Administration

   The Programme Committee decided to invite one or two outstanding people to future conferences to make presentations to plenary sessions. Professor Nagel may make a very good candidate, including a microcomputer workshop. (Wendell Schaeffer, IASIA and NASPAA)

3. International usage

   I am writing to express my warm appreciation for the excellent job you did during the IASIA Conference at the session on the use of microcomputers for decision analysis. I know from all reports that I speak for the many people who participated in the session when I say that the session was a very successful one. (Kenneth Kernaghan, Vice-President, International Association of Schools and Institutes of Administration)

Government Personnel

1. Chief of the Management Analysis Branch of the
   Centers for Disease Control

   To help in this complex task of drawing conclusions from a long
   list of qualitative and quantitative data, the study team used
   P/G% Best CHoice microcomputer software. (Ronald Martin,
   Chief)

2. The Training Institute of the United States
   General Accounting Office

   The material you sent is very helpful in laying out our program.
   (Kenneth Hunter, GAO Training Institute)

Public Policy

1. Reviewer for the book on *Policy Studies:
   Integration and Evaluation*

   I strongly recommend publishing this book . . . I especially like
   the discussion of software alternatives. (Greenwood Press)

2. A researcher and teacher in the public policy field

   A major contribution to quantitative decision-making is part/
   whole percentages. (C. E. Teasley, University of West Florida)

Political Science

1. American politics teaching

   Students were unanimous in their praise of the program as it gave
   them a positive introductory experience in the use of the microcomputer as an aid in policy decision-making. The ease with which
   this program can be used makes it a useful addition to any introductory or advanced American Politics or Public Policy course.
   (Len Faulk, SUNY-Fredonia, "Policy/Goal Percentaging Analysis", paper presented at the June 1986 Conference on "Using Microcomputers in Political Science Teaching" at Gettysburg College)

2. International relations

> I liked Best Choice so much, both at the APSA demonstration and here in the leisure of my own PC, that I applied for a small University of Hawaii grant to develop some international relations policy options for our introductory IR course. Today I learned that I am to receive the grant. (Michael Haas, Professor of Political Science, University of Hawaii)

LEGAL DECISION-MAKING

Lawyers

1. A prominent Philadelphia lawyer

> I think it is fair to say that your seminar was the first that I have ever genuinely enjoyed attending during my more than 20 years of practicing law. I have attended a lot of seminars in which I learned a great deal, but this is the first in which I really enjoyed the learning process. Interestingly, on my return to the office on Monday I had a major meeting scheduled with a client who was having difficulty with a trial/settlement decision and I put several of the techniques I picked up at the seminar to work with positive effect. (C. Howard Thomas, Jr, of Saul, Ewing, Remick and Saul)

2. Chair of the Lawyer Microcomputer Users Group
   in Chicago

> Dear Professor Nagel:
> BRAVO!!!!!!
> The program was simply great!
> To say you did a fantastic job is the understatement of the decade!
> I too believe that the need for your technology is present now and that its use in law offices and business is close at hand. If I were you, I'd pursue the financing vehicles that exist in Illinois. If you need some references to lawyers and/or firms that could help you, I'd be pleased to pass that information on to you.
> I enjoyed being a small part of your program. I trust I made

some contribution. It was my honor and pleasure to be a part of the program. (Paul Bernstein)

3. A prominent West-Coast lawyer

I am fascinated with the decision-making software and its applications to the legal profession. (J. Patrick Huston of Morgan, Lewis, and Bokius)

Judges

1. An arbitrator and Law Professor

The author is definitely on the leading edge of a movement which will eventually and inevitably blend law and technology. (John Cooley, Loyola University of Chicago)

2. A distinguished Federal Judge

I want to thank you for the considerable effort you put in the successful settlement of the above-entitled cause. We ought to meet sometime to discuss whether your experiences in this case can be utilized to develop computer-aided settlement procedures on a broader scale. With warmest personal regards. (Marvin E. Aspen, United States District Court)

3. A State Judge

The most important applications for judges facilitate judicial research, analysis and decision-making, rather than the mere search, manipulation or retrieval of large volumes of stored data. (Judge George Nicholson, Sacramento Municipal Court in his report on "The Courthouse of the Future"; the only judicial decision-making book he cites is Nagel, *Microcomputers as Decision Aids in Law Practice* (Westport, Conn.: Greenwood-Quorum, 1987))

Law Publishers

1. *Computer Law Newsletter*

The program can be applied to such law practice problems as deciding (1) whether to go to trial or settle out of court in civil and criminal cases, (2) how to allocate time or other resources across a set of cases, (3) which of the various laws should be adopted for achieving a set of goals, (4) what decision should be reached in resolving a legal dispute, (5) what level of activity should be engaged in for a given matter where doing too much or too little may be undesirable, and (6) other decision problems that involve goals, alternatives, and relations between goals and alternatives.

2. *Law Practice Newsletter*

"Policy/Goal Percentaging: A Lawyer Aiding Program" LOGIC (1986)
Can help firms develop models for software programs and mini-computer systems to help in legal decision-making . . . covers court cases predictions, decision on whether or not to take cases, allocation of attorney time, allocation of money, and decisions as to which lawyers to assign to various cases. *Of Counsel: The Legal Practice Report* (December 1987)

3. *Attorneys Computer Report* (February 1988)

The decision-making technique known as decision analysis can be a powerful tool for the lawyer familiar with its nature and use. (John Burns, Attorney Management Consultant).

4. Law book publisher

Here they are, a contractor for *Using Computers in Litigation Strategy* and a contractor *Using Computers in Legal Resources Allocation*. (Eric Valentine, Executive Editor and Manager, Greenwood Press)

Law Professors

1. A review essay

    If anyone can create judicial prediction and lawyer decision-making services at this time, surely Dr. Nagel is a prime candidate. (Professor David A. Funk, *Indiana Law Review*: 617–24 (1988))

2. Canadian Law Professor

    Anyone interested in improving and understanding the legal process would find [Nagel's work] challenging and provoking. (Professor D. J. MacDougall, Faculty of Law, University of British Columbia)

3. US Law Professor

    Your article on dispute resolution is important work and will advance the overall cause of negotiation. (Bryan Johnston, Director, Center for Dispute Resolution, Willamette University College of Law)

4. Dispute Resolution Professor

    It was the consensus of the Dispute Resolution Research Colloquium of Northwestern University, in which I share, that you provided us with one of our most interesting meetings. (Stephen B. Goldberg, author of *Dispute Resolution* (Boston: Little, Brown, 1987))

Administrators of Continuing Legal Education (CLE) Programs

1. CLE Program of the District of Columbia Bar and the Georgetown University Law Center

    We have received your course materials and found them to be most impressive. Our assistant Director will be contacting you shortly with prospective dates. (Lawrence Center, Executive Director)

2. Committee on Continuing Professional Education
   of the American Law Institute and the American Bar Association

   We shall continue to forge ahead with you. . . . (Paul Wolkin,
   Executive Director)
   Thanks once again for your able chairmanship of the course.
   (Alexander Hart, Director of the Office of Courses of Study)

GENERAL DECISION-MAKING

Decision Theory

1. The International Institute for Applied
   Systems Analysis

   P/G is rather easy on operation . . . and could be successfully
   used for the purpose of teaching managerial personnel as well as
   for the solution of problems arising in everyday life of decision
   makers at all levels. . . . (Iuri Tchijov and A. Alabian, both
   from the USSR)

2. A Professor of Economics and
   Decision Sciences

   My students who used to work with Expert Choice have found
   P/G% more user friendly and more useful for sensitivity analysis
   than Expert Choice. I look forward to getting an upgraded
   version of PG Lotus for use in my Fall '88 classes. (Alain Albert,
   University of Quebec)

3. Reviewer for the book on *Evaluation*
   Analysis with Microcomputers

   I am keen to look at the software with a view to using it with
   MBA students in particular. (Abacus Press)

4. The Editor of *Knowledge: Creation, Diffusion,*
   Utilization

   Nagel's project marks an important step towards creating new
   and improved decision aids for practical problem solving. The

proposed set of decision aids – which represents a kind of "procedural expert system" based on Nagel's very considerable knowledge and experience – has unique features. The system yields equivalent results to those produced by mathematically similar routines (for example, Saaty's Analytic Hierarchy Process), but does so in a simple and user-friendly fashion. This means that Policy/Goal Percentaging Analysis is likely to be widely adopted by instructors, trainers, and decision-makers, thus contributing towards the resolution of urgent practical problems and giving Nagel and the Center for Advanced Study the visibility and credit deserved. (William Dunn, University of Pittsburgh)

5. The Director of the National Collegiate
Software Clearinghouse

New statistical technologies will spread more quickly through the impact of microcomputing. An example is policy percentaging analysis, an alternative to cost-benefit analysis developed by Stuart Nagel at the University of Illinois. (G. David Garson, "The Impact of Microcomputing on Political Science" (APSA Annual Meeting 1984))

6. *Comparative Software Review*

Without question P/G% is the best of the available software; no other program is as versatile and powerful (or as inexpensive). Prefcalc is a second choice, whose utility function approach makes it especially suitable for some problems (e.g. those in which diminishing returns are a primary factor). The remaining packages are interesting only in their oddities and recommendable only under very limited circumstances. Decision Analyst may appeal to those who like its report style outputs. Confidence Factor has the advantage of including 4 MS/OR routines on the same disk. Electre and Lightyear are amazingly easy to use. (Benjamin Radcliff, "Comparing Multi-Criteria Decision-Making Programs", *Social Science Microcomputer Review* (Spring 1986))

7. Book on aids for personal decision-making

P/G% is logically structured. The user approaches each problem with the same steps. It is nevertheless very flexible and useful for multicriteria decision making. (Holger Schutz and Helmut Jungermann, *Aids for Personal Decision Making* (Technical University of Berlin, 1988))

Natural Science

1. President of the AAAS Western Region

   Found the workshop at AAAS Chicago well done, interesting, and useful. Anxious to work with the software (A. Leviton, Computer Services, California Academy of Sciences)

2. Director of a University Extension Program

   I will be offering your workshop to Eastern Michigan University faculty and staff through the Science Service Center. We might be able to offer similar workshops to a wider community in Michigan. (O. Bertrand Ramsay, Professor of Chemistry)

Computer Science

1. Evaluation from the Wisc-Ware Software
   Distribution System

   Easy to use program . . . Covers a complex topic well. . . . No significant errors were noted in testing. . . . A complete user guide is provided . . . Supporting print materials are very extensive and supportive. (Chuck Bilow, Software Evaluator)

15 Bibliographies for the Software

This set of materials includes bibliographies on P/G% applied to evaluation analysis, political science, public administration, law, and the judicial process as of approximately July 1988.

METHODS OF POLICY/GOAL PERCENTAGING

The items below emphasize the methodological aspects of Policy/ Goal Percentaging, as contrasted to applications like public policy evaluation and law practice. Those subjects are covered in other bibliographies. The items below are authored by Stuart Nagel.

General Books

Evaluation Analysis with Microcomputers (Greenwich, Conn.: JAI Press, 1989) with John Long and Miriam Mills.
Public Policy: Goals, Means, and Methods (New York: St Martin's Press, 1984).

General Articles

"P/G% Analysis: A Decision-Aiding Program", *Social Science Microcomputer Review*, 3: 243–7 (1985); *Evaluation Review*, 9: 209–14 (1985); *Evaluation News*, 6: 21–24 (1985); *Legal Software Review*, 2: 205–7 (1985); *Proceedings of the American Institute for Decision Sciences*: 165–7 (1985); *TIMS Public Programs and Processes Communications*, 7: 2–4 (October 1984); *Facet: Newsletter of the MCDM SIG*: 5–6 (June 1985).
"Microcomputers to Overcome Problems in Program/Policy Evaluation", *Evaluation and Program Planning*, 10: 159–68 (1987).
"Problems in Doing Systematic Policy Analysis", in Naomi Lynn, *Public Administration: The State of the Discipline* (Chatham, N.J.: Chatham House, 1990).

**Items Relevant to the Multi-dimensionality
Aspects of P/G%**

"Part/Whole Percentaging in Policy/Program Evaluation", *Evaluation and Program Planning*, 8: 107–20 (1985).
"Economic Transformations of Nonmonetary Benefits in Program Evaluation", in James Catterall, (ed.), *Economic Evaluation of Public Programs* (San Francisco, Calif.: Jossey-Bass, 1985).
"Nonmonetary Variables in Benefit-Cost Evaluation", *Evaluation Review*, 7: 37–64 (1983).

**Items Relevant to the Missing Information
Aspects of P/G%**

"Dealing with Unknown Variables in Policy/Program Evaluation", *Evaluation and Program Planning*, 6: 7–18 (1983).
"New Varieties of Sensitivity Analysis", *Evaluation Review*, 9: 209–14 (1985).
"Lawyer Decision-making and Threshold Analysis", *University of Miami Law Review*, 36: 615–41 (1982).

**Items Relevant to Multiple Alternatives
and Allocation**

"Optimally Allocating Money to Places and Activities", in Patrick Humphreys and Janos Vecsenyi (eds), *High Level Decision Support: Lessons from Case Studies* (Amsterdam: North-Holland (1989).
"Using Percentaging Analysis to Aid in Allocating a Budget", *Public Productivity Review*, 44: 65–92 (1987).

Items Relevant to Constraints and Simplicity

"Comparing MCDM and P/G% with Traditional Optimizing", in Yoshikazu Sawaragi (ed.), *Multiple Criteria Decision Making: Toward Interactive and Intelligent Support Systems* (Kyoto, Japan: Kyoto Matsugosaki, 1986).
"Microcomputers, Risk Analysis, and Litigation Strategy", *Akron Law Review*, 19: 35–80 (1985).

Other General Uses of P/G%

"Microcomputers and Improving Social Science Prediction", *Evaluation Review*, 10: 635–60 (Symposium on "Microcomputers and Evaluation Research" 1986).
"Sequencing and Allocating Attorney Time to Cases", *Pepperdine University Law Review*, 13: 1021–40 (1986).
"Microcomputers, P/G%, and Dispute Resolution", *1985 Proceedings of the Society of Professionals in Dispute Resolution*: 229–58 (1986).

POLICY/GOAL PERCENTAGING APPLIED TO POLITICAL SCIENCE

The items below emphasize the political science aspects of policy/goal percentaging. There are separate P/G% bibliographies dealing with policy evaluation methods and law. The items below are authored by Stuart Nagel.

General Books

Evaluation Analysis with Microcomputers (Greenwich, Conn.: JAI Press, 1989) with John Long and Miriam Mills.
Super-Optimum Solutions in Public Controversies (Champaign, Ill: Decision Aids, Inc., 1989)
Public Policy: Goals, Means, and Methods (New York: St Martin's Press 1984).

Predicting and Explaining Political Behavior

"Using Microcomputers and P/G% to Predict Cases", *Akron Law Review*, 18: 541–74 (1985).
"Case Prediction by Staircase Tables and Percentaging", *Jurimetrics Journal*, 25: 168–96 (1985)
Causation, Prediction, and Legal Analysis (Westport, Conn.: Greenwood Press, 1986).

Evaluating and Making Political Decisions

Law, Policy, and Optimizing Analysis (Westport, Conn.: Greenwood Press, 1986).
"Using Microcomputers to Choose Among Government Structures", *International Political Science Review*, 7: 27–37 (Symposium on "Government Structures and Public Policy", 1986).
"Policies, Goals, and Criminal Justice Problems", *Law and Policy Studies* (Greenwich, Conn.: JAI Press, 1986).

Bargaining and Advocacy

"Microcomputers, P/G%, and Dispute Resolution", *1985 Proceedings of the Annual Meeting of the Society of Professionals in Dispute Resolution*: 229–58 (1986).
Multi-Criteria Dispute Resolution and Decision Aiding Software (Westport, Conn.: Greenwood-Quorum Press, 1990).

Teaching Political Science

"Using Microcomputers and P/G% for Teaching Policy Analysis and Public Policy", in Peter Bergerson and Brian Nedwek (eds), *Teaching Public Administration* (Southeast Missouri State University Public Administration Program, 1985).
"Using Microcomputers to Teach Political Science Substance", *News for Teachers of Political Science*, 5: 10–14 (1986).
"Teaching Public Policy from a Perspective of Goals, Means, and Methods", in Josephine LaPlante (ed.), *Teaching Public Policy Studies* (Croton-on-Hudson, N.Y.: Policy Studies Associates, 1986).

POLICY/GOAL PERCENTAGING APPLIED TO PUBLIC ADMINISTRATION

The items below emphasize the public administration aspects of Policy/Goal Percentaging. There are other bibliographies dealing with other P/G% applications. The items below are authored by Stuart Nagel.

General Books

Evaluation Analysis with Microcomputers (Greenwich, Conn.: JAI Press, 1989) with John Long and Miriam Mills.
Public Policy: Goals, Means, and Methods (New York: St Martin's Press, 1984).

Budgeting and Financial Management

"Optimally Allocating Money to Places and Activities", in Patrick Humphreys and Janos Vecsenyi (eds), *High Level Decision Support: Lessons from Case Studies* (Amsterdam: North-Holland, 1989).
"Using Percentaging Analysis to Aid in Allocating a Budget", *Public Productivity Review*, 44: 65–92 (1987).

Personnel Management and Labor Relations

"Using Management Science to Assign Lawyers to types of Cases", *Capital University Law Review*: 223–42 (1986).
"Can and Should There Be Systematic Assignment of Judges to Casetypes?", *Judicature*, 20: 73–5 (1986).
"Microcomputers, P/G%, and Dispute Resolution", *1985 Proceedings of the Society of Professionals in Dispute Resolution*: 229–58 (1985).

Management Science and Policy Analysis

"Microcomputers to Overcome Problems in Program/Policy Evaluation", *Evaluation and Program Planning*, 10: 159–68 (1987).
"Problems in Doing Systematic Policy Analysis", in Naomi Lynn and Aaron Wildavsky, *Public Administration; The State of the Discipline* (Chatham, N.J.: Chatham House, 1990).
"MCDM and P/G% as Improvements on Traditional Optimizing", in Yoshikazu Sawargi (ed.), *Decision Making with Multiple Alternatives* (Berlin:Springer-Verlag, 1987).

Administration of Specific Programs

Super-Optimum Solutions in Public Controversies (Champaign, Ill: Decision Aids, Inc., 1989).

Criminal Justice Administration

"Optimum Sequencing of Court Cases to Reduce Delay", *Alabama Law Review*, 37: 583–638 (1986).

"Sequencing and Allocating Attorney Time to Cases", *Pepperdine University Law Review*, 13: 1021–40 (1986).

Law, Policy, and Optimizing Analysis (Westport, Conn.: Greenwood Press, 1986).

"Policies, Goals, and Criminal Justice Problems", *Law and Policy Studies*, 1: 37–56 (Greenwich, Conn.: JAI Press, 1987).

Organizing Administrative Structures
Including Intergovernmental

"Using Microcomputers to Choose Among Government Structures", *International Political Science Review*, 7: 27–37 (Symposium on "Government Structures and Public Policy", 1986).

POLICY/GOAL PERCENTAGING APPLIED TO LAW

The items below are especially relevant to using personal computers for decision-making in law practice. They are authored by Stuart Nagel.

General Books

Microcomputers as Decision Aids in Law Practice (Westport, Conn.: Greenwood Press, 1987).

Evaluation Analysis with Microcomputers (Greenwich, Conn.: JAI Press, 1989) with John Long and Miriam Mills.

Applying Decision Science to Law Practice (Philadelphia, Pa.: American Law Institute American Bar Association, 1984).

Public Policy Goals, Means, and Methods (New York: St Martin's Press, 1984).

Litigation Strategy

"Applying Decision Science to the Practice of Law", *Practical Lawyer*, 30: 13–22 (April 1984).

"Microcomputers, Risk Analysis, and Litigation Strategy", *Akron Law Review*, 19: 35–80 (1985).

"Microcomputers, P/G%, and Dispute Resolution", *1985 Proceedings of the Society of Professionals in Dispute Resolution*: 229–58 (1986).

"Lawyer Decision-Making and Threshold Analysis", 36 *University of Miami Law Review*, 56: 615–42 (1983).

Judicial Prediction

"Using Microcomputers and P/G% to Predict Cases", *Akron Law Review*, 18: 541–74 (1985).

"Case Prediction by Staircase Tables and Percentaging", *Jurimetrics Journal*, 25: 168–96 (1985).

Allocating Attorney Resources

"Sequencing and Allocating Attorney Time to Cases", *Pepperdine University Law Review*, 13: 1021–40 (1986).

"Allocating Attorneys to Casetypes", *Capital University Law Review*, 15: 223–42 (1986).

"Attorney Time Per Case, Finding an Optimum Level", *University of Florida Law Review*, 32: 424–41 (1980).

Improving the Judicial Process

"Using Management Science to Assign Judges to Types of Cases", *Miami Law Review*, 40: 1317–36 (1986).

"Optimum Sequencing of Court Cases to Reduce Delay", *Alabama Law Review*, 37: 583–638 (1986).

Legal Policy Evaluation

Legal Decision-Making and Microcomputers (Westport, Conn.: Greenwood-Quorum Press, 1990).

Law, Policy, and Optimizing Analysis (Westport, Conn.: Greenwood Press, 1986).

Causation, Prediction, and Legal Analysis (Westport, Conn.: Greenwood Press, 1986).

POLICY/GOAL PERCENTAGING APPLIED TO THE JUDICIAL PROCESS

The items below emphasize applications of Policy/Goal Percentaging
to making decisions relevant to the substance and procedures of the
judicial process. The items below are authored by Stuart Nagel.

General Books

Microcomputers as Decision Aids in Law Practice (Westport, Conn.:
Greenwood Press, 1987).
Public Policy: Goals, Means, and Methods (New York: St Martin's
Press, 1984)

**Deciding More Effectively and Consistently
on Substance Matters**

Synthesizing Prior Cases

"Using Microcomputers and P/G% to predict Cases", *Akron Law
Review*, 18: 541–74 (1985).
"Case Prediction by Staircase Tables and Percentaging", *Jurimetrics
Journal*, 25: 168–96 (1985).

Synthesizing the Facts in a Case

Causation, Prediction, and Legal Analysis (Westport, Conn.: Greenwood Press, 1986).

Decisions Under Conditions of Risk

"Decision Theory and the Pretrial Release Decision in Criminal
Cases", *University of Miami Law Review*, 31: 1433–91 (1977)
"Decision Theory and Juror Decision-Making,", in B. Sales (ed.),
The Trial Process (New York: Plenum, 1981).

Mediating Disputes

"Plea Bargaining, Decision Theory, and Equilibrium Models", *In-
diana Law Journal*, 51 and 52: 987–1024, 1–61 (1976)
"Microcomputers, P/G%, and Dispute Resolution", *1985 Proceedings of the Annual Meeting of the Society of Professionals in
Dispute Resolution*: 229–58 (1986).

Legal Policy Evaluation or Explanation

Legal Decision-Making and Microcomputers (Westport, Conn.: Greenwood-Quorum Press, 1990).
Law, Policy, and Optimizing Analysis (Westport, Conn.: Greenwood Press, 1986).

Deciding More Efficiently on Administrative Matters

Judicial Assignment

"Using Management Science to Assign Judges to Types of Cases", *Miami Law Review*, 40: 1317–36 (1986).
"Time-Oriented Models and the Legal Process: Reducing Delay and Forecasting the Future", *Washington University Law Quarterly*: 467–527 (1978).

Allocating Court Resources

"Using Microcomputers for Evaluating Legal Policies and Decisions", submitted to *Harvard Law Review*.
"Optimally Allocating Money to Places and Activities", in Patrick Humphreys and Janos Vecsenyi (eds.), *High Level Decision Support: Lessons from Case Studies* (Amsterdam: North-Holland, 1989).

ARTICLES REFERRING TO POLICY/GOAL
PERCENTAGING BY AUTHORS OTHER THAN S. NAGEL

Richard Brunelli, "Breakthrough Program: Computer Analysis Can Predict Court Rulings", *The Recorder* (15 January 1986).
Richard Brunelli, "Coin-Flip or Computer?: Systemization of Legal Hunches Could Be the Ultimate Litigation Tool", *Chicago Daily Law Bulletin* (21 August 1986).
Sean Butler, "Software Aids Lawyers in Selection of Judges, Arbitration Panels", *United States Law News*, 1: 23 (October 1986).
Richard Diennor, "How Case Evaluation Can Improve Your Practice", *The Profitable Lawyer*, 2: 13 (October 1985).
Len Faulk, "Policy/Goal Percentaging Analysis", in William Wilson (ed.), *Computing in Undergraduate Political Science* (Gettysburg, Pa.: Gettysburg College, 1987).

258 — Decision-aiding Software

Timothy Martin, "Computer-Aided Counseling", *Attorneys Computer Report*, 5: 6–8 (October 1986).

Timothy Martin, "Computer-Aided Negotiation Helps Put Risks into Perspective", *Attorneys Computer Report*, 5: 11–14 (November 1986).

Timothy Martin, "Computer-Aided Advocacy Helps Attorney Promote His Position", *Attorneys Computer Report*, 5: 1–4 (December 1986).

Benjamin Radcliff, "Comparing Multi-Criteria Decision-Making Programs", *Social Science Microcomputer Review*, 4 (1986).

Beverly F. Salbin, "Increased Profits Through Case Allocation: A Systematic Approach", *Of Counsel: The Monthly Legal Practice Report*, 5 15–16 (January 1986).

Robert Wilkins, "Policy/Goal Percentaging Analysis", *The Lawyer's PC*: 8 (1 May 1985).

THE POLICY/GOAL PERCENTAGING OR BEST CHOICE DATA FILES

There are now approximately 400 data files available for use within the Policy/Goal Percentaging or Best Choice system. The data files cover a great variety of evaluation problems and other problems that relate to political science, public policy, public administration, law, criminal justice, social science, methodology, and other fields. There are now data files for all the tables and figures in each of the following S. Nagel books:

Teach Yourself Decision-Aiding Software (Champaign, Ill.: Decision Aids, Inc., 1989).

Public Policy: Goals, Means, and Methods (New York: St Martin's Press, 1984).

Evaluation Analysis with Microcomputers (Greenwich, Conn.: JAI Press, 1989).

Microcomputers as Decision Aids in Law Practice Champaign, Ill.: x 51 Greenwood 1987).

Decision Aiding Software and Legal Decision-Making (Westport, Conn.: Greenwood-Quorum Press, 1989).

Super-Optimum Solutions in Public Controversies (Champaign, Ill.: Decision Aids, Inc., 1990).

Political Science and Multi-Criteria Decision-Making (Champaign, Ill.: Decision Aids, Inc., 1987).

Multi-Criteria Decision-Making and Criminal Justice (Champaign, Ill.: Decision Aids, Inc., 1987).

Public Administration and Multi-Criteria Decision-Making (Champaign, Ill.: Decision Aids, Inc., 1987).

The Judicial Process: Litigation and Public Policy (Champaign, Ill.: Decision Aids, Inc., 1987).

Evaluation Problems in Health, Education, and Welfare (Champaign, Ill.: Decision Aids, Inc., 1987).

Note:

Further details can be found concerning each of the approximately 400 data files in the P/G% Data Files Manual (Champaign, Ill., Decision Aids, Inc., 1987). Copies of the data files themselves are available on the P/G% floppy disks and the forthcoming PG Lotus floppy disks.

16 A Tutorial Introduction to the P/G% Software

It is the purpose of this tutorial to guide new users of the P/G% software through an example problem which involves most of the analytic situations that one is likely to encounter in other examples. This example presupposes no prior contact with the P/G% program, microcomputers, multi-criteria decision-making, spreadsheet analysis, or related techniques. Only the ability to read is presupposed, and an interest in learning about the P/G% decision-aiding software.

This tutorial emphasizes a step-by-step approach to demonstrating the P/G% software. The steps include whatever keys are necessary to hit and whatever typing is necessary to do in order to reproduce all the screens shown in each tutorial. The introductory version elaborates on the main menu, including its five parts of file management, data management, initial analysis, sensitivity analysis, and the creating/ saving of new files.

The outline of this tutorial is as follows:

Preliminaries

> Getting started
> The main menu
> The file management sub-menu

The data management sub-menu

> The budget and the alternatives
> The criteria
> The relations between the alternatives and the criteria

The primary and intermediate analysis

> Primary analysis
> Intermediate analysis

The threshold and convergence analysis

> Threshold analysis
> Convergence analysis

Creating and completing files

Some conclusions
For further information
Appendix : Pointers for the smooth working of the P/G% program

PRELIMINARIES

Getting Started

1. Put Disk #1 into Drive A and Disk #2 into Drive B. If you have only one drive, then put Disk #1 into Drive A. Turn on the microcomputer. After the microcomputer warms up, the *title page* should appear on the screen which says *"POLICY EVALU-ATION : P/G%"* (see Screen 1). If the title page does not appear or if the screen goes blank at any time, press the combination of the *Control, Alternative*, and *Delete* keys simultaneously, or turn the computer off and then on with Disk #1 in Drive A. The screen can be moved up, down, to the left, or to the right when the title page is showing by hitting the shift key and any of the arrows at the right of the keyboard. One can always return to the title page by either hitting *Return* or hitting *F9* to go to the main menu and then hitting *F6*.
Note:
If the P/G% disk does not self-boot, then type *"Policy"* in response to the A prompt with a graphics adapter and *"Tpolicy"* without a graphics adapter.

Screen 1   The title page

POLICY EVALUATION
P/G%
F8 for assistance
© 1984, 1985 Nagel & Long r&dv8.7

---

2. For a starter, hit *F8* for assistance. Then hit a little "*b*" to see the main *purposes* of the program and why it is called Policy/Goal Percentaging. In addition to choosing the best alternative or combination, the program can be helpful for allocating scarce resources, developing predictive decision rules, making decisions under conditions of risk, dealing with missing information, making optimum level decisions, dealing with multiple dimensions on multiple goals, resolving conflicting constraints, simplifying complicated decision-making problems, and other useful purposes to be discussed in the intermediate and advanced tutorials (see Screen 2).

Screen 2   Help screen: introduction to P/G%

This program is mainly designed to process a set of

   (1) goals or criteria to be achieved
   (2) policies or alternatives for achieving the goals
   (3) relations between goals and alternatives

in order to choose the best alternative or combination
for maximizing benefits minus costs

   The program is called Policy/Goal Percentaging Analysis
as it relates alternative policies to goals, and it makes use of
part/whole percentages to handle the problem of goals being
measured on different dimensions.

---

3. Hit *Return* to return to the title page. Then hit *F8* again and a little "*a*" to see what the *function keys* do (See Screen 3).

Screen 3   Help screen: function key definitions

   Function keys

F10 – (or carriage return)
        used for entering information or
        moving to the next display
F6   – (Back)
        used to return to selection menus
F7   – (Data)
        used to branch between results presentation
        and the rawscore display

F8   –   (Help)
          used to initiate help sequences
F9   –   (Menu)
          returns you to the menu last accessed
F1   –   (Quit)
          This key is only active in conjunction with
          the shift key – used to exit to DOS

---

(1) The *F10* key is the same as the carriage return key, but it is available to the left hand. It is mainly used to go to the next display. The carriage return key is also referred to as the "*Enter*" key or the "*Next*" key.

(2) The *F9* key is mainly used to go back to the main menu when one is using the program. If you are at the title page, you go forward to the main menu by hitting *Return*.

(3) Hitting the *F1* key or *Shift-F1* will give you an A prompt. In response to the A prompt type "*Policy*" and hit *Return* if you have a color computer, or a monochrome computer with a graphics adaptor. Type "*TPolicy*" and hit *Return* if you have a monochrome computer without a graphics adaptor. You need to access the *TPolicy* program if the title page has many short horizontal lines on the left and right border. Otherwise, the program may not behave properly. "*Policy*" is the default version and self-booting version of the program on the assumption that most microcomputers can handle graphics software.

(4) Hitting the *F6* key is useful for going back to the title page from the main menu.

Hit *Return* to go back to the title page when you are looking at the help display about the function keys. Then hit *Return* to go to the main menu.

The Main Menu

The main menu has five options: (see Screen 4):

Screen 4   The main menu

POLICY EVALUATION P/G%

1. File management
2. Data management

3. Primary analysis
4. Threshold/Convergence
   analyses
5. Save present data

F6 for Title page
F9 to return to this menu

---

1. *"File management"* enables the user to make changes in existing data or to create a new file.
2. *"Data management"* enables the user to make changes in existing data or to create new data mainly regarding (1) the goals or criteria to be achieved, (2) the alternatives for achieving them, or (3) the relations between goals and alternatives.
3. *"Primary analysis"* shows the initial conclusion as to the overall scores or the allocation percentages of the alternatives.
4. *"Threshold analysis"* tells the user what it would take to bring a second-place alternative up to first place. *"Convergence analysis"* tells the user at what point the weight of a goal becomes high enough that the goal dominates the other goals.
5. *"Save present data"* is the option exercised in order to preserve for the future whatever new criteria, alternatives, or relations one has recently created in a data file.

The File Management Sub-menu

1. Hit a *1* to access the *file management sub-menu*. The file management sub-menu in effect asks three questions (See Screen 5). There is generally no need to hit *Return* where there is no ambiguity as to what option one is referring to. If there were an option 1.1 or 11, then one would have to hit *Return* to indicate the entry is completed. If an extra *Return* is hit, the computer may move beyond the point where one wants to go, although it should be easy to go back generally by hitting *F9* to go through the main menu.
2. Option 3 wants to know on what *disk drive* is the data file that you want to access, or on what disk drive do you want to create a new data file. The default is Drive A. One normally has Disk #1 in Drive A. Disk #1 contains the P/G% program, two sets of demonstration data files, and one set of policy analysis data files. Additional data files are on Disk #2 and #3. To access those additional disks, put them into Drive B and then hit a *3* (in response to

Screen 5   The file management sub-menu

POLICY EVALUATION P/G%

FILE MANAGEMENT
1. Master file selection
   Current file =
2. Data file selection
   Current file =
3. Disk drive – A

---

the file management sub-menu) to inform the computer to work with Drive B, or whatever letter you want.
3. Option 1 wants to know the *master file* you want to select. A master file is a group of specific files that deal with a common subject matter, although the common subject matter may be rather loosely defined. Hit a *1* to see what the master files are on Drive A. There are three master files there named "demo1", "demo2", and "policy". Type *"demo1"*, and hit *Return* (see Screen 6).

Screen 6   The master files on disk drive A

POLICY EVALUATION P/G%

Disk drive = A
Available files:
demo1   demo2   policy
File to attach:

SHIFT F10 to create
SHIFT F8 to delete

---

4. The computer returns to the file management sub-menu and shows that demo1 has been successfully accessed. The second option wants to know what *specific data file* you want to access. Hit a *2* to see the specific data files on the demo1 master file. There are as many as 20 specific data files on each master file. The data files relate to a variety of policy, legal, personal, predictive, and other problems. Type *"diversn"* to access the data file that we would like to use for illustrative purposes, and hit *Return*. To access a specific data file, it is necessary only to type enough characters to distinguish it from the other data files on the screen. (For the floppy disk which corresponds to this book, use the *"diversn"* file on master file DAS1, as indicated at the bottom of page x.)

Thus "*di*" would have been sufficient. One, however, does have to match the characters on the screen with regard to being upper or lower case. The names of master files should be spelled out in full, but can be either upper or lower case (see Screen 7)

Screen 7 The specific data files on the DAS1 master file

POLICY EVALUATION P/G%

Current data file =
Available files:
ASPA   diversn police crime
damages health SEQUENCE AFFIRM
JURYINST OPTBOND GEOALLOC OPTSENT
FP/FT SENTDISC +LAWYER EXPVAL2
NEWTRIAL FARMERS5 DIVERSN2

File to get:

SHIFT F10 to create
SHIFT F8 to delete

The Data Management Sub-Menu

1. After hitting *Return*, the computer goes back to the file management sub-menu to show that the DEMO1 master file and the diversn data file have been accessed. The next step is to hit *F9* to go back to the main menu. Then hit a 2 to access the *data management sub-menu* (see Screen 8).

Screen 8 The data management sub-menu

REVIEW / MODIFY

1. Total Budget
   Currently set at $ = 0.00
2. Alternatives
3. Criteria
4. Alternatives / Criteria
    scores
5. Method = Percentaging

---

2. The data management sub-menu has *five options* that one could exercise. They cover:

(1) Changing the total *budget*, where one is allocating scarce resources.

(2) Changing the *alternatives*, their minimum allocations, or their previous actual allocations.

(3) Changing the *criteria*, their measurement units, or their relative weights.

(4) Changing the *scores* of the alternatives on the criteria.

(5) Changing the method for dealing with *multi-dimensional* criteria from raw score analysis to percentaging analysis, or back.

The Budget and the Alternatives

1. Since we are not working with an allocating problem, there is no need to change the *budget* from its default figure of $0 or $10,000. The resources being allocated could be dollars, time, money, people, or any quantity, not just dollars. To change the budget, hit a *1* when Screen 8 is showing. The bottom of the screen will ask what you want the budget to be changed to. Type the new number, and hit *Enter*. The new number will then register on Screen 8 under option 1. For the purposes of this tutorial, however, leave or return the budget at $0 or at 100 for 100% of the cases.

2. Hit a *2* to see what the *alternatives* are. Three alternative ways of disposing of criminal cases appear on the screen. They are trials, plea bargains, and diversion out of the judicial system. Other alternatives could include dismissal, a subdividing of trials into bench trials and jury trials, or a subdividing of pleas into guilty pleas based on either explicit bargaining or an implicit understanding that pleading guilty will result in a lighter sentence than being found guilty after a trial (see Screen 9).

Screen 9   The alternatives for the diversion example

| | Budgets | |
Alternative	Minimum	Actual
1 trials	0.00	0.00
2 pleas	0.00	0.00
3 diversion	0.00	0.00

Select a number to modify –
SHIFT F10 to add, F10 to proceed

3. Since this is not an allocating problem, there are no *minimum amounts* assigned to each alternative. Likewise, there is no *previous actual amount* for each alternative to be compared with the optimum amounts which are calculated by the program in light of the goals, their weights, and the relations between the alternatives and the goals. The use of minimum amounts is discussed in the section on constraints. If previous actuals were inserted, then the primary analysis would show the differences or residuals between the actuals and the optimums. Doing so helps understand why the actuals differ from the optimums which usually relates to the analyst not accurately indicating the values and perceptions of the decision-makers. The difference could also be partly attributed to the decision-makers not accurately perceiving the relations between alternatives and criteria, or relations between criteria and higher criteria.

4. If we wanted to *change* the name of an alternative, we would hit a *1, 2*, or *3*, depending on the number of the alternative, and then hit *Return*. The cursor arrow would move up to that row so we could type a changed name minimum, or actual.

5. If we wanted to *add another* alternative, we would hit a *4* and *Return*. The cursor would then move to row 4 so we could type a new name, minimum, and actual. The default is zero on the minimums and actuals.

6. After observing and possibly experimenting with the alternatives, hit *Return*. We now see the second alternatives display. It allows the user to *activate or deactivate* any of the alternatives by hitting their numbers and *Return*. An active alternative is shown by a star, bigger letters, green letters, or brighter letters. A deactivated alternative is shown by no star, smaller letters, red letters, or dimmer letters. In this example, only trials and pleas are activated in order to keep the example simple to start with. The diversion alternative could be activated by hitting a *3*, and *Return*, and then deactivated by hitting a *3* and *Return* again.

The Criteria

1. From the second alternatives display, hit *Return* when no alternative is in the process of being activated or deactivated. The screen then changes back to the data management sub-menu. Hit a *3* to see what *the criteria* look like. A lot of criteria appear on the screen for deciding whether trials or pleas are more desirable, and

later for deciding the percentage of the cases to allocate to trials or pleas (see Screen 10).

Screen 10   The criteria for the diversion example

Criterion	Meas. Unit	Weight
1 – delay	days	–1.00
2 + respect	0–10 scale	2.00
3 – expense	dollars	–1.00

Select a number to modify –
Shift F10 to add, F10 to proceed

2. The first column shows the *names of the criteria*. For now, we are interested only in the criteria of reducing delay in criminal cases and increasing respect for the legal system. Other criteria such as reducing expense could be considered later. The minus signs in front of "delay" and "expense" are designed to show that those criteria are negative criteria, meaning that low scores on them are desirable. The minus signs do not mean that the goals are delay reduction and expense reduction, since those would be positive goals. The plus sign in front of "respect" is designed to show the respect criterion is a positive criterion, meaning the high scores on it are desirable.
3. The second column shows the *measurement units* for each criterion. Delay is measured in days. Respect is measured on a 0–10 scale, and expense is measured in dollars.
4. The third column or *weight* column shows the direction and the relative importance of each criterion. Delay and expense have negative direction because they are like golf scores in that it is desirable to have a low score on delay and expense. Respect has a positive direction because respect is like bowling or basketball scores. It is desirable to have a high score on respect. For the sake of discussion, delay and expense are considered equally important, and respect is considered twice as important as either of them.
5. Anything in the criteria display can be *modified or added* to the same way as the alternatives display. One indicates the criterion number to be modified and hits *Return*. That moves the cursor up to the appropriate row so a changed or new criterion, measurement unit, or weight can be typed. After doing so, hit *Return* to move the cursor back to the bottom of the display.
6. Hitting *Return* again will bring on the second criteria display. It

allows the user to *activate or deactivate* any specific criteria from the total set. This specific example uses only the delay and respect criteria.

The Relations Between the Alternatives and the Criteria

1. Hitting *Return* again will bring back the data management sub-menu. Now hit a *4* to see the *relations* between the alternatives and the criteria. Those relations are as follows (see Screen 11):

Screen 11 The data matrix showing relations between alternatives and criteria

---

ALTERNATIVE / CRITERIA SCORING

	– delay	+ respect
trials	120.00	6.00
pleas	30.00	2.00

F6 to exit	F4 to rescale an entry
F8 for assistance	SHIFT F4 to set rescaling factors

---

(1) The average trial in this analysis takes 120 days from arrest to conclusion.
(2) The average plea bargain takes 30 days from arrest to conclusion.
(3) Trials received an average score of 6 on respect for the law on a 0–10 scale in an informal survey of lawyers.
(4) Plea bargains received an average score of 2 on respect in the same informal survey.

2. Any number in that data matrix can be *changed* by moving the cursor arrow to the right, left, down, or up by hitting the cursor arrow buttons on the number pad at the right-hand side of the keyboard. When the cursor is pointing at the number one wants to change, one should then type whatever new number one wants, and then hit *Return*, *F9*, or another arrow button. Any of those hits will register the number.
3. Numbers can be typed to a large number of *decimal places* for either the relations scores or the criteria weights. The computer only displays those number to two decimal places, but is capable of storing them to many places. Large numbers like $1,000,000,000 can be expressed as 1,000 units where each unit is a $1,000,000.

4. When the data matrix appears on the screen, one can hit *Shift-F4* to access a set of procedures that allow the numbers in the table to be *transformed* by a multiplier for probabilistic discounting. That, however, is better handled by using the probabilities as weights or partial weights in the criteria display. The transformations are more useful for time discounting to show the present value of future benefits or costs, or the future value of present benefits or costs. Some transformation are easier to make with a calculator such as getting reciprocals or logarithms of the numbers for dealing with some negative goals or non-linear relations. Hit *F6* to exit from the data transformations back to the data matrix.

5. When inserting scores into the data matrix, be sure that all the alternatives and criteria are at least temporarily activated. Otherwise, there may be confusion as to where a score is supposed to go in terms of the correct row, column, and cell. The saving option on the main menu may sometimes need to be exercised in order to get data to appear in the data matrix when there are many rows and/or columns.

THE PRIMARY AND INTERMEDIATE ANALYSIS

Primary Analysis

1. With the data matrix on the screen, one should *hit F9 twice* to return to the main menu. The first hit stops off at the data management sub-menu to provide the user with an opportunity to make further possible changes in the alternatives, criteria, or relations scores. One can also check to see if the proper alternatives and criteria have been activated. Hit F9 a second time, and when the main menu appears on the screen, hit 3 to access the primary analysis. (See Screen 12).

Screen 12 The primary analysis for the diversion example

Alternative	Combined W P/W	%
1 trials	70.00	70.00
2 pleas	30.00	30.00
F7 for Score matrix		
SHIFT F10 for P/Ws		

2. The *primary analysis* shows that trials is the better of the two alternatives between trials and pleas. It has an overall score of 70 versus an overall score of only 30 for pleas. One could interpret the results as meaning that the optimum allocation to trials is 70% of the cases, and the optimum allocation to pleas is 30% of the cases. That, however, would not be an accurate interpretation, as will be indicated later when we discuss allocation analysis. Here we are just trying to choose the better alternative.

Intermediate Analysis

1. To see where 70 and 30 came from, one should hold down the shift key with the left hand and then hit the *Return* key briskly with the right hand. On the screen will appear the data matrix with the numbers transformed into *part-whole percentages* to take into consideration that delay is measured in days and respect is measured on a 0–10 scale (see Screen 13).

Screen 13   The part/whole percentage transformations of the raw data

	PART/WHOLE %	
	− delay	+ respect
trials	80.00	75.00
pleas	20.00	25.00

SHIFT F10 for weighted P/Ws
F6 to proceed

(1) To calculate the part/whole percentages for the delay column, the computer adds the 120 days and the 30 days to get a whole of 150 days. The 120 is then divided by 150 to get a part/whole percentage (p/w%) of 80%. The 20 is also divided by 150 to get a p/w% of 20%.

(2) To calculate the p/w% s for the respect column, the computer adds the score of 6 and the score of 2 to get a whole of 8. The 6 is then divided by 8 to get a p/w% of 75%. The 2 is also divided by 8 to get a p/w% of 25%.

2. Again hold down the shift key with one finger, while briskly hitting the *Return* key with another finger. On the screen will appear the *weighted part/whole percentages*. They are the same as

the part/whole percentages except they have been multiplied by the weights of the goals. The weight of the delay goal is -1.00. Thus the 80% becomes -80%, and the 20% becomes -20%. The weight of the respect goal is 2.00. Thus the 75% becomes 150%, and the 25% becomes 50% (see Screen 14).

Screen 14   The weighted part/whole percentages of the raw data

	WEIGHTED PART/WHOLE %	
	– delay	+ respect
trials	–80.00	150.00
pleas	–20.00	50.00

3. Looking at the weighted part/whole percentages, the overall trial score is 70% by *adding across* the trials row. Likewise, the overall pleas score is 30% by *adding across* the pleas row. That is where the 70% and the 30% come from in the primary analysis.
4. There are *two columns* in the primary analysis. The first column is called the combined weighted part/whole percentages. In this situation, those amounts are 70% and 30%. The second column consists of percentages that are made to add to 100%, partly for allocation purposes. The numbers in the second column equal the numbers in the first column divided by the sum of the weights. In this situation, the sum of the weights is -1 plus 2, which is 1. Thus, the last column is the same as the second to the last column because here we are dividing by *1*.

THE THRESHOLD AND CONVERGENCE ANALYSIS

Threshold Analysis

1. Hit *F9* to go back to the main menu. Then hit a *4* to access two important kinds of sensitivity analysis. Then hit a *1* to access the *threshold analysis*. That kind of analysis is designed to determine what it would take to bring a second or other-place alternative up to the desirability level of the first-place alternative.
2. After exercising the threshold analysis option, the screen refreshes our memory as to the primary analysis. It shows that trials won over pleas by a score of 70 to 30. That means there would have to

be changes in the relations scores or the weights big enough to overcome that 40 point spread or *gap*.
3. The bottom of the screen for the threshold analysis asks us to *select a pair* of alternatives to contrast. Normally we would compare the first- and second-place alternatives. We might compare the first-place alternative with the eighth-place alternative if we have a special interest in the eighth-place alternative. We might compare the twelfth-place alternative with the fifth-place alternative if the first five alternatives are all going to be considered winners and we are the twelfth-place alternative. In this example, there are only two alternatives. We therefore hit *1* and *Return*, and then *2* and *Return*.
4. There are six input items which determine the 70–30 split. A change in any one of those items may be capable of generating a tie between the two alternatives. The interpretation of the *threshold scores* for the relations between the alternatives and the criteria are as follows (see Screen 15):

Screen 15 The threshold analysis for the diversion example

	THRESHOLD ANALYSIS		
	trials	pleas	Weight
− delay	??	0.00	−1.667
+ respect	3.71	3.23	1.200

(1) No change in the amount of trial delay will make pleas into a winner so long as respect has a weight of 2 and trials does three times as well as pleas on the goal of respect.
(2) If trials were to drop on the respect goal from a 6.00 to a 3.71, then there would be a tie. A judicial administrator is unlikely to encourage a drop in the respect for trials just to justify having more plea bargains. Another way to read the 3.71 is to say that pleas would become the winner if the 6.00 estimate of trial respect could be wrong by about 2.29 points. This tells us how much room for error we have.
(3) Pleas would become the winner if the delay on pleas could be reduced from 30 days to 0 days. That is impossible since it would mean that people would have to plead guilty at the time they are arrested. The police officer would have to be authorized to be a judge, which would violate fair procedure.

(4) If the score of pleas on respect could be raised from 2.00 to 3.23 on the average, then there would be a tie between pleas and trials on their overall scores, as shown in Screen 12. The new overall scores would be 50 points or 50% apiece. That can be tested by inserting the 3.23 in place of the 2.00 in the data matrix shown in Screen 11, and then asking for a new primary analysis. The respect of plea bargains could be increased by giving more resources to public defenders so they would not be pressed to unnecessarily plead their poor clients guilty. There is also a need for more resources to prosecutors so they would not be so pressed to accept guilty pleas to lesser charges by rich defendants.

(5) If more weight were given to delay by changing its weight from a negative 1.00 to a negative 1.67, then there would also be a tie.

(6) If less weight were given to respect by changing its weight from 2.00 to 1.20, there would also be a tie. Any of those threshold values can be helpful in dealing with missing information. For example, if we do not know what weight to give respect relative to delay, Screen 15 tells us that any weight above 1.20 will make trials a winner and any weight below 1.20 will make pleas a winner. Thus all we need to decide is whether the weight of respect is more than 1 or no more than 1, assuming this is a problem of choosing between trials and pleas.

5. Suppose raw scores (rather than percentaging) are used and the weights are all equal to 1. The threshold scores of the winning alternative would then all be X lower than the original scores, and the threshold scores of the losing alternative would all be X higher than the original scores. X is the size of the gap between the winner and the loser in the primary analysis. Suppose the weights are all equal to 1 and there are only two criteria. The threshold weight of one criterion will then be equal to the reciprocal of the threshold weight of the other criterion. No matter what the scores or weights are, any one threshold value is capable of causing a tie between the two alternatives if it is substituted for the corresponding original value.

Convergence Analysis

1. *Convergence analysis* tells us at what weight a goal becomes so important that we are within 5 percentage points of what the

allocation would be if that goal were the only goal. For example, if respect were the only goal, the allocation would be 75% to trials and 25% to pleas according to Screen 13, assuming a true zero on the 0–10 respect scale.

2. Before doing the convergence analysis, it is desirable to go back to the first criteria display (Screen 10) in order to *change all the weights* to a magnitude of 1.00. See point 5 under "The Criteria" above to see how to modify a weight on the criteria display, such as changing the weight of 2 for respect to a weight of 1. Otherwise it is too difficult to interpret the meaning of the convergence analysis. The analysis will change the weight of respect one unit at a time until the overall allocation percentages are within 5 percentage points of 75% and 25%. To change the weight of respect from 2.00 to the better starting point of 1.00, follow the procedure mentioned in the text that accompanies Screen 10.

3. Hit *F9* to return to the main menu. Hit *4* to go to the threshold/ convergence sub-menu. Hit *2* to choose the convergence option. The computer then asks if we want to *increment* the weight of respect more or less than one unit at a time. We hit *Return* if the one-unit default is acceptable. Otherwise we specify a larger or smaller increment and then hit *Return* (see the top part of Screen 16).

4. The computer then asks if we want to work with a *percentage-points difference* or a percentage ratio. We prefer a percentage-points difference. We therefore hit *1* (see the middle part of Screen 16).

Screen 16 The convergence questions for the diversion example

---

CONVERGENCE ANALYSIS

Enter a delta for incrementing the weights.
(default = 1.00)
Select a stopping rule
    1. Percentage point difference.
    2. Percent of desired.

Enter a stopping difference
(default = 5 percentage points)

---

5. The computer then asks *how big a difference* do we want to work with. We say *5.1* so the computer will stop at 5.0. If we said 5.0,

the computer would find a weight that will produce a deviation under 5 percentage points (see the bottom part of Screen 16).

6. After typing *5.1*, then hit *Return*. The screen shows that when respect reaches a *convergence weight* of 2.00, the allocation to trials and pleas is within 5 percentage points of what it would be if respect had a weight of infinity or if respect were the only goal. We know that is true because we know that with a weight of 2.00, the allocation is 70% and 30% according to the primary analysis of Screen 12. We also know that if respect were the only goal, the allocation would be 75% and 25% according to the part/whole percentages of Screen 13 (see Screen 17).

Screen 17 The convergence results for the diversion example

CONVERGENCE ANALYSIS

	Weight	
delay	−2.00	
respect	2.00	Stopping difference set at:
		5.1 percentage points.

CREATING AND COMPLETING FILES

Creating a Data File

1. Thus far we have been working with an existing file called *Diversion*. We now want to provide the experience of creating a new file. To do that, put Disk #1 in Drive A and *Disk #3 in Drive B*. Disk #3 has the most room for new files. When inserting or removing disks, be sure the red light on the disk drive is not on.

2. Turn the computer on. When the title page appears, hit *Return* to go to the main menu. Hit a *1* to go to the file management sub-menu. Hit a *3* to inform the computer that we want to work with Drive B. Hit a *1* to see what the *master files* are on Disk #3. Type "*Misc2*" to access that master file as being appropriate for an experimental data file. Hit *Return*. See Screen 6 to see what a previous list of master files looks like.

3. The file management sub-menu returns to the screen. It shows that we have successfully accessed the Misc2 master file. Hit a *2* to see what specific *data files* are on that master file. For your first

file, you might name it after yourself. If your name is Sam Jones, call it the Jones file, although that is not very descriptive of the subject matter. Type "*JONES*". Then while holding down the *Shift* key, hit the *Return* key. Doing so creates the data file called *JONES*, although as of now there is nothing in the data file. See Screen 7 to see what a previous list of data files look like.

4. After hitting *Shift-Return* to create the *JONES* file, the screen briefly shows that the file has been created. The screen then asks whether this new file should be a *prescriptive or predictive* file. A prescriptive file is one that is designed to arrive at a conclusion as to which alternative or combination should be adopted or prescribed. A predictive file is one that is designed to arrive at a conclusion as to what quantities of points lead to various decisions. Type the letter A to choose a prescriptive model (see Screen 18).

Screen 18   Model specification in creating your own file

MODEL SPECIFICATION

Please select the model which is
appropriate for your needs.

A. Prescriptive
B. Predictive

Creating a Master File or Deleting Files

1. To *create a master file*, as contrasted to a specific data file, hit *F9* to go to the main menu. Hit a *1* to go to the file management Sub-menu. Hit another *1* to see what the master files are on that disk. Type the name of the new master file that you want to create. Then while holding down the *Shift* key, hit *Return*. Doing so will create a new master file, assuming there is room on the disk for a new master file. If you want a Disk #4 for additional data files, insert a formatted blank disk into Drive B with Disk #1 in Drive A, and then proceed to create master files and data files on Disk #4. If you want a Disk #4 that contains the program, then duplicate a copy of Disk #1 and delete the master files so there is room for new files. See below on duplicating and deleting.

2. To *delete a master file*, hit *F9* to go to the main menu. Hit a *1* to go

to the file management sub-menu. Hit a *1* again to see the names of the master files on that disk. Now type the name of whatever file you want to delete. Then while holding down the *Shift* key, hit the *F8* function key. That will delete the master file specified. All the master files on a given disk can be deleted in order to have a clean disk for creating a whole new set of master files. That can be done with a duplicate copy of Disk #3 in order to create a Disk #4. A Disk #5 can be created which will contain the P/G% program and no master files by deleting the master files from a duplicated copy of Disk #1. Disk #5 will then be available for new master files and new data files along with the P/G% program.

3. To *delete a specific data file*, hit *F9* to go to the main menu. Hit a *1* to go to the file management sub-menu. Hit a *1* again to see the master files. Type the name of the relevant master file, such as *Misc2*. Hit *Return*. Hit a *2* to see the specific data files. Type the name of the data file you want to delete. Then while holding down the *Shift* key, hit the *F8* function key. That will delete the data file specified.

4. To make a *duplicate copy* of any one of the P/G% disks, put the DOS disk into Drive A, hit *Control-Alternate-Delete*. Then hit *Enter* twice, and type *"Diskcopy A: B:."* Then put the source disk in Drive A and a blank disk in Drive B, and hit *Enter*. To copy a master file from one disk to another, do the same thing except type *"Copy A: Demo1.NAM B:,"* inserting the name of the file in place of *"DEMO1"*. One can use similar commands to go to or from Drive A to hard Drive C on a hard disk machine.

5. To *rename* a master file, put the disk operating system into Drive A. Put the disk containing the master file into Drive B. When you obtain an A prompt, type *"Rename b:. Nam. Nam"*. The original name goes on the first blank, and the new name goes on the second blank. This will result in changing the name of the master file with its contents preserved. To change the name of specific data file, one needs to delete the file and re-enter it. For now, there is no way to move a data file from one master file to another. The program is in the process of being rewritten for use with Lotus 1–2–3 spreadsheets which will allow such changes and others.

Completing a New Data File

1. After typing *"A"* in response to the request to specify a model in Screen 18, a blank *alternatives* display will appear on the screen.

Hit a *1* and *Return* to move the cursor up to row 1. For the sake of simplicity, we can recreate the file that deals with trials versus pleas. Therefore, type the word *"TRIALS"*. Put the *Caps Lock* key in for typing with all capital letters if you want type that is more readable at a distance. Hit *Return* to register the word, then hit *Return* twice to record the default zeros for minimum and actual budget. That brings the cursor back to the bottom. Then hit a *2* and *Return*. Then type *"Pleas"*, and hit three *Returns*. That brings the cursor back down for adding a third alternative if we had one. Hit *Return*. Doing so activates both alternatives (see Screen 9)

2. Hit *Return* again. Doing so causes a blank *criteria* display to appear on the screen, although it might cause the data management sub-menu to appear. If so, then hit *3* to access the criteria display. Hit a *1* and *Return* to move the cursor up to the top row. Type *"Delay"*, and hit *Return*. Type *"Days"* as the measurement unit, and hit *Return*. Type -1 as the weight, and hit *Return*. Type a *2* and *Return*. Type *"Respect"* and *Return*. Type *"0–10 Scale"* and *Return*. Type *2* for the weight, and hit *Return*. Hit another *Return* to activate both criteria (see Screen 10). In creating a new file, we would normally give all the criteria equal weight of +1 or −1 and then allow the threshold analysis to be helpful in indicating where it might be worthwhile to use differential weights.

3. Hit *Return* again to either go directly to the *data matrix* or indirectly by way of the data management sub-menu. Type *"120"* for trials on delay. Then hit the *down arrow* on the number pad at the right. Hit *30* for pleas on delay. Then hit the *right arrow* on the number pad. Hit a *2* for pleas on respect. Hit the *up arrow*. Hit a *6* for trials on respect (see Screen 11).

4. Hit *F9* to go back to the *data management* sub-menu. Hit a *1* to reset the budget. Hit *zero* and *Return* to show that this is not a budgeting problem. Hit *F9* to go to the main menu. Hit *5* and *Y* to save the present data.

5. Now hit *3* to see the *primary analysis* which should be the same as Screen 12. There is no difference in working with the primary, intermediate, threshold, or convergence analysis as to whether an old file has been accessed or whether we are working with a newly created file.

6. Hit *F9* either once or twice to go back to the main menu. Then hit a *5* to exercise the *saving option*. Answer *Y* when the computer

asks whether you really want to save everything that is currently in the data file. That option can be exercised at any time to preserve new material, not just when a data file is being completed. Saving may sometimes be necessary to get entered data to appear in a big data matrix.

Printing P/G% Tables

1. One can obtain a printing of any table or other material that appears as a screen as a result of creating changes or a new data file. To do so, attach the computer to a printer. Turn the printer on. *Press Shift-PrintScreen* when the desired screen appears on the computer monitor.
2. To obtain especially fast printing, use the *TPOLICY program*, rather than the POLICY program. That involves hitting *Shift-F1*, and then typing *"TPOLICY"* in response to the A-prompt. The TPOLICY program is also capable of printing any screen even when one does not have a graphics printer, although the printing may not be as aesthetic as with a graphics printer.

SOME CONCLUSIONS

You have just completed the Introductory Tutorial. The most important *points we have covered* are:

(1) Preliminaries, like getting started, the main menu, and the file management sub-menu.
(2) The data management sub-menu, including the alternatives, the criteria, and the relations between alternatives and criteria.
(3) The primary and intermediate analyses, including part/whole percentages, weighted part/whole percentages, and the sums of the weighted part/whole percentages.
(4) Threshold and convergence analysis to show critical points in the weights of the criteria and in the relation scores of the alternatives on the criteria.
(5) How to create files and save data for future use. Those five points correspond to the five options in the main menu.

FOR FURTHER INFORMATION

For further information concerning the P/G% or Best Choice software, see the following items by S. Nagel:

(1) *Evaluation Analysis with Microcomputers* (JAI Press, 1987), available in manuscript form from Decision Aids, Inc., 1720 Parkhaven Drive, Champaign, Ill., 61820.
(2) *Using Microcomputers as Decision Aids in Law Practice* (Greenwood Press, 1987).
(3) "A Microcomputer Program for Evaluation Analysis", *Evaluation and Program Planning*, 10 (1987), 159–68.

NOTE: Copies of the Intermediate and Advanced Tutorials can be obtained from the author for $10 which is the price of photocopying, postage, and handling. The Intermediate Tutorial discusses how the decision-aiding software can deal with (1) multiple dimensions on multiple goals, (2) multiple missing information, (3) multiple alternatives especially allocating, and with (4) multiple and possibly conflicting constraints. The Advanced Tutorial discusses working with (1) predictive criteria, (2) decision-making under risk, (3) decision-making where doing too much or too little is indesirable, (4) decision-making where sequencing is a concern, and (5) group decision-making. Write to Stuart Nagel, Political Science Department, University of Illinois, Urbana, Illinois, 61801, USA.

Appendix: Pointers for the Smooth Working of the P/G% Program

1. In dealing with file creation, access, or deletion, be sure to give a **file name** before you indicate what is to be done with that file.
2. If an instruction says "hit *Shift-Next*", that means hit both keys **simultaneously**, not sequentially.
3. If the program gets stuck and does not seem to want to move, then hit (1) *Next* (also known as the Carriage Return or Enter key), (2) *Back* (also known as the *F9* key), (3) *Control-Alternate-Delete* simultaneously, or, as a last resort, (4) turn the computer off and then back on again.
4. Before entering the name of an alternative, be sure to give it a **number** and hit *Enter*. Doing so moves the cursor up to the correct row number for entering the alternative. The same thing must be done for each criterion.
5. After listing your alternatives, then indicate you have no more alternatives by hitting *Next*. Doing so will bring forth the second alternative display. That display should show asterisks next to each alternative that you want actively considered. If you want to **deactivate an alternative**, then type its number and hit *Carriage Return*. Do the same thing after listing your criteria.
6. In order to enter your data in the data matrix, use the **cursor arrows** at the right of the keyboard to move the cursor to the left, right, up, or down. If you have more than five criteria, then move the right arrow to the right after the fifth criterion, and the screen will display the sixth through the tenth criterion.
7. When you are **listing each alternative**, hit *Next* twice to bypass the minimum and previous budget allocations if you are not doing a budgeting problem.
8. Avoid hitting *Next* more times than you want. Otherwise, you will be propelled further into the program than you want to be.
9. The above pointers and others can be learned by reading the manual, reading the screen, or through practice, but they are put here to save time and frustration.
10. Access an **existing file** by selecting a master file and then selecting

a data file. Hit *Carriage Return* between each selection. Create a **master file** or a **specific data file** by typing the new name and then hitting *Shift-Next*.

11. Give the budget **$0** if you are not allocating a budget on the data management menu.

12. Choose **raw score analysis** by hitting *option 5* on the data management menu. Do so when all your criteria are measured in the same units, or if you can indicate how much more one unit or one criterion is worth compared to one unit on a second criterion. Choose **percentaging analysis** for dealing with multi-dimensionality when your criteria are not measured in the same units.

13. Anytime you want to see the A-prompt, hit *F1* or *Shift-F1*. When the A-prompt appears, type *"POLICY"* if you are at a terminal that has a graphics adapter. Type *"TPOLICY"* (for text policy) if you are at a terminal that lacks a graphics adapter.

14. You can use the regular or default version of the P/G% program if your IBM-compatible computer has a color monitor, or has a monochrome monitor but shows big letters on the title page of the program. If, however, your computer is monochrome and does not show big letters on the title page, then your computer does not have a graphics capability. You then need to use the *"TPOLICY"* version of the program by following the instructions in point 13 above. Otherwise, the program will not function well.

15. To create a new file, call up the **file maintenance sub-menu**. Decide what master file has some space. Type a name for the new file, and then hit *Shift-Return* when the display shows the data files on the master files with which you were working.

16. When first beginning the creation of new files, keep them **simple**. That means (1) few alternatives and few criteria; (2) a choosing problem rather than an allocation problem; (3) simple scoring without multi-dimensionality such as 1–5 scales; (4) no probability discounting; (5) no missing information; (6) prescriptive rather than predictive analysis; and (7) no constraints. Add those additional features as you acquire a little more experience.

17. Begin a new file with **equal weights for the criteria**. Then change the weights in light of what the threshold analysis shows would make a difference.

18. Be sure to **turn the stars on** to activate all the alternatives and all the criteria before inserting relation scores. Otherwise the computer will not know what alternatives and criteria you want to work with.

Bibliography

American Bar Association *Standards Relating to Trial Courts* (Chicago: American Bar Association, 1976).

Bartholomew, P. "Supreme Court and Modern Objectivity", *New York State Bar Journal*, 33: 156–64 (1961).

Barzun, Jacques and Henry Graff *The Modern Researcher* (New York: Harcourt, Brace, 1957).

Bodily, Samuel "Spreadsheet Modeling as a Stepping Stone", *Interfaces*, 16: 34–42 (1986).

Boyer, R. and D. Savageau *Places Rated Almanac: Your Guide to Finding the Best Places to Live in America* (Chicago: Rand McNally, 1985).

Bridgeman, P. W. *Dimensional Analysis* (New Haven, Conn.: Yale University Press, 1922).

Buffa, Elwood and James Dyer *Management Science/Operations Research: Model Formulation and Solution Methods* (New York: Wiley, 1981).

Bui, X. T. *Evaluation Planning with Basic* (Berkeley, Calif.: Sybex, 1981).

Carr, Robert *The Supreme Court and Judicial Review* (New York: Rinehart, 1942).

Chen, Fiona "Teaching Computer Application in Public Administration" (Eastern Washington University, School of Public Affairs, 1984).

Clark, R. *The Birth of the Bomb* (New York: Horizon, 1961). Compton, Arthur. Atomic Quest (New York: Oxford University Press, 1956).

Conway, R. *et al. Theory of Scheduling* (Reading, Mass.: Addison-Wesley, 1967).

Cooper, George, *et al. Law and Poverty: Cases and Materials* (St Paul: West, 1977).

Easton, A. *Complex Managerial Decisions Involving Multiple Objectives* (New York: Wiley, 1973).

Edwards, Ward and Robert Newman *Multi-Attribute Evaluation* (Beverly Hills, Calif.: Sage, 1982).

Erickson, Warren and Owen Hall *Computer Models for Management Science* (Reading, Mass.: Addison-Wesley, 1986).

Evaluation Review Symposium (June 1986).

Frank, J. *Courts on Trial: Myth and Reality in American Justice* (Princeton, N.J.: Princeton University Press, 1950).

Friedman, L. and S. Macaulay (eds) *Law and the Behavioral Sciences* (Indianapolis: Bobbs-Merrill, 1977).

Gibbons, H. "Using Computers to Analyze Legal Questions", in Thomas Rasmusson (ed.), *System Science and Jurisprudence* (Lansing, Mich.: Spartan Press, 1986).

Gramlich, Edward *Benefit–Cost Analysis of Government Programs* (Englewood Cliffs, N.J.: Prentice-Hall, 1981).

Guilford, J. *Psychometric Methods* (New York: McGraw-Hill, 1954).

Haines, Charles E. *The Role of the Supreme Court in American Government and Politics 1789–1835* (Berkeley, Calif.: University of California Press, 1944).

Harris, Clifford *The Break-Even Handbook* (Englewood Cliffs, N.J.: Prentice-Hall, 1978).

Henderson, T. *Spreadsheet Software: From VisiCalc to 1–2–3* (Indianapolis, Ind.: Que, 1982).

Jones, H. (ed.) *Legal Method: Cases and Text Materials* (Mineola, (N.Y.: Foundation, 1980).

Kerr, N. and R. Bray (eds) *The Psychology of the Courtroom* (New York: Academic Press, 1982).

Key, V. "The Lack of a Budgetary Theory", *American Political Science Review*, 34: 1137–44 (1940).

Kotler, Philip *Marketing Decision Making: A Model Building Approach* (New York: Holt, 1971).

Kraemer, Kenneth "Curriculum Recommendations for Computers in Public Management Education" (Washington, D.C.: NASPAA, 1984).

LaFave, Wayne and Austin Scott *Handbook on Criminal Law* (St Paul: West, 1972).

Landis, C. and R. Park *Teaching Law with Computers: A Collection of Essays* (Denver: Westview, 1979).

Lawlor, R. "Stare Decisis and Electronic Computers", in G. Schubert (ed.), *Judicial Behavior: A Reader in Theory and Research* (Chicago: Rand-McNally, 1964).

Lee, Sang and Laurence Moore *Introduction to Decision Science* (Princeton, N.J.: Petrocelli/Charter, 1975).

Levine, James, Michael Musheno and Dennis Palumbo *Criminal Justice in America: Law in Action* (New York: Wiley, 1985).

Lindblom, Charles *The Policy-Making Process* (Englewood Cliffs, N.J.: Prentice-Hall, 1980).

Lindsay, Peter and Donald Norman *Human Information Processing* (New York: Academic Press, 1972).

Lindzey, Gardner (ed.) *Handbook of Social Psychology: Theory and Method* (Reading, Mass.: Addison-Wesley, 1954).

Llewelleyn, K. *The Common Law Tradition: Deciding Appeals* (Boston: Little, Brown, 1960).

Loftus, G. "Say It Ain't Pittsburgh", *Psychology Today* 19(6): 8–10 (1985).

MacRae, Duncan and James Wilde *Policy Analysis for Public Decisions* (N. Scituate, Mass.: Duxbury, 1979).

Mason, Mary Ann *An Introduction to Using Computers in the Law* (St Paul: West, 1984).

McMillan, C. *Mathematical Programming: An Introduction to the Design and Application of Optimal Decision Machines* (New York: Wiley, 1970).

Money Magazine, "The Best Places to Live in America", 34–44 (August 1987).

Moore, C. *Profitable Applications of the Break-Even System* (Englewood Cliffs, N. J.: Prentice-Hall, 1971).

Nagel, S. "Case Prediction by Staircase Tables and Percentaging", *Jurimetrics Journal*, 25: 169–96 (1985).

————*Causation, Prediction, and Legal Analysis* (Westport, Conn.: Greenwood Press, 1986).

————*Evaluation Analysis with Microcomputers* (Greenwich, Conn.: JAI

Press, 1989) with John Long and Miriam Mills.

———*Policy Evaluation: Making Optimum Decisions* (New York: Praeger, 1982).

———*Public Policy: Goals, Means, and Methods* (New York: St Martin's Press, 1984).

———"Using Microcomputers and P/G% to Predict Court Cases", *Akron Law Review*, 18: 541–574 (1985).

———*Using Personal Computers for Decision-Making in Law Practice* (Westport, Conn.: Greenwood Press, 1986).

———"A Microcomputer Program for Dealing with Evaluation Problems", *Evaluation and Program Planning*, 9: 159–68 (1987).

———"A Microcomputer Program for Evaluation Analysis", *Evaluation and Program Planning*, 9: 159–68 (1987).

———"Applying Decision Science to the Practice of Law", *Practicing Lawyer*, 30: 13–22 (1984).

———"Attorney Time Per Case: Finding an Optimum Level", *University of Florida Law Review*, 32: 424–41 (1980).

———"Economic Transformations of Nonmonetary Benefits in Program Evaluation", in James Catterall (ed.), *Economic Evaluation of Public Programs* (San Francisco, Calif.: Jossey Bass, 1985).

———"Evaluation Analysis with Microcomputers", *Public Productivity Review*, 42: 67–80 (1987).

———"Lawyer Decision-Making and Threshold Analysis", *University of Miami Law Review*, 36: 615–642 (1983).

———"Microcomputers, Risk Analysis, and Litigation Strategy", *Akron Law Review*, 19: 35–80 (1985).

———"Microcomputers and Improving Social Science Prediction", *Evaluation Review*, 10: 635–60 (Symposium on "Microcomputers and Evaluation Research", 1986).

———"Microcomputers and Public Policy Analysis", in Don Calista (ed.), *Microcomputers and Public Productivity* (Special issue of the *Public Productivity Review*, 1985).

———"Multiple Goals and Multiple Policies", in Nagel, *Public Policy: Goals, Means, and Methods* (New York: St Martin's Press, 1984).

———"New Varieties of Sensitivity Analysis", *Evaluation Review*, 9: 772–9 (1986).

———"Nonmonetary Variables in Benefit-Cost Evaluation", *Evaluation Review*, 7: 37–64 (1983).

———"Optimally Allocating Federal Money to Cities", *Public Budgeting and Finance*, 5: 39–50 (1985).

———"Part/Whole Percentaging as a Useful Method in Policy/Program Evaluation", *Evaluation and Program Evaluation*, 8: 63–8 (1985).

———"Problems in Doing Systematic Problem Analysis", *Public Policy Analysis and Management* (Greenwich, Conn.: JAI Press, 1988).

———"P/G% Analysis: A Decision-Aiding Program", *Social Science Microcomputer Review*, 3: 243 (1985).

———"P/G% Analysis: An Evaluation Aiding Program", *Evaluation Review*, 9: 209–14 (1985).

———"Sequencing and Allocating Attorney Time to Cases", *Pepperdine*

Law Review, 13: 1021–39 (1986).

——"Using Management Science to Assign Judges to Casetypes", *Miami University Law Review*, 40: 1317–36 (1986).

——"Using Microcomputers and P/G% for Teaching Policy Analysis and Public Policy", in Peter Bergerson and Brian Nedwek (eds), *Teaching Public Administration* (Program in Public Policy Analysis and Administration: St Louis University, 1985).

——"Using Microcomputers and P/G% to Predict Court Cases", *Akron Law Review*, 19: 541–74 (1985).

Nagel, S., M. Beeman, and J. Reed "Optimum Sequencing of Court Cases to Reduce Delay", *Alabama Law Review* (1986).

Nagel, S. and M. Mills "Microcomputers, Policy/Goal Percentaging, and Dispute Resolution", in Cheryl Cutrona (ed.), *Bringing the Dispute Resolution Community Together* (Washington, D.C.: Society of Professionals in Dispute Resolution, 1986).

——"Allocating Attorneys to Casetypes", *Capital University Law Review* (1986).

Posner, Richard *Economic Analysis of Law* (Boston, Mass.: Little, Brown, 1977).

Quade, Edward *Analysis for Public Decisions* (Amsterdam: North-Holland, 1983).

Radcliff, Benjamin "Multi-Criteria Decision Making: A Survey of Software", *Social Science Microcomputer Review* (Spring, 1986).

Remer, D. *Computer Power for Your Law Office* (Berkeley, Calif.: Sybex, 1983).

Richmond, Samuel *Operations Research for Management Decisions* (New York: Ronald Press, 1968).

Saaty, Thomas *Decision Making for Leaders* (Belmont, Calif.: Wadsworth Publishing Co., 1982).

Saaty, Thomas *The Analytic Hierarchy Process: Planning, Priority Setting, Resource Allocation* (New York, McGraw-Hill, 1980).

Sales, B. (ed.) *The Trial Process* (New York: Plenum, 1981).

Sawaragi, Yoshikazu (ed.) *Multiple-Criteria Decision Making* (Berlin: Springer-Verlag, 1987).

Schubert, Glendon *Quantitative Analysis of Judicial Behavior* (Riverside, N.J.: Free Press, 1942).

Smyth, H. *Atomic Energy for Military Purposes: The Official Report on the Development of the Atomic Bomb* (Princeton, N.J.: Princeton University Press, 1947).

Spezzano, Charles "Decision Support Software", *Popular Computing* (October 1985).

Statsky, W. and J. Wernet *Case Analysis and Fundamentals of Legal Writing* (St Paul: West, 1977).

Thode, W. *et al.* (eds) *Introduction to the Study of Law: Cases and Materials* (Mineola, N. Y.: Foundation, 1970).

Thompson, Mark *Benefit–Cost Analysis for Program Evaluation* (Beverly Hills, Calif.: Sage, 1980).

Thompson, Mark *Decision Analysis for Program Evaluation* (Cambridge, Mass.: Ballinger, 1982).

Tullock, Gordon   *The Logic of the Law* (New York: Basic Books, 1971).

Warren, Charles   *The Supreme Court in United States History* (Boston: Little Brown, 1935).

Weisberg, Herbert F.   "Microcomputers in Political Science" *News for Teachers of Political Science*, 2 (Summer 1983).

Wildavsky, Aaron   *Speaking Truth to Power: The Art and Craft of Policy Analysis* (Boston, Mass.: Little, Brown, 1979).

Zeleny, Milan   *Multi-Criteria Decision-Making* (New York: McGraw-Hill, 1982).

Decision-aiding Software Packages

ACIDRAIN   Cambridge Decision Analysts, Management Studies Group, University Engineering Dept., Mill Lane, Cambridge, UK.

ARBORIST   The Scientific Press, 540 University Avenue, Palo Alto, CA 94301.

AUTOMATIC DIAGNOSIS   Jose Bernardo, Dept. Bioestaoistica, Fac. Medicina, Ave Blasco Ibanez 17, 46010 Valencia, Spain.

BRAINSTORMER   Soft Path Systems, c/o Cheshire House, 105 N. Adams, Eugene, Oregon 97402.

BUDGET PRIORITY SYSTEM   Tina Bamford, User Manager, Work Sciences, 26 Southwood Lawn Road, Highgate, London N6 5SF, UK.

CEIS   D. P. Cenas, Woodcroft, Weston-in-Gordano, Bristol BS20 8PZ, UK.

COMBINED ARBITRATION   S. Brams, Dept. of Politics, New York University, New York, NY 10003.

CONAN METAGAME ANALYSIS PROFRAM   Nigel Howard Systems, 10 Bloomfield Road, Moseley, Birmingham B13 9BY, UK.

CONFIDENCE FACTOR   Simple Software, Inc., 2 Pinewood, Irvine, CA 92714.

CONSULTANT   Organization Development Software, 1605 South Garden St., Palatine, IL 60067.

COPE   Bath Software Research Ltd., 40 Park Street, Bristol BS1 5JG, UK.

CYBERFILTER   Raul Espejo, Management Centre, Aston University, Birmingham B4 7ET UK.

DECAUD. G.F.   Pitz, Dept. of Psychology, University of Southern Illinois at Carbondale.

DECIDE   Public domain software, Software Express Direct, Box 2288, Merrifield, VA 22116.

DECISION AIDE   Kepner-Tregoe, Inc., Research Road, P.O. Box 704, Princeton, NJ 08540-0704.

DECISION AID   DSI Micro Inc., 519 Dutchess Turnpike, Poughkeepsie, NY 12603.

DECISION ANALYSIS SYSTEM   Armada Systems, P.O. Box 637, Station A, Downsview, Ontario, Canada, M3M 3A9.

DECISION ANALYST   Executive Software, Inc., 2 North State St., Dover, DE 19901.

DECISION MAKER   S. G. Pauker, New England Medical Centre, Boston, MA.

DECISION MAKING   NCSU Software Clearinghouse, Box 8101, NC State Univ., Raleigh, NC 27695.

DECISION TREE ANALYSIS OF LITIGATION   George Siedel, 526

Bus. Ad., Univ. of Michigan, Ann Arbor, MI 48109.
DECISIONMAKER Niall Fraser, Dept. of Systems Design Engineering, Univ. of Waterloo, Waterloo, Ontario, Canada.
DECISIONMASTER Syntonic Software Corp., 10428 Westpark, Houston, TX 77042.
DECISION Once Begun Computations, Seasport, ME 04974.
DECMAK Bohanec, Efstathiou and Rajkovic, "J. Stefan" Institute, Jamova 39, 61000 Ljubljana, Yugoslavia.
DEMAND/SUPPLY PLANNING SUPPORT SYSTEM Nicholas Hadwick, MIS-Advanced Technology, 1 Burroughs Place Room 2E24, Detroit, MI 48232.
DSS-UP Charles C. Holt, Management Dept., University of Texas, Austin, TX 78763.

EIRES Elie C. Harel, 11937 Foxboro Drive, Los Angeles, CA 90049.
ELECTRE X. T. Bui, Operations Research, New York University, Washington Square, New York, NY 10278.
EQUITY Scott Barclay, Decision Analysis Unit, London School of Economics, Houghton Street, London WC2A 2AE, UK.
ESSI N. Nikkinen, University of Jyvaskyla, Dept. of Computer Sciences, Seminaarinkatu 15, SF-40100 Jyvaskyla, Finland.
EXPECT Szenteleki, c/o Janos Vecsenyi, H-1125 Budapest, Diosarok ut 16/II, Hungary.
EXPERT CHOICE Decision Support Software, 1300 Vincent Place, McLean, VA 22101.
EXPERT Magic7 Software Co., Los Altos, CA.

FACILITATOR Floyd Lewis, Decision Science Dept., Western Washington Univ., Bellingham, WA 98225.
FAZANTWEG3 E. J. Stokking, 9765 JL Paterswolde, The Netherlands.
FLEXIGRID Finn Tschudi, Univ. of Oslo, Norway.

GOAL PROGRAMMING Part of the Sang Lee textbook software – MICRO MANAGEMENT SCIENCE available from W. C. Brown of Dubuque, IA.

HEURISCO Institut für Kernenergetik und Energiesysteme, c/o Dr. A. Engemann, University of Stuttgart, 7000 Stuttgart 80, West Germany.
HIVIEW Scott Barclay, Decision Analysis Unit, London School of Economics, Houghton Street, London WC2A 2AE, UK.
HOPIE Martin Weber, Institut für Wirtschafts, RWTH Aachen, Templergraben 64, D-5100 Aachen, West Germany.

IDEA GENERATOR Experience in Software, 2039 Shattuck Avenue, Suite 401, Berkeley, CA 94704.
IDEAL/PET J. Whelan, c/o School of Economic Studies, University of Leeds, Leeds LS2 9JT, UK.
INFORMATION PLANNER Knowledge Ware, Inc., 2006 Hogback Road, Ann Arbor, MI 48105.
IRIMS H. Otway, Joint Research Centre Ispra, Commission of the European Communities, C. C. R. Ispra (Varese), 21010 Ispra, Italy.

JAVELIN   Javelin Software Corp., Cambridge, MA.

JOBBER BUSINESS SIMULATION   Dennis P. Slevin, Innodyne, Inc., 734 Orchard Hill Dr., Pittsburgh, PA 15238.

KNOWLEDGE CRAFT   Mike Chambers, Carnegie Group, Inc., 650 Commerce Court, Station Square, Pittsburgh, PA 15219.

LIGHTYEAR   Lightyear, Inc., 2465 Bayshore Rd., Suite 301, Palo Alto, CA 94303.

LINEAR SCORING MODELS   P. Lovie, Dept. of Mathematics, University of Keele, Keele, Staffordshire, ST5 5BG, UK.

LOGSIM   Software and Support for Population Data Processing, United Nations, Room DC2-1570, New York, NY 10017.

MACCHOICE   Superex Business Software, 151 Ludlow Street, Yonkers, NY 10705.

MASS   Shimon Schocken, Dept. of Decision Sciences, University of Pennsylvania, Philadelphia, PA 19104.

MAUD   Decision Analysis Unit, London School of Economics, Houghton Street, London WC2AE, UK.

MICROLAY   Gerhard Wascher, Betriebsmirtschaftliches Institut Universitat Stuttgart-Abt IV, Keplerstr. 17, D-7000 Stuttgart 1, West Germany.

MIDAS   Robert de Hoog, Social Science Informatics, University of Amsterdam, Herengracht 156, 1016 BS Amsterdam, The Netherlands.

NORMA   R. Stamper, London School of Economics, Houghton Street, London WC2A 2AE, UK.

ODS SOLUTION CENTER   ODS, Inc., 1011 East Touhy Ave., Suite 535, Des Plaines, IL 60018.

OPCOM   Ayleen Wisudha, Decision Analysis Unit, London School of Economics, Houghton Street, London WC2A 2AE, UK.

ORDO   J. C. Courbon, CUI, Univ. of Geneva, 10 Rue du Lac, 1211 Geneva 4, Switzerland.

PERSONAL CONSULTANT   M. Bulder, European Marketing Division, Texas Instruments, 1101 CB Amsterdam, The Netherlands.

PLEXPLAN   J. F. Nunamaker, Dept. Management Info. Systems, Coll. Business and Pub. Admin., Univ. of Arizona, Tucson, AZ 85721.

POLICY PC   Executive Decision Services, P.O. Box 9102, Albany, NY 12209.

POWER'S DECISION AID   Daniel Power, 9002 Gettysberg Lane, College Park, MD 20740.

PREFCALC   Euro-Decision, B.P. 57-78530, BUC-FRANCE.

PRIORITIES   Tina Bamford, Work Sciences, 26 Southwood Lawn Road, Highgate, London N6 5SF, UK.

PRIORITY DECISION SYSTEM – PDS   Work Sciences Associates, 26 Southwood Lawn Rd., Highgate, London, N6 5SF, UK.

PROLOGA   Katholieke Universiteit Leuven, Dept of Applied Economics, Dekenstraat 2, 3000 Leuven, Belgium.

P/G%   Stuart Nagel, 361 Lincoln Hall, Univ. of Illinois, Urbana, IL 61801.

QSB   Yih-Long Chang, 301 Hagerty Hall, Faculty of Management Science, Ohio State Univ, Columbus, OH 43210.

RANK MASTER   Exemplary Software, 6039 Collins Ave, Room 525, Miami Beach, FL 33140.

SAFETI PACKAGE TECHNICA   M. Seaman, Lynton House, 7/12 Tavistock Square, London WC1H 9LT, UK.

SELSTRA   Stuart Wooler, Decision Analysis Unit, London School of Economics, Houghton Street, London WC2A 2AE, UK.

SERIATIM   NCSU Software, Nat'l Collegiate Software Clearinghouse, Box 8101, NC State University, Raleigh, NC 27695.

SMALL GROUP DECISION-MAKING   SSMR Software Department, Box 8101, NC State Univ, Raleigh, NC 27695.

SPAT   P. F. Lourens, Traffic Research Centre, University of Groningen, Netherlands.

STRATATREE.   Decision Support Software, Inc., 1300 Vincent Place, McLean, VA 22101.

STRATEGIC INTERVENTION PLANNING   G. van den Wittenboer, I. W. A., Grote Bickersstraat 72, 1013 Ks Amsterdam, The Netherlands.

STRATMESH   P. R. Dickson, Academic Faculty of Marketing, Ohio State Univ., 1775 College Road, Columbus, OH 43210.

SUPER TREE   300 Saud Hill Road, Menlo Park, CA 94025.

SYSTEM   W. Comshare, 32–34 Great Peter Street, London SW1P 2DB, UK.

THE DECISION MAKER   Alamo Learning Systems, 1850 Mt. Diablo Blvd., Suite 500, Walnut Creek, CA 94596.

TRIGGER   Thoughtware, Inc., 2699 South Bayshore Drive, Suite 1000a, Coconut Grove, FL 33133.

TROUBLE SHOOTER   Kepner-Tregoe, Inc., P.O. Box 704, Princeton, NJ 08542.

VALUE ANALYSIS   Mr. John Plummer, 43 Buena Vista Terrace, San Francisco, CA 94117.

VIG   P. Korhonen, Helsinki School of Economics, Helsinki, Finland.

VIMDA   P. Korhonen, Helsinki School of Economics, Helsinki, Finland.

WEIGHTED POINT RATING SOFTWARE   Personal Software Company, P.O. Box 776, Salt Lake City, Utah 84110.

ZAPROS   Oleg Larichev, UN IISI, 9Pr 60 Ler Ocrjabrya, Moscow 117312.

Name Index

Subject Index